Best Friends at the Bar

What Women Need to Know about a Career in the Law

ASPEN PUBLISHERS

Best Friends at the Bar

What Women Need to Know about a Career in the Law

Susan Smith Blakely, Esquire

Wolters Kluwer
Law & Business

AUSTIN   BOSTON   CHICAGO   NEW YORK   THE NETHERLANDS

Aspen Publishers
Attn: Permissions Department
76 Ninth Avenue, 7th Floor
New York, NY 10011–5201

To contact Customer Care, e-mail customer.care@aspenpublishers.com,
call 1-800-234-1660, fax 1-800-901-9075, or mail correspondence to:

Aspen Publishers
Attn: Order Department
PO Box 990
Frederick, MD 21705

Printed in the United States of America.

2 3 4 5 6 7 8 9 0

ISBN 978-07355-9385-5

Library of Congress Cataloging-in-Publication Data

Blakely, Susan Smith, 1946-
    Best friends at the bar : what women need to know about a career in the law / Susan
Smith Blakely.
        p. cm.
    Summary: "This book addresses the realities of law firm practice and gives pre-law
students, law students, and attorneys a realistic view of the opportunities and hazards
encountered by women and advice about how to deal with them"—Provided by
publisher.
    ISBN 978-0-7355-9385-5
    1. Women lawyers—United States. 2. Law—Vocational guidance—United States.
    3. Women—Vocational guidance—United States. I. Title.

KF299.W6B59 2009
340.023'73—dc22

                                                        2009033426

About Wolters Kluwer Law & Business

Wolters Kluwer Law & Business is a leading provider of research information and workflow solutions in key specialty areas. The strengths of the individual brands of Aspen Publishers, CCH, Kluwer Law International and Loislaw are aligned within Wolters Kluwer Law & Business to provide comprehensive, in-depth solutions and expert-authored content for the legal, professional and education markets.

CCH was founded in 1913 and has served more than four generations of business professionals and their clients. The CCH products in the Wolters Kluwer Law & Business group are highly regarded electronic and print resources for legal, securities, antitrust and trade regulation, government contracting, banking, pension, payroll, employment and labor, and healthcare reimbursement and compliance professionals.

Aspen Publishers is a leading information provider for attorneys, business professionals and law students. Written by preeminent authorities, Aspen products offer analytical and practical information in a range of specialty practice areas from securities law and intellectual property to mergers and acquisitions and pension/benefits. Aspen's trusted legal education resources provide professors and students with high-quality, up-to-date and effective resources for successful instruction and study in all areas of the law.

Kluwer Law International supplies the global business community with comprehensive English-language international legal information. Legal practitioners, corporate counsel and business executives around the world rely on the Kluwer Law International journals, loose-leafs, books and electronic products for authoritative information in many areas of international legal practice.

Loislaw is a premier provider of digitized legal content to small law firm practitioners of various specializations. Loislaw provides attorneys with the ability to quickly and efficiently find the necessary legal information they need, when and where they need it, by facilitating access to primary law as well as state-specific law, records, forms and treatises.

Wolters Kluwer Law & Business, a unit of Wolters Kluwer, is headquartered in New York and Riverwoods, Illinois. Wolters Kluwer is a leading multinational publisher and information services company.

DEDICATION

I dedicate this book to my father, Rex M. Smith, Esquire, now deceased, who encouraged me to follow him into the legal profession and who taught me the true meaning of ethical and honorable behavior. Without his encouragement and example, none of this would have been possible.

In addition, I dedicate this book to my mother, Virginia Treganza Smith, the only nonlawyer in the family, who often is heard to say that one lawyer is enough for *any* family. She made sure that we children—and all of our friends—practiced correct grammar and effective writing skills. At an age that she will not allow me to disclose but that is not far from the centennial mark, she continues to tutor English grammar and can conjugate with the best of them. She has my greatest love and admiration.

I also dedicate this book to the new generation of women lawyers, including my daughter Elizabeth, through whose eyes we see the future and put the past in perspective. I wish them all good fortune in making the law profession work for them, one career at a time and with a cooperative voice.

ABOUT
THE AUTHOR

Susan Smith Blakely is an attorney and former teacher whose experiences
include practicing law, with a specialty in construction contract litigation
and land use, serving as chief of staff to an elected official, and teaching in
public school systems throughout the United States. She holds a Bachelor
of Science degree from the University of Wisconsin and a Juris Doctorate
from Georgetown University Law Center, where she was a teaching fellow
for legal research and writing. Although Ms. Blakely has published in
professional law journals in the past, this is her first book.

Ms. Blakely lives in Great Falls, Virginia, with her husband Bill, also an
attorney. They have two children: Elizabeth, 25 years old, a graduate of the
University of Virginia and currently a law student at Seton Hall University
School of Law and Derick, 23 years old, a recent graduate of the University
of Virginia who works in the defense industry. Ms. Blakely enjoys reading,
playing the piano, gardening, skiing, traveling, walking her dog, and being
with family and friends when she is not writing.

CONTENTS

Chapter 5: Critical Lessons   169

Chapter 6: The Working Bar Speaks Out: As Heard From the Best Friends   193

Chapter 7: The Solution   219

Epilogue: The Male Perspective by Sheldon Krantz, Esquire   223

FOREWORD

Although the title more than suggests the topic of this remarkable and continuing timely guide, Susan Smith Blakely provides us a thoughtful and informative work replete with concrete and practical advice for those interested in beginning a career in the law. It is, on a certain level, quintessentially female in the sense that it reflects one of the best aspects of the female character: cooperatively sharing insights. Woman to woman, these vignettes about specific life experiences prepare the reader to avoid the pitfalls too often encountered by her predecessors. Thus, the poem "The Bridge Builder" by Will Allen Dromgoogle, shared with us in the Preface, which was delivered at the Centennial celebration of the founding of the Portia Law School in Boston (now New England Law | Boston), is so apt.

Similarly, this collection of insights provides an invaluable tool for the practicing lawyer who is finding it difficult to chart her own course through tempestuous legal waters. Thus, *Best Friends at the Bar: What Women Need to Know About a Career in the Law*, documenting the diverse experiences of women in both the private and public sectors, as different in their age, race, and ethnic backgrounds as in their professional experiences, examines the unique challenges faced by women in the law, for the edification and improvement of the entire profession.

Although the so-called glass ceiling, or as the esteemed 1935 Portia Law School graduate, Eleanor Burke, referred to it, the "cement ceiling," has been shattered, the robust demands of balancing professional and home life remain. As described in this book, the demands and challenges confronted by women in our profession are many. Ms. Blakely's and her contributors' sage and unflinching advice on achieving a healthy professional and home life is delivered to the reader with both pride and encouragement, coupled with a healthy dose of reality (a successful law practice surely requires some sacrifice). Every profession, of course, has its unique demands, but those particular to the legal profession—long hours, demanding clients, intellectual battle, "courtroom performance," and time sheets—can strain all of one's resources: financial, mental, and emotional.

Consequently, as detailed in this work, a romantic and unrealistic approach to a career in the law is a sure-fire recipe for frustration, disappointment, and failure. The stories assembled by Ms. Blakely provide concrete, practical advice to focus an aspiring lawyer on self-knowledge and introspection long before even beginning the application process for law school. Given the expense and time commitment of achieving a Juris Doctorate, a prospective law student, gender notwithstanding, should take a sober approach to the practice of law prior to the expenditure of time, talent, and tuition. Ms. Blakely has selected some of the trailblazers of our profession (albeit without attribution); these contributors in turn describe how sensibilities have changed, barriers have been swept away, and boundaries have been dissolved. Nonetheless, she cautions quite sensibly, merely because the path has been prepared, it need not necessarily be followed by every woman mulling over a career in law.

The contributors' stories describe the problems they encountered individually and what worked and did not work for them. Newer attorneys might not encounter similar experiences or face the choices they faced. The stories inform the reader of choices that were available at a certain time and place and how earlier female lawyers overcame particular hurdles. The critical questions, then, for the reader are, "What is the best path for me? From what professional course will I derive the most professional satisfaction and stimulation?" The answers to those questions require self-awareness and honesty. Only the reader holds the answers to these questions, but this book is significant because it frames issues as other works have not and provides candid and serious treatment to very personal issues confronted by female lawyers.

To put a new spin on the old legal maxim, *caveat emptor*, I suggest strongly that the buyer embrace the accumulated wisdom found in this work. As Ms. Blakely aptly reminds the reader, just as in many other areas of life, there is no substitute for preparedness.

Let me add my personal words of advice to the young women who read this book: Whatever course you chart, remember: choose knowingly and willingly. Refrain from going down a path because you think that by doing so you will make others happy. Be honest in your assessment of the kind of professional life that will feed and nourish your professional soul. Never base your decisions on fear. Do not choose a career in law solely because you think it will please or honor a parent or spouse. You would be doing yourself, as well as the person you believe you are pleasing, a disservice. If you choose a law career, do not forget to be an advocate for yourself, not just for your clients. As contributors to this book counsel, advise your superiors of your needs when appropriate. Take this sage advice. Worthwhile firms will make accommodations for worthwhile associates. Suffering in silence serves no purpose other than generating and storing resentment and dissatisfaction—hardly any manager's model for lawyer productivity. By alerting your firm to your needs in a measured, professional manner, you allow management to respond in an effective manner, which could well have positive repercussions for others in the firm, as well as ultimately leading you to occupy a management role.

Whatever your path, maintain your integrity through your honesty and authenticity. Law can be a wonderfully fulfilling profession. And we need you! To all I wish every happiness, success, and Godspeed.

Judge Margaret Sweeney
U.S. Court of Federal Claims

At the centennial celebration of Portia Law School in Boston on September 23, 2008, a 1935 graduate of the school, Eleanor Burke, took the stage at almost 100 years of age to tell the young women in the audience about her experiences at America's first law school for women. Her remarks were poignant and moving, as she described a time of such limited professional opportunities for women that most of the audience could not even imagine. She emphasized that the women lawyers of today "stand on the shoulders of the women who have come before them" and compared the "concrete ceiling" of her day to the "glass ceiling" that exists today. As she explained, The Portia Law School story started with Arthur Winfield MacLean, a Boston attorney, who began a "quiet revolution" by agreeing to tutor two women who wanted to become lawyers and write the Massachusetts bar exam. MacLean believed that women had the intelligence and temperament to excel in the profession, and in 1908 he and others founded Portia Law School for women who could not obtain an education in the law elsewhere because of their gender. The school derived its name from the character Portia in Shakespeare's *The Merchant of Venice*, who disguised herself as a man to gain entry to the court to argue her case. The efforts in founding the law school were successful and, after 30 years as the only law school in the nation founded exclusively for the education of women, Portia Law School opened its doors to men in 1938, changing its name to New England School of Law. Known today as New England Law | Boston, it remains a shining example of the independent law school started over a century ago for the education of women.

Fittingly, United States Supreme Court Justice Ruth Bader Ginsberg and former United States Supreme Court Justice Sandra Day O'Connor were distinguished guest speakers at the centennial celebration of Portia Law School during 2008 and 2009. They both offered encouragement and commendation to young women lawyers, and Justice O'Connor spoke of the challenge of teaching young women to build bridges for other women to follow like their predecessors had done. She read a poem entitled "The Bridge Builder" by Will Allen Dromgoole to illustrate her point.

An old man going a lone highway
Came at the evening cold and gray
To a chasm vast and deep and wide.
The old man crossed in the twilight dim;
The sullen stream had no fears for him.
But he turned when safe on the other side
And built a bridge to span the tide.

"Old man," said a fellow pilgrim near,
"You are wasting your time with building here.
You never again will pass this way—
Your journey will end with the closing day.
You have crossed the chasm deep and wide;
Why build you this bridge at eventide?"

The builder lifted his old gray head.
"Good friend, in the way that I've come" he said,
"There followeth after me today
A youth whose feet must pass this way.
This stream that has been as naught to me,
To the fair-haired youth might a pitfall be.
He, too, must cross in the twilight dim;
Good friend, I'm building the bridge for him.

I was honored to be in the audience to witness this important history lesson and the moving remarks by women pioneers in the profession. In this setting and in my research for this book, I have learned so much that makes me even more proud to be a woman attorney. I hope that this book will help you as much in reading it as it has helped me in writing it. I know that we will continue to learn together as time marches forward and that the knowledge that we gain will help us in building bridges for the women attorneys to follow.

ACKNOWLEDGMENTS

I owe a debt of gratitude to the remarkable women who have contributed to this book. They gave interviews, filled out questionnaires, and e-mailed in the middle of the night with important thoughts that could not wait until morning. Many of them are not only my colleagues at the legal bar, but also my best friends for solving career problems over a cup of coffee or a glass of wine. We laughed, and we cried, as we tried to figure out how to fit into a profession that had all the trappings of a male bastion. Each of these women has encountered at least some of the pitfalls that are detailed in this volume and has survived in the profession to help tell the story. These women have been a great inspiration to me. I toast each and every one of them and applaud their enthusiasm for making things easier for the next generation of women lawyers.

I could not have written this book without the invaluable input from these contributors. As will become obvious from the descriptions of the individual contributors that follow, many of them are women who have risen to the top levels of law practice and management and the judiciary, and the value of their contributions is extensive and unparalleled in a book of this nature. These women not only understand the problems and offer valuable insight and advice, but they also have a special capacity to empathize with young women in the profession. They support the mission of the book and wish to lend helping hands to improve the legal profession for women and to keep more women in the practice. If there is an Old Girls Network in the legal profession, this might just be it. In addition, I am indebted to the young women contributors, whose new-generation stories also are critical to my mission.

If I am successful, you will come to think of these women lawyers, young and older, as your best friends at the bar. It is my hope that you will find yourselves engaged in "conversations" with them that will help lead you out of the morass of career dilemmas toward successful careers in the law.

My function has been a combination of contributor and conduit, and I am very pleased to be able to bring this information to you. Collectively, my observations and those of the contributors will present insightful and valuable advice on the subjects addressed.

The contributors were all guaranteed anonymity to protect their professional reputations and to assure the most valuable and candid advice possible. As a result, contributory material from a member of this group typically will be identified in the text as coming from "one of my contributors" or, to create a more personal conversation with the reader, a fictitious name has been attached to the contribution. In these instances, I have included the approximate age of the contributor to enhance the personal connection between contributor and reader. In certain instances, where I believe it is valuable to the reader, I identify material as part of my own story. However, many of my own experiences are also anonymously intertwined throughout the text.

The contributor pool is diverse and includes women from a variety of races, ethnic backgrounds, and religions; both single and married women; women with children and those without; women from the North, South, East, West, and areas in between; young women and older women; and women from a variety of practice areas. In addition to these women, I am also indebted to the deans and directors of career counseling at law schools throughout the country who gave generously of their time and opinions to make this book as complete and useful as possible. I came away from these interviews confident that the next generation of female lawyers is in good hands. I also have been fortunate to have contributions from my friend Jackie Finn, principal in Finn & Associates, a legal search firm in the Washington, DC area. Last, but not least, I am grateful to the male managing partners who generously lent their voices. Their perspectives are critical to a thorough treatment of the subject, and I thank them for their time and advice—and not billing me for it!

I am particularly grateful for the participation of the Honorable Margaret Sweeney, Judge, U.S. Court of Federal Claims, who contributed the Foreword to the book, and to Sheldon Krantz, a partner at DLA Piper and a former law school dean and professor, who assisted me in bringing you the male perspective in the Epilogue. Their enthusiasm for this project, from the high perches where they reside, gave me confidence and assurance that this book is not only valuable to you but necessary for you.

I also am blessed to have another very special best friend at the bar. My husband, Bill Blakely, Managing Partner of the Washington, DC office of Polsinelli Shughart, deserves top scores as a lawyer, husband, father, and colleague. Bill and I married shortly after college and put each other through law school with the help of the GI Bill. We have practiced law together and separately, and Bill totally "gets" the issues addressed in this book and has observed the work-life issues up close and personal as we raised our two children while keeping our careers alive and thriving. He has been a great sounding board and voice of reason for me throughout my career, and I believe that he has been a better male supervisor of young women lawyers as a result. We, too, have addressed many of these problems over a cup of coffee or a glass of wine, and he has never failed to tell me the truth about winning the battle and losing the war. He has a more refined sense of fairness than anyone I know, and he uses it to improve the lives of those less fortunate. He has my greatest love, respect, and gratitude.

The contributors to this book are as follows:

Private Sector Attorneys

Cathy Dean, Esq., Senior Partner, Polsinelli Shughart PC, Kansas City, MO, commercial litigation

Anita Estell, Esq., Shareholder, Polsinelli Shughart PC, Washington, DC, attorney/lobbyist

Elizabeth Lewis, Esq., Partner, Cooley Godward Kronish LLP, Reston, VA, employment and labor

Cathy A. Hinger, Esq., Member, Womble Carlyle Sandridge & Rice, PLLC, Washington, DC, business litigation

Annie Khalid Hussain, Esq., Associate, Arnold & Porter, Washington, DC, international arbitration

Marjory G. Basile, Esq., Principal, Miller Canfield Paddock and Stone PLC, Detroit, MI, intellectual property and litigation

Mary Gately, Esq., Partner, DLA Piper, Washington, DC, complex product liability litigation

Sharon Pandak, Esq., Partner, Greehan Taves Pandak & Stoner, Woodbridge, VA, public entity law

Pamela Beck Danner, Esq., Owner, Danner & Associates, McLean, VA, business, wills and trusts, associations and foundations

Mara V. J. Senn, Esq., Partner, Arnold & Porter, Washington, DC, white collar litigation

Monica P. McCabe, Esq., Partner, Vandenberg & Feliu LLP, New York, NY, intellectual property

Caroline Petro Gately, Esq., Partner, Venable, Washington, DC, commercial litigation

Patricia Maher, Esq., Partner, King & Spalding LLP, Washington, DC, litigation

Lauren DeSantis-Then, Esq., Associate, Polsinelli Shughart PC, Washington, DC, commercial litigation

Marjorie J. Burchett, Esq., Partner, Luce, Forward, Hamilton & Scripps, San Diego, CA, real estate

Kathryn T. Harris, Esq., Vice President and General Counsel, DLT Solutions, Inc., and Founder & Sr. Principal, Resolution Law Group, plc, Herndon, VA, general corporate, commercial and government contracts, employment, technology, copyright and trademark

Anita Herrera, Esq., President, OTC Legal LLC and Chief Compliance Officer, Nodal Exchange, LLC, Washington, DC and Vienna, VA, finance and energy

Muriel Nichols, Esq., Vice President and Senior Wealth Strategist, Eaton Vance Investment Counsel, Boston, MA, asset management

Dorothy E. Terrell, Esq., Partner, Smith Pachter McWhorter PLC, Vienna, VA, construction and government contracts law

Kathleen Harney Smith, Esq., Associate, Walsh Colucci Lubeley Emrich & Walsh, PC, Arlington, VA, commercial real estate

Abby C. Denham, Esq., Associate, Miles and Stockbridge PC, McLean, VA, business litigation

Carol Guy-Jackson, Esq., Shareholder, Polsinelli Shughart PC, Washington, DC, business lawyer

Deborah Bouchoux, Esq., Adjunct faculty, Georgetown University, Washington, DC

Amy Natterson Kroll, Esq., Partner, Bingham McCutchen LLP, Washington, DC, securities

Katherine Posner, Esq., Partner, Condon & Forsyth LLP, New York, NY, insurance and aviation law

Patricia Gillette, Esq., Partner, Orrick, Herrington & Sutcliffe LLP, San Francisco, CA, employment law

Andrea S. Kramer, Esq., Partner, McDermott, Will & Emery, LLP, Chicago, IL, financial products, trading and derivatives

Barbara Portwood, Esq., Shareholder, Leonard, Street and Deinard PC, Minneapolis, MN, bond counsel for tax-exempt financing and government subsidies

M. Maxine Hicks, Esq., Managing Shareholder of the Atlanta Office, Epstein, Becker & Green, PC, Atlanta, GA, Chair of the National Real Estate Practice

Natalie Prescott, Esq., Associate, Latham & Watkins LLP, San Diego, CA, litigation

Jordan Y. Crosby, Esq., Associate, Ugrin, Alexander, Zadick & Higgins, PC, Great Falls, MT, insurance defense and insurance bad faith

Regina Lennox, Esq., Associate, McKee Nelson LLP, New York, NY, business litigation

Elizabeth S. Ryan, Esq., Associate, Patton Boggs LLP, Washington, DC, public policy

Chandra Emery, Esq., Former Associate, Tonkon Torp LLP, Portland, OR, commercial litigation

Robin Meguire, Esq., Founder, meguirelaw.com, Great Falls, MT, contract, appellate and public interest law

Amy Yeung, Esq., Assistant General Counsel, ZeniMax, and Former Associate, WilmerHale, Washington, DC, securities law

Pamela Moore, Esq., Partner, McCarter & English, LLP, labor and employment law

Law Firm Managing Partners

Francis B. Burch, Jr., Esq., Co-Chairman of DLA Piper, LLP (US)

ACKNOWLEDGMENTS

Andrew D. Ness, Esq., Howrey LLP and Former Managing Partner, Washington DC Office, Thelen LLP

W. Russell Welsh, Esq., Chairman and Chief Executive Officer, Polsinelli Shughart PC

Richard Leveridge, Esq., Managing Partner, Washington, DC Office, Dickstein Shapiro LLP

Kim Koopersmith, Esq., Managing Partner-United States, Akin Gump Strauss Hauer & Feld LLP

Public-Sector Judges and Attorneys

Honorable Margaret M. Sweeney, Judge, U.S. Court of Federal Claims

Honorable Cecilia Altonaga, Judge, U.S. Federal District Court, Southern District of Florida

Honorable Ann Walsh Bradley, Justice, Wisconsin Supreme Court

Honorable Joanna Fitzpatrick, Judge, retired, Court of Appeals of Virginia

Honorable Rosemarie Annunziata, Senior Judge, Court of Appeals of Virginia

Honorable Leslie Alden, Judge, Fairfax Circuit Court (VA)

Honorable Jan Brodie, Judge, Fairfax Circuit Court (VA)

Kathlynn Fadely, Esq., Assistant Director of Aviation, Aviation and Admiralty Litigation, Torts Branch, Civil Division, U.S. Department of Justice

Karen J. Harwood, Esq., Deputy County Attorney, Office of the County Attorney, Fairfax County (VA), land use and legislation (retired)

Mary Grad, Esq., United States Attorney, U.S. Attorney's Office, Sacramento, CA, criminal prosecutor

Shiva V. Hodges, Esq., Career Law Clerk to the Honorable Joseph F. Anderson, Jr., Judge, U.S. Federal District Court, District of South Carolina

Law School Faculty

Kathleen Boozang, Esq., Associate Dean and Professor of Law, Seton Hall University School of Law

Paula A. Monopoli, Esq., Professor of Law and Founding Director, Women, Leadership & Equality Program, University of Maryland School of Law

Law School Directors of Career Development and Career Counselors

Maura J. Kelly, Esq., Assistant Dean for Career Development and Public Service, Boston University School of Law

Mary Karen Rogers, Executive Director, Career Development Office, Suffolk University Law School

Mandie R. Araujo, Esq., Director of Career Services, New England Law|Boston

Gihan Fernando, Esq., Assistant Dean, Office of Career Services, Georgetown University Law Center

Carole Montgomery, Esq., Director, Career Development Office, George Washington University Law School

Traci Mundy Jenkins, Esq., Director, Office of Career & Professional Development, American University Washington College of Law

Joan King, Esq., Retired Director of Career Center, Brooklyn Law School

Stacey Lara-Kerr, Esq., Associate Director, Center for Professional Development, Seattle University School of Law

Sonia Cunha, Director of Career Services, Seton Hall University School of Law

Stephanie Richman, Esq., Assistant Dean, Office of Career Services, Rutgers School of Law, Newark

Sheldon Krantz, Esq., Partner, DLA Piper, Washington, DC, contributed to "Epilogue: The Male Perspective." Mr. Krantz is a specialist in corporate and white collar criminal defense and the Director of New Perimeter, DLA Piper's unique affiliated nonprofit that provides global pro bono services. He is the former Dean of the University of San Diego School of Law and, prior to that, a professor of law and the Director of the Center for Criminal Justice at Boston University School of Law. Mr. Krantz was named the DC Bar Pro Bono Lawyer of the Year in 2004 and a District of Columbia Super Lawyer in 2008.

I also would like to thank the people at Wolters Kluwer/Aspen Publishers. Working with each of them was a true pleasure. Richard Kravitz was my first contact there, and he conveyed confidence in my manuscript and moved it on to the next level. I will always be grateful to him for his enthusiasm and encouragement. Carol McGeehan continued that level of enthusiasm and provided me with excellent editors in Richard Mixter, who advocated for this project in a very effective manner, and Dana Wilson, who oversaw the fine-tuning and presented me with an excellent product. I am also grateful to Jen Armstrong for her marketing strategies and innovative approach to assuring that this book reaches the greatest number of readers.

Prologue

Emily had dreamed of being a lawyer all of her life. She came from a family of lawyers, and, as a child, she loved milling around her father's law office. She liked the smell of the leather-bound books, and she especially liked the days when her father took her to the courthouse with him to file a paper or to meet with the judge. Emily prepared herself well. She succeeded in high school, went to an Ivy League college, and attended a first-tier law school. She graduated from law school at the top of her class and was hired by a national law firm where she made a six-figure salary and had excellent opportunities for advancement.

Two years into Emily's legal career, she resigned from the law firm, where she worked around the clock. She had no social life, no prospects for marriage, and she knew that marriage and family would be very important to her some day. She did not feel like she fit into what seemed like a man's profession, and she did not know how to change that. She was riddled with debt from her student loans, and she felt that she had disappointed herself and her family. She told her friends that practicing law was not what she had expected.

How could this have been avoided? What would have helped Emily to be better prepared for law practice?

Hopefully, a book like this one would have helped Emily. This book is for young women in law schools and undergraduate colleges and universities across America who are considering careers in the law and pursuing those careers. It is also for young female practitioners who are passionate about their careers as attorneys, who want challenging and stimulating professional lives, and who also want complete personal lives without compromising their professional hopes and dreams. These are admirable professional and personal goals, but they often can be on a collision course.

You are probably one of these women. By reading this book, you will have the chance to gain insight into the challenges of the legal profession for women and to learn valuable lessons from some of the most accomplished women attorneys in the business. The contents of this book can change your life by assisting you in planning a successful and satisfying legal career and helping you to avoid the pitfalls that can derail those plans. One of my contributors, a federal judge, has compared the book to Ariadne's story in Greek mythology. You might recall that Ariadne provided her lover Theseus with the skein of thread that enabled him to find his way out of the labyrinth after killing the Minotaur. It is my fervent hope that this book will become your skein of thread and will help you to successfully find your way through the challenge of modern law practice.

Another of my contributors has compared the challenges and the failings of young women lawyers to those of Dorothy in the Wizard of Oz. "Dorothy was a true leader," according to Patricia Gillette of Orrick, Herrington & Sutcliffe. "[Dorothy] identified the tasks at hand, formulated a plan, and overcame obstacles to reach her goals: a brain for the scarecrow, a heart for the tin man, and courage for the cowardly lion. [But] when push came to shove, what did Dorothy ultimately ask for herself from the Wizard? Nothing." Gillette believes that too many women lawyers are like Dorothy. They ask for no credit, reward or recognition and, as a result, they are not thought of as leaders. She says that women need to take more active roles in managing and advancing their careers, including courting clients, socializing with firm leaders, touting their capabilities and pressuring firms to expand leadership opportunities for women ("Too Many Women Lawyers are Like Oz's Dorothy, Partner Says," *ABA Journal Law News Now*, July 8, 2009). To reach these goals, Gillette has co-founded the Opt-In Project, first at Heller Ehrman and later at Orrick, to address how firms can do a better job retaining women lawyers. For more information on Opt-In and other similar programs, see "Legal Field Struggles to Retain Women," *San Francisco Daily Journal*, June 29, 2006.

You should be aware that this book does not address a thorough history of women in the law, the mechanics of practicing law, the substantive issues encountered in the law, or the day-to-day routines of a law practice and its lawyers. Much of that information is gained in law school, and there are many other books that address those subjects. You will read many of those books as part of your comprehensive preparation for your future professional experiences. In addition, by the time you read this book, many of you will have had legal internships, clerkships, and summer associate positions, and you will have gained the information that you need from those experiences. A combination of your legal education, those experiences, and the contents of this book will put you in a position to make excellent choices for your personal and professional life.

This book also does not address women lawyers who are working in business settings outside the traditional practice of law. Those jobs, as corporate counsel and in positions related to business, can offer greater flexibility in terms of schedule and the absence of billable hour requirements, but they also include challenges associated with traditional business structures. These issues are worthy of consideration but are not appropriate for inclusion in this book. For more information on legal jobs in those settings, see *So You Want To Be Corporate Counsel* by Mark Harris (Infinity Publishing.com, 2002) and *The New Corporate Counsel* by Sally Gunz and Robert V. A. Jones (Carswell Legal Publications, 1991).

There are other books for young women lawyers, and some of them are excellent resource materials and are recommended to you wherever appropriate. Some are scholarly and historical, and some are just plain trite. This book is none of those things. Rather, this book is a combination of realism about the profession and good, sound advice. To the best of my knowledge, the anecdotes presented here are true, and they are included as real-life experiences that my contributors and I consider valuable and instructive.

Learning the lessons included in this book might not be equally important for all women aspiring to a legal career. There are always the superstars who have the right combination of attributes to help them rise to the top without the need for a book like this. We all know them. They are the very brightest and highest achievers at the best law schools, who have been taken under the wings of powerful and effective mentors and who succeed, notwithstanding the odds that normally affect women in the profession. However, these women are in the minority, and most of the women who read this book will not have the superstar profile. As a result, the book will be a valuable assist to most of you in developing successful careers and compatible personal lives.

You should not envy the superstars. You should thank them. They continue to open doors for all of us. It is the superstars who prove themselves so valuable to employers that they gain concessions that would not be gained by the rest of us under the same circumstances. Over time, those concessions have proved to be successful, and employers have become willing to address them for other women attorneys who are not necessarily superstars.

I recall a time in 1983 when I was negotiating a part-time schedule with my law firm in anticipation of the birth of my first child. The most difficult issue was part-time partnership. I believed that I was entitled to the reward of partnership because of my past performance, and I was willing to be realistic on the salary. As preparation for discussions with the partners, I researched part-time policies for a variety of firms in the geographic area, and I found only one woman who had been selected to a partnership as a part-time attorney. She was a superstar. She had graduated first in her class at a very prestigious law school, had performed admirably at a government agency prior to private practice, was married to a high-profile man who gained her entry into circles of power, and she had a great mentor supporting her for part-time partnership. I was happy for her, although I knew that I did not possess all of those same qualities to be treated similarly. In some respects she had established a new baseline, and other women would soon be allowed to follow in her footsteps. Fortunately, that has become the case. There are many more part-time women partners in firms throughout the country today. It is still a steep climb, but not as steep as it would have been without the superstars. The superstars have helped to open up many additional choices for women in the profession.

This brings me to, perhaps, the most important message that I have to convey to you. It needs to be one of your main focuses as you read the book. It is about choices. My purpose is to inform you about the choices that you will face in pursuing a legal profession, the importance of having well-informed choices as your goal, and the imperative that those choices be your own—made by you and for you. In the end, it is all about choices and the limitations of some career paths and the opportunities of others. It is about safeguarding your career and keeping yourself in the legal arena even while you are "off ramp" so that you will have future choices to reenter the profession if and when you choose to.

Women attorneys have these choices today because law is not a man's profession anymore. Yes, it is still dominated by men, but women are very much a part of the legal world, and concessions to women's schedules and recognition of their unique roles in child care and family issues has brought about that result. We are far beyond the days when women could not get hired in prestigious law firms or become members of the bench. Women can choose to be in law firms or they can choose to be in the other myriad legal settings. They can choose to have flexible time or they can choose to work full time. Men are not keeping them out. However, for women lawyers who want marriage and family and also want successful and satisfying legal careers, the choices are much harder than for men with similar aspirations.

These are serious issues that require serious consideration. The discussion and recommendations contained in this book will assist you in that endeavor. Reading the book will develop awareness that can make or break a woman's legal career and can turn what might be a disappointing experience into something much more satisfying. In the end, I hope that this book will have the effect of adequately preparing young women for the realities of a legal career and keeping talented women in a profession that has played such an important role in my life and in the lives of my best friends at the bar. I hope that it will help women attorneys avoid the pitfalls that have adversely affected so many women lawyers of my generation, who had few positive role models and who encountered senior women in the practice who preferred competing with them to mentoring them.

Choices, choices, choices. Keep that as your focus, and you will gain the maximum benefit from the discussions that follow. The best choices are the ones that are made by you and for you, with adequate information and with an eye to the future. So, let's get on with it. There are so many choices!

Millenial Generation lawyers are more
inclined than their predecessors to
abandon unsatisfactory work circum-
stances and to derail careers without
planning ahead. Career strategies are
not only advisable, they are essential.
—Law School Career Counselor

The Problem

According to the American Bar Association (ABA), there were 1,143,358 lawyers licensed to practice in America in 2007, and 30.1 percent of those were women. Although the number of women licensed to practice has increased steadily over the years, women as a percentage of total law students is beginning to decline. Although it is true that the number of both men and women choosing law as a profession have decreased in recent years, it is the women who are deciding in larger numbers not to apply to law school (Law School Admission Counsel (LSAC), Volume Summary Applicants by Ethnic & Gender Group). Although this has been the trend in the recent years, it should be noted that the number of students applying to law school was up 3.8 percent for the Fall 2009 semester. According to the LSAC, the likely reason for the unexpected increase is the economic downturn. As stated by LSAC president, Daniel Bernstine, "In recessionary periods, people tend to go back to school if they are out of work . . . to upgrade their current education" (*ABA Journal Law News Now*, www.abajournal.com, April 29, 2009). Whether this increase in interest in law school is an anomaly or not remains to be seen. For more on the effects of the troubled economy on the legal profession, see "The Economy Matters—A Lot" in Chapter 2.

The recent trend in decreased numbers of applicants to law schools has not always been the case. ABA figures show that, from 1963 to 1990, the enrollment of women in ABA-approved law schools rose each consecutive year. In the academic year 1963-1964, only 3.7 percent of law school students were women, compared with 42.5 percent in the academic year 1990-1991. In the academic year 1992-1993, for the first and only time since 1963, women outnumbered men at 50.4 percent. Again, from the academic year 1993-1994 to the academic year 2002-2003, female enrollment climbed steadily. Since that time, however, although the enrollment numbers for female law students increased for the academic years 2006-2007 and 2007-2008, the percentage of women among the total of students in law schools has declined each year.

In the academic year 2002-2003, women made up 49 percent of law school enrollment, whereas in the academic years 2006-2007 and 2007-2008, only 46.9 percent and 46.7 percent, respectively, of law school students were women (ABA Legal Education Statistics, Enrollment and Degrees Awarded, 1963-2007 and First Year and Total J.D. Enrollment by Gender, 1947-2001). Although there is a minority view that the reason fewer women, as compared to men, are applying for, enrolling in, and graduating from law school might be due to the perceptions of broader business options for women and a strong economy during those time periods, whatever the reasons, the general decrease in the percentage of women law students is a reversal of the long-running trend.

In addition to the declining law school statistics for women, each year many talented women attorneys leave the practice of law because of unrealized expectations and disillusionment. According to statistics from the

LAW STUDENTS

Academic Year	Total JD Enrollment	Gender	
		Male	Female
2000-01	125,173	52%	48%
2001-02	127,610	51%	49%
2002-03	132,885	51%	49%
2003-04	137,676	51%	49%
2004-05	140,376	52%	48%
2005-06	140,298	53%	48%
2006-07	141,031	53%	47%
2007-08	141,719	53%	47%

Source: ABA Section of Legal Education & Admissions to the Bar
http://www.abnet.org/legal/statistics/stats.html

ABA and National Association of Women Lawyers, approximately 42 percent of women leave the profession midcareer, and the attrition rate for women at major law firms is currently at 76 percent by their fifth year of practice (National Association for Law Placement (NALP) Foundation for Law Career Research and Education, 2008; *Working Mother Magazine*, Focus on the Best Law Firms-Part-time Partners, November 16, 2008). Surprisingly, most of these women do not leave because they lack interest in practicing law, and relatively few of these women leave the workforce to be at-home moms. Rather, these women leave for more family-friendly jobs, and statistics show that only 9 percent of women law graduates were not working 15 years after graduation. "A fair assessment of the experience of women who have left [law firm practice] is likely to reveal that the highly credentialed and motivated women lawyers who were hired leave not to stay at home, but to work for other legal employers" (*Creating Pathways to Success, Advancing and Retaining Women in Today's Law Firms*, Women's Bar Association of the District of Columbia Initiative on Advancement and Retention of Women, May 2006). Many women law graduates, who are smart and capable attorneys, want to be in the workforce but are discouraged by the restrictions of the legal profession and dissatisfied with their career development and prospects for promotion. These women leave a profession that they have taken years to prepare for and, in many cases, before they have repaid the debts accumulated to attend high-priced law schools. Many of these women were top performers in law schools and had promising positions in their practices. Although many of them have chosen family life over practicing law, some have left the practice for other reasons that rendered it unacceptable for them. Whatever the specific reasons for these decisions, it appears to evidence a great deal of dissatisfaction for women in the profession.

According to the findings of a commission on women in the law profession, in the academic year 2006-2007 there were 66,085 women attending law school in America (46.9 percent of the total law school enrollment) and approximately 343,000 women in the legal profession throughout the United States (Commission on Women in the Profession, ABA, *A Current Glance at Women in the Law*, 2007). Although these appear to be impressive numbers, the most current attrition figures for women attorneys are more discouraging. Between 1980 and 2000, the percentage of females in the profession increased from 8 percent to 27 percent, but the percentage of women in practice between the ages of 29 and 34 decreased considerably (ABA Lawyer Demographics, 2008).

The rate at which female associates leave firms increases with the length of tenure—from 3 percent of associates leaving within one year of hiring to 76 percent for associates who had been with a firm five years. Female associates were nearly twice as likely as males to depart to pursue a better work-life balance. (NALP Foundation for Law Career Research and Education, 2008). The conclusion from these statistics is that we are producing more women lawyers in America but retaining fewer during the early years of practice when the work-life challenges are likely to be the greatest for women with small children. According to the Center for WorkLife Law at the University of California Hastings College of the Law,

42 percent of women lawyers leave the profession at some point during their careers, and the figures are of even greater concern for women of color. The NALP Foundation for Law Career Research and Education in 2005 reported that 81 percent of minority female associates leave law firms within five years of being hired (NALP, *Toward Effective Management of Associate Mobility*).

Male and female attorneys, alike, generally agree that the alarmingly high attrition rates for women lawyers do not bode well for the profession, and employers cannot be counted on to pay adequate attention to the problem. Real attention to this problem of retention and related issues for women in the law was brought in 1987 with the founding of the ABA Commission on Women, first chaired by Hillary Rodham Clinton, to assess the status of women in the legal profession. That first Commission issued a groundbreaking report in 1988 showing that women lawyers were not advancing at a satisfactory rate. The report included information to support the findings that a variety of discriminatory barriers remained a part of the professional culture, that the significant increase in the number of women attorneys would not eliminate these barriers, and that a thorough reexamination of the attitudes and structures in the legal profession was needed. Fifteen years later, impressive women lawyers, judges, and academics from around the country gathered at a Women's Power Summit on Law & Leadership at Harvard University to address these same issues and to reassess. Again in 2009, a similar group of women lawyers, judges, and academics gathered at a follow-up Women's Power Summit at the University of Texas School of Law to assess the progress that had been made, identify the end goals, and set an agenda for future change. In a video advertising the 2009 conference, Hannah Brenner, Executive Director of the Center for Women in Law at the University of Texas School of Law, summed up the concerns of attendees and the status of women in the law. She stated that the movement to improve the status of women in the law is stalled and that not much progress has been made in the last 20 years. As a result of this concern and the agenda for change agreed to by the attendees, this conference issued an "Austin Manifesto," which can be viewed at *www.utexas.edu/law/academics/centers/cwl/summit*, framing the problems and pledging their efforts to bring about positive change.

The urgency of this retention issue was addressed recently by United States District Court Judge Nancy Gertner, as quoted in the Report On The Conference "Advancing Women in the Profession: Action Plans for Women's Bar Associations," June 11-12, 2007 in Boston:

> Ten years from now, if we don't do anything about it, the ranks of senior women will, in fact, thin out. Fewer and fewer women will be ready to assume the positions of leadership. The purpose of this [conference] is to make certain that this will not be true.

These concerns were further underscored by a May 2008 conference at George Washington University sponsored by the Project for Attorney Retention, an initiative of the Center for WorkLife Law at the University of California Hastings College of the Law, and entitled "Positioning Law Firms for Long-Term Success: New Strategies for Advancing Women Lawyers." This conference outlined the issues with retention and the efforts of private firms and public corporations to address those issues. For more information on the Hastings Law project, go to *www.worklifelaw.org* and *www.pardc.org.*

Another resource on this subject was prepared by Yale Law Women in cooperation with *Working Mother Magazine* and Deborah Epstein Henry, Esquire, founder and president of Flex-Time Lawyers LLC. This study provides an annual list of the 50 best law firms for women lawyers raising children and discusses those findings. For the most current list, go to *www.workingmother.com.* In an August 21, 2007 edition of *Working Mother Magazine*, Epstein Henry stated:

> I have watched as the numbers of women partners at law firms, the numbers of women leaders at law firms, the numbers of women rainmakers, the numbers of women working flexibly and the numbers of women advancing while working flexibly, have remained exceedingly low and stagnant. It is long overdue to create a baseline of law firms not only to let them know where they stand today but, more importantly, to help them improve their future

standing. Many firms are poised to start devoting significant attention and resources to improve their retention and promotion of women. However, they do not even know their strengths and weaknesses or where to start.... The ultimate objective of the Best Law Firms for Women list is to invigorate a dialogue, measure where we are, arm firms and lawyers with information to change, create a competition and compulsion among firms, and continue to raise the bar of what makes a best law firm for women.

A more thorough discussion of the survey methodology and its findings can be found at *www.flextimelawyers.com/best/why.pdf.* For more information on the initiative, go to *www.flextimelawyers.com/best.asp.*

As you can see, the issues that will affect you in your future practice are being addressed in a variety of ways, and I urge you to become involved in these efforts at your law school, your law firm, your local bar association, and the ABA. It will take the efforts of more than just a few women to bring about positive change. The real push for positive change will come from women like you, who not only view addressing work-life issues as a priority and as good business, but who also view it as a necessity to make their professional lives and family lives compatible and to safeguard the future of their careers.

Law schools and law firms should embrace retention of women lawyers as a goal and should endorse the kind of mentoring that will be necessary to address the problem and improve circumstances for women in their schools and practices. Firms must not only make it worthwhile for women to join the firm, but they also must make it worthwhile for women to stay at the firm. After all, women attorneys make up at least half of the talent pool and, based on their standings in law schools, it might be the top echelon of the talent pool.

Although law firms will articulate that retention of good lawyers is just good business sense and that top management has to view work-life issues as a priority, the real test is not whether they talk the talk but whether they walk the walk. The jury is still out on that result.

Here is the large firm management mantra. One of my contributors, a managing partner in a large law firm, maintains that finding ways to retain and develop young lawyers is key to the well-being of a law firm and that it is very important for law firms to keep up with the industry and to look different over time, as the market requires. He further states that firms need to be proactive in getting women and minorities into management and executive committee positions so that all the necessary firm members are included in the important conversations that will make the industry evolve correctly over time. In addition, he emphasizes that the presence of women in management positions sends a strong message to the industry and to clients, where women hold positions of power, and provides a very pragmatic reason for firms to pay the appropriate attention to these issues.

This all sounds very good. However, it is not clear that all firms have this same orientation and approach to the problem. The critical questions are how many firms earnestly address the issues of retention and work-place issues for women and how many make adjustments to remedy the disparities that they may discover in that process? Of course, we do not know the answer to those questions. All we do know is that the news is not good on retention of women in the legal profession. In fact, the news is very bad. However, the reasons behind the grim retention figures are not altogether clear. The District of Columbia Women's Bar Association 2006 study, *Creating Pathways to Success*, included unexpected conclusions about the reason that so many women attorneys are opting out. Although it recognized the pressures of work-life issues, it also noted that many women, who use work-life as a reason for leaving a particular practice, immediately join another practice. This suggests that the work-life justification for leaving an employer might have become an acceptable excuse that is being used to mask other more significant problems for women in law firms—problems that they are not willing to address for reasons of privacy and to protect future relationships with the firm and its members. On the other hand, economics and the high costs of raising a family in our society today might cause some women to exchange one work-life nightmare for another.

Law schools are also beginning to look at this retention issue and are stressing the need to invest in women lawyers at an early stage in their careers. The University of Maryland School of Law is a leader in this effort, and its program Women, Leadership, and Equality is reported to be the first and only one of its kind at any American law school. Professor Paula Monopoli, one of my contributors and the founding director of the program, describes it as follows:

> We give [young women law students] the ability to have their ideas heard and implemented within their organizations at every stage of their careers. Building credibility, expertise, and the ability to get their ideas heard—even as first-year lawyers—enables them to exercise informal leadership as they move along the path to formal leadership. It helps them to be valued by their employers, and my hypothesis is that women will stay where they are valued. Our students are able to hit the ground running when they enter the profession and are at a significant advantage in terms of understanding the dynamics of the workplace as well as bringing excellent analytical skills to the table. Law schools teach students how to think like lawyers, but have traditionally taught them little about the organizations within which they use those analytical skills. Our program tries to bridge the gap. (*Raising the Bar*, Women's Bar Association of the District of Columbia, 2008-2009, Issue IV, "Investing in Women Lawyers' Success Begins in Law School," page 4)

I am so pleased that such a program exists. According to Professor Monopoli, the success of the University of Maryland School of Law program is that it has been "imbedded" in the curriculum and has been given course status and recognition by the faculty and the law school. It is a two-year program that includes a second-year theory seminar and a third-year applied skills workshop. The program is in its fifth year, and Professor Monopoli reports that the students who have been through the program are very positive about the benefits of the program as applied to their chosen practices. This is an excellent result, and I hope that other law schools will recognize the same responsibility to their students and establish similar theoretical and skills-based programs in the near future. The need is great, and the time is now.

Although retention is a major concern, this book is not meant to judge those women who have left the legal profession. Rather, it is meant to assist women preparing for the profession to enable them to begin their legal careers with open eyes and with more of a level playing field than women lawyers of prior generations. Women will have to level that playing field themselves because, historically, men are not going to do it for them. Armed with the collective experience of the contributors to this book, leveling that playing field should become easier. That is certainly my hope. If that means that more women lawyers continue in the profession and gain satisfaction from their experiences and that more women lawyers ascend to top leadership and management positions in their practices, that will be a good thing, and I will have achieved my goal.

For women lawyers with family responsibilities, however, remaining committed to their practices is much more than just a professional goal. It is very personal. For them, the investment is in their futures, and it is a battle for career and job satisfaction. In the past, too many women attorneys had career paths not unlike my own: full-time litigation associate at a law firm; part-time litigation associate at a law firm after having a child; part-time counsel at a second law firm after having a second child; interruption of career to stay at home to care for children for an extended time period; return to work in a law-related field until children were in middle school; and return to law practice as a partner in a third firm. In that scenario, our careers were continuously interrupted, and it took us many years beyond the norm to achieve partnership or a similar feeling of success in our profession. My contributors and I hope that you will all avoid this result, and we are here to lend a hand.

With this background in mind, be prepared for the stark realities of law practice, and arm yourself with research and a solid goals assessment. You are likely to find that the early years of practice can be an eye-opening experience for all lawyers, male and female alike. According to law school career counselors, the current generation of young lawyers is more inclined to walk out of unsatisfying circumstances and to derail careers without planning ahead. This is rarely an acceptable result. It is imperative to have a career plan—something like a mosaic that creates a pattern. It is really a simple case of developing building blocks for the future. Having a career strategy is different from having a job, and it takes different skills.

One contributor, a law school career counselor, has a contemporary art poster of a block pattern in her office for a reason. She uses it to demonstrate that the blocks, which look random at first glance, actually display a pattern when more closely examined. She tells her students that this is the same process that they will go through if they give time and attention to developing a career plan. According to her, the most important blocks in the career plan are job satisfaction blocks, but getting to the ultimate goal of job satisfaction might require a series of choices, detours, and skill-based acquisitions. In other words, Rome was not built in a day! It takes patience and a deliberate approach to get what you want.

This can be a problem for members of the "millenial generation," who have been raised on technology like cell phones, instant messaging, and Blackberries, and often view things in terms of instantaneous responses and results. Instant gratification has become part of our culture, and the patience to develop a plan might not come as easily for young people today or seem as important. However, for young women attorneys, especially, many of whom will desire children and require a balance of work and life, it is critically important to go through this process to view a career prospectively to determine what is needed to stay in the profession and to succeed.

So, let's embark. Presumably, by now you have decided that you want a career in the law. You have at least addressed the issues of long hours, sacrifice of personal and family time, possible delay of having children and the issues of the female biological clock, stress inherent in the practice, and other obstacles that prevent most women lawyers from "having it all." And, you still want to be a lawyer. That is good! You go, girl!

If you have not given these things much thought, I would advise you to get to a library or bookstore. Pronto. There are a variety of research books out there that provide a realistic view of what you can expect. My personal favorite is *Women-at-Law: Lessons Learned Along the Pathways to Success* by Phyllis Horn Epstein. It is a thoughtful and thorough examination of women's experiences in the legal profession, including interesting historical and statistical materials, and is replete with testimonials from contemporary women attorneys.

Women-at Law and other books of the kind are excellent resource materials, but they are no substitute for the information that I hope to communicate to you. The book you are holding is a how-to book, presented in a format that is concise and easy to read. It can be viewed as a checklist of the "do's" and "don'ts" and is designed to be a quick reference. It includes a variety of anecdotes addressing these issues and valuable advice from women in the practice today and yesterday. It is a handbook, and I hope that you will use it that way to a successful result.

Undergraduate school was fun. I took a lot of interesting courses and gained a lot of perspective. I did not specialize in a narrow course of study because I believe in a broad liberal arts education. Now I am wondering what to do next. I do not like the sight of blood, I am not good with numbers, and business and commerce do not interest me. I think I'll go to law school.
—*Female Undergraduate History Major*

The Starting Point

The following points are what I like to think of as axiomatic to the discussion of success for women in the law. An understanding of these concepts is essential to gaining the greatest value from the lessons that follow. Wherever it is relevant and appropriate, I include observations, comments, and advice from my contributors. There is no substitute for this kind of practical information and personal story, and you should filter it all through an overlay of your own goals and objectives.

Chart Your Career Plan Early

If you are serious about a career in the law, your planning should start in college. Excelling in college will be critical to whether or not you will be accepted into a law school of your choice. For the most part, law schools look at two criteria: grade point averages (GPAs) and Law School Aptitude Test (LSAT) scores. It is becoming increasingly difficult to be accepted to a law school of your choice, and, therefore, you should be doing everything possible in college to maximize your GPA. Your choice of major is not as important, although law schools likely will recognize the difference between a major in sociology or communications and one in history, philosophy, or English where the curricula emphasize analysis and persuasive writing. For the same reasons, your choice of studies also might have some influence on how well you perform on the LSAT. Check with your college career counseling office to determine which majors might be most advantageous in preparing for law school.

You also should be looking for opportunities to get involved in campus and community activities relevant to the law or that demonstrate a commitment to social and political issues that are influenced by the law. Law school admissions offices will typically view these activities as "make weights" once you have met their GPA and LSAT requirements.

Unless you are a phenomenal standardized test-taker, it is advisable to do some preparation for the LSAT during the spring semester of your junior year of college in anticipation of taking the test at the end of the junior year or in the fall of the senior year. An exception to this general rule is for students who have a known history of difficulty with standardized tests. Those students should start test preparation earlier. There are books you can purchase for self-preparation, and there are a variety of courses available for tutorial preparation. Although I do not agree with the extreme emphasis on the LSAT results as a criterion for admission to law school, it is a fact of life and one that warrants your very close attention.

If you have not paid attention to these matters in college, do not despair. There are plenty of postgraduate opportunities to enhance your résumé. Many law schools, like graduate business schools, put a high value on work experience, and some prefer students who have been out in the "working world" to those right out of college. Choosing relevant work experience and obtaining excellent references from those jobs will also be helpful in applying to law school.

The Law School Decision

Law school career counselors offer the following advice about the law school decision. Law school is not something that you want to do as a default option because you cannot think of anything else to do after graduation from college. Too often, the analysis among bright and motivated undergraduate students goes something like this: "I am not interested in medical school; accounting, finance, and business are not for me; I think I might go to law school because it will open up some options later." Under these circumstances, the decision to go to law school becomes a way of delaying *real* decision making and keeping options open for the future. According to the law school career counselors, this is the wrong approach and one that can end up being very expensive and very unsatisfying. Law school is too expensive for a whim. The decision to go to law school should be very deliberate, based in reality, and fully researched with the end game in mind.

One contributor emphasizes the importance of self-assessment and research for undergraduate prelaw students. She describes many post-graduate decisions that are made for the wrong reasons, like practicing law is exciting (it isn't—most of the time it is tedious detail work), practicing law is glamorous (it isn't—except on television shows and in the movies), and lawyers make a lot of money (some do, some don't). She says that undergraduate students need to take time to really consider their strengths and weaknesses, the lifestyle they want, and the work environment that suits them best to make good career decisions, and she recommends some good tools that are available to help prelaw students determine if their skills and interests are compatible with being a successful lawyer (see *www.Decisionbooks.com*). She describes "the tragedy" of some of the law students she counsels who did not take the time to fully understand their own interests and goals and what it would take to be a successful lawyer. These students might figure out that the law is not for them after a year or so of law school, but, by that time, they are so far invested in a law degree, both financially and in terms of time, that they cannot bring themselves to quit. You do not want this to happen to you, so do your homework up front.

Perhaps surprisingly, some of the career counselors advise that the law school decision should be analyzed in terms of money—cold, hard cash. Such an analysis, they say, is the most effective way to keep the evaluation on target. They know that this will run against the ideology of many undergraduate students, who view the societal "good" that can be accomplished with a law degree as preferable to the money that can be earned. However, the experts point out that the choice of a career in the law is really all about money. It is about the money that, in many cases, must be borrowed to pay for law school and about the money that has to be earned to pay off the student loans. It is about the lack of options during the time that associate lawyers are trying to maximize income to pay back those loans as quickly as possible. They emphasize that law school today costs a minimum of $100,000, and it takes years of income at the median salary for most entry-level lawyers to earn that amount of money. So, it is about money, and you must keep that in mind in making the decision of whether to go to law school.

My contributors are consistent in their advice that young women take a realistic view of the demands of a career in the law before making a decision. One contributor observes that a legal career is not for everyone but that she would recommend a legal career to a young woman who is not afraid of hard work and long hours and will know the importance of finding the proper balance between work and family life. Several contributors stress the importance of being realistic about the commitment necessary and the unpredictable hours, demanding clients, and challenges of difficult legal problems. Another contributor recommends that you work in a law office or in a law-related environment first before making the decision to go to law school and emphasizes that a legal career can be very rewarding if it is developed deliberately.

Another contributor with very diverse practice experience agrees that she would recommend the field of law to a woman but that she would temper that recommendation with a "good dose" of honesty about the sacrifices and hurdles that all but a few women face as lawyers. According to her, choosing the right field of law and the right type of practice is not easy, and, unless you enter law school with a specific interest or expertise or come from a legal family, it is very hard for a young person to fully appreciate the varied legal career paths and how to select the right one. She believes that career decisions for most young law school graduates often result from serendipity and circumstance. Although that can work in some cases, she believes that it is one of the reasons why many young women leave the practice of law after only a few years. Similarly, another contributor, a veteran of large and small firms and in-house corporate counsel, recommends a legal career for a woman but with a "huge caveat." She points out that the profession is extremely demanding and that, although it is not impossible to be a working mother and to practice law, law firms generally do not truly support the needs of their attorneys who are mothers. In her words, "The reality lags behind the lip service."

This is not intended to discourage you. Despite this counsel for caution, almost without exception, the contributors report very satisfying, diverse, and successful careers. Law is not only an honorable and worthy profession, but it also opens up myriad opportunities for you to expand your intellect and to contribute to society in very important and valuable ways. One contributor states, "It is never dull, and you learn something new every day." Another contributor, a partner in a high-visibility national practice, points out that, "A law degree prepares your mind to do many things, not just practice law or give advice as a lawyer. It provides you with credibility that other graduate degrees do not necessarily provide." This contributor said that she was struck by how many of the accomplished men and women poised to become a part of the new administration after the November 2008 presidential election were lawyers, and she presumed that they had reached such high levels of government at least partially because of their legal training.

Several other contributors also emphasize that there are many options available with a legal career, far beyond life in a law firm, and that the opportunities for leadership abound. Others emphasize the opportunities for providing financial self-sufficiency, security, stability, and the sense of power that comes with being capable of ascertaining, knowing, and understanding the law. A state appellate court judge says that it has been an extremely rewarding career that she has loved. She has been a public servant for more than 30 years and feels that she has made a contribution to the law and especially to people who have appeared in her courtroom. Similarly, another contributor observes that the nature of a lawyer's work is to help people, whether that is a paying client or a pro bono client, and another contributor, a minority woman who specializes in lobbying, says that a legal career is a wonderful way for a young woman to strengthen her intellectual and analytical skills. She chose a career path to affect public policy and shape law from its inception. Another contributor, the mother of two, chose a career in estate planning and managed wealth, has risen to senior woman planner at her current very prestigious firm, and was elected only the second woman president of a major metropolitan estate planning council. Still another contributor, with years of practice experience in large national firms, has gained great personal satisfaction from blending a busy family life with an interesting career in teaching and writing about the law. She particularly loves staying in touch with former students and tracking the success of their legal careers.

One of my contributors describes the tremendous honor and privilege of working for the Department of Justice. She says that she still feels a lump in her throat whenever she rises before the bench and states, "I represent the United States of America." She describes the positive experience of her 33 years of public service and the extraordinary luck of having been the Federal Aviation Administration's "token" woman lawyer in 1976 prior to joining the Department of Justice. Another contributor chose a completely different path and, after years of practice in large national firms, founded her own firm, which she has built to a very competitive position over the last ten years. She points out that, despite the lean times, it is the single most personally satisfying accomplishment of her life.

Another of my contributors stresses the importance and satisfaction of a career in not-for-profit, public interest, and legal services practices. She believes that people gravitate to these practices because it gives greater meaning and significance to their lives. It is a way to make a real difference in the lives of others by reducing human suffering, righting a wrong, stopping an unfair practice, or ensuring that justice is not just for some but for all. These practices demand a high level of creativity, hard work, and devotion and can provide great professional and personal satisfaction. (See the Seattle University School of Law Web site, *http://www.law.seattleu. edu/Careers/Public_Interest.xml*, for more information.)

These are very different career paths and represent the vast opportunities open to women with a law degree. There is no one career path that is better than others, but one might be better for you than another at different stages of your life. It is all about choices, and there are so many. The many and varied types of law practices are explored in greater depth in Chapter 4.

In addition to overwhelmingly supporting the decision of women to go to law school, my contributors believe that women are uniquely equipped for careers in the law and make exceptionally fine lawyers. The contributors list the following as important qualities possessed by many women and that make them very proficient at the law: patience and the ability to be active listeners with the goal of building bridges and gaining trust; ability to create a cooperative and less threatening atmosphere for consensus building; attention to detail and thoroughness; ability to multitask and organize; a keen sense of the value of relationship building; receptiveness to new ideas and approaches to problem solving without emphasis on "turf" or ego; a sense of humor; superior interpersonal skills and the ability to work with a variety of personality types; high level of emotional intelligence and compassion; discipline in a variety of settings; ability to be direct with clients and adversaries; tenacity; inclusive and exceptional leadership style; good listening skills; diplomacy; common sense; a deference for utilitarian approaches; a strong sense of justice and the importance of fairness; efficiency and superior ability at time management that comes from experience as working women with children and household responsibilities; empathy and understanding; and a tenacious drive to succeed.

Although it is never a good idea to generalize, it is important to pay close attention to this list. It is impressive and should give you a good sense of which of your skills will serve you well in the profession. I agree with all of those observations and especially appreciate the attributes of problem solving and organization. As pointed out by one of my contributors, a law school friend of mine and a partner in a national law firm, women are instinctive problem solvers. Women seem compelled to find a solution and "not discuss an issue to death, or worse, to paralysis." That quality is additionally valuable because the cost of legal services to clients is significant, and the direct approach that is comfortable to women helps to keep those costs in line.

The value of these attributes can be significant. One of my contributors, a law firm managing partner, tells this story about a woman's important contribution to his practice. He was involved in litigation with an opposing counsel, who he found very difficult to work with. Uncharacteristically, he found himself in screaming matches with this other attorney over most issues, and it became a very frustrating experience. In reflecting on the situation, he determined that there was just too much testosterone between the two male lawyers and that the communication was not going to improve. As a result, he put his female associate in charge of all the communications for the case. Staff was instructed to put all calls from opposing counsel through to the associate, and she handled all the logistics of the case. She worked well with opposing counsel, the screaming subsided, and the working conditions improved all around.

Choosing the Right Law School

Once you have made the decision to pursue a career in the law, choosing the best law school for you also is important. Although I recognize that getting accepted to *any* law school today is very difficult for many applicants, those who have choices for schools should consider where they want to practice after graduation. With the exception of what are regarded as national law schools (mostly those in what has come to be known as the "top tier"), many law schools emphasize the law of the region where the school is located and concentrate on studies that might become very beneficial as preparation for the bar exam for that state.

Additionally, by practicing in the area where you attended law school, you will be able to take the best advantage of networking with former classmates and positioning yourself for case referrals. Generation of new work is the bread and butter of law practice, and you should always be thinking about opportunities to maximize generation and business development opportunities.

The experts recommend that you ask hard questions of both yourself and of the law schools that you are interested in and that are interested in you. Do your research, and find out what the courses of study include and whether there is something in a particular curriculum that especially appeals to you and your interests. To your surprise, it might be human rights or nonprofit work that typically does not pay high salaries but presents very interesting and stimulating practice. Some of the career counselors also admit, against their own interests, that the law school admission staffs most likely will not help you with this analysis. If they are competing with other schools for you, they will tend to put a positive gloss on the rewards of their law school. That is not to say that they will give you inaccurate information, but the information might be delivered with a degree of nuance that is not necessarily in your best interest.

For example, when speaking with admissions staff, you might inquire about the average income of recent graduates of that particular school. The response will most likely be delivered in terms of the high end (currently annual salaries of up to $160,000 for the largest law firms) and a median annual salary of $40,000, with very little emphasis on the low-end salaries. To help you better understand the salary distribution, the National Association for Law Placement (NALP) has analyzed and graphed the distribution of full-time salaries for the classes of 2006 and 2007, including the salary figures for the public sector and nonprofits as well as the private-sector large, medium, and small law firms. Assuming that the trend continues, the graphs make it clear that there are two very different legal employment markets facing current law graduates. This information graphs as a "bimodal curve" and is what many law schools use to convey salary information and to report a median entry-level salary of $40,000. According to this graph, whereas 16 percent of starting salaries were $160,000, 38 percent were $55,000 or less. Collectively, salaries in the $40,000 to $60,000 range accounted for 42 percent of salaries. The NALP explanation of the graph states that this bimodal distribution of starting salaries was not always the case for law school graduates, and that, as recently as 1999, starting salaries for law school graduates showed a much more traditional bell curve. (See *www.NALP.org.*)

As you can see, there are many things to consider in deciding where to attend law school. A law school career counselor points out that it is also imperative that you visit the law school of your choice and sit and talk to students about their curriculum, their professors, student life, and other subjects of interest. If the students are too busy or reluctant to talk to you, that is also an important bit of information.

Some of you might have done all the right things to choose the right law school for you, but your decision turns out to be the wrong one. And, because of the extreme competition for law school admission, some of you will find yourselves in situations where you had to settle for a law school that was not a first choice. This is not the end of the world, and you might not be out of options. There is always the possibility of transferring law schools, and it should not be overlooked. The number of law students transferring to another law school after the first year has increased considerably in recent years, and this result has been described by law school observers as a "dynamic" transfer market. It might not be advisable to stay in an academic setting where you are not happy or comfortable, and transferring could be the answer. However, transferring can be challenging in terms of "fitting in" to a new environment, especially when you have not experienced the bonding with the first-year class that is a very important component of the law school experience. Challenges are meant to be met and overcome, however, and it might be the right choice for you. Go in with your eyes open and realize that the correct standard of measure for the success of your experience is probably not "perfection."

As a law student, you will become very busy, and the temptation will be to forget about further career planning for the three or four years that you are in law school. Do not do this. Keep your eyes on your career objectives during law school and learn from the professionals around you. Part of your law school experience may include employment as a law clerk and summer associate in law firms, and you will be interfacing with legal professionals in these environments as well as in clinical studies as a part of your coursework. You will meet many lawyers and judges who will visit your law school as guests, speakers, and adjunct professors. Ask them questions about their experiences and use that information to enrich your educational journey. They all have been in your situation, and they are not only flattered to be asked, but they also are very willing to be helpful.

Your quest for a career plan throughout law school should be as specific as possible. Take every opportunity to gain experience to help you decide your preferred specialty and employment setting. Explore law clerk positions, internships, and externships, which can be for credit, as vehicles to gain experience and valuable insight. These externships, which are cooperative efforts between law schools and willing employers, can include very interesting jobs at United States Attorney offices, agencies of government, hospitals, and prosecutor's offices, to name just a few. The summer after your first year of law school can be particularly challenging in terms of employment. Most law firms do not hire law students until they have completed the second year of law school, and the opportunities for legal internships and clerkships are limited for first-year students. The first-year course load is difficult and takes rigorous study and discipline, and, after exams are finished in the spring, the most alluring option might be to take off for an extended vacation or a secluded environment to rejuvenate before the fall semester. However, come back to your senses!

It is a tough job market out there. Take advantage of any legal-related summer job or internship to enhance your opportunities for permanent employment later.

If you do all of these things, you will be well on your way to developing a good career plan that you will hone and revise as necessary throughout the years of your education and your practice. To further assist you with advice from your contemporaries, I also recommend an interesting new Web site for gaining information and participating in dialogue with other young women law students and practicing attorneys. Ms. J.D. at *www. ms-jd.org* was created in 2006 by a group of female law students from Boalt Hall (University of California, Berkeley), Cornell, Georgetown, Harvard, NYU, Stanford, UCLA, University of Texas at Austin, the University of Chicago, the University of Michigan, the University of Virginia, and Yale law schools. The online service provides a forum for dialogue and networking among women lawyers and aspiring lawyers and addresses concerns about retention, the role of gender in the progression of many women's legal careers, the lack of representation of women in the highest courts and echelons of the legal community, and other issues facing young women in the profession. It could become a valuable resource for you in developing a career plan, and I encourage you to check it out.

Define Yourself

Women professionals, in general, must learn to define themselves, not be defined by others, especially men who dominate the professions. Trying to level the playing field by becoming one of the boys usually does not work. Women are not going to be accepted at the boys' clubs by acting like men. Believe me, the men know the difference. The aspiring woman might provide some form of entertainment, but she rarely will be accepted in ways that will further her career. As pointed out by one of my young contributors, "Too often woman lawyer trailblazers that preceded us had to curse like sailors and swill scotch to hang with the boys.

Our generation of women lawyers can embrace our natural attributes and, not only survive, but thrive!" Well said. A woman lawyer today will gain acceptance if she is a force to be reckoned with on her own terms. Quite simply, by a good show of competence and perseverance, the male lawyers would rather have her with them than against them. Embrace the differences and make them work for you, but don't dress like them and don't smoke their cigars. You will look foolish doing both.

Defining yourself is especially important for law students as they look forward to choosing a practice after law school. It is a temptation to look at a job description, view it with intrigue and excitement, and allow it to influence your decision about a situation that might not be right for you. Remember to define yourself and stay true to your objectives. One of my contributors, a law school career counselor, also warns against allowing peer pressure from fellow law students to affect your choices or to undermine your self-definition. She reports that she sees this often and regrets that the pressure to "achieve the prestige" interferes with good personal and professional choices for law students. Another of my contributors, a male managing partner, simply says, "Do not try to be what you are not." He urges you to define your skill set and to find an employer where your skills can work to the advantage of the firm or organization. Choose the setting where you want to practice and do not let someone else "put" you there.

Another law school career counselor recommends that women law students seek out conversations with women practitioners in appealing areas of practice and professional settings. Young women law students must be willing to ask the tough questions about day-to-day life as a woman lawyer in a particular practice setting, including questions about work-life balance if that is a concern. If you take this honest and candid approach, those conversations can be very instructive and valuable.

The most important consideration in defining yourself is deciding what will make you happy so that you will continue in the practice to satisfy your own goals and to benefit the profession. Happiness, however, is relative and should not be confused with perfection. The culture of law practice is founded on work as its own reward. As such, it is very demanding work, but it can be immensely gratifying. My work experience tells me that there is no perfect work situation in the law. No matter how satisfying the job situation, it is still "work" and not "play." The most that you can hope for is an enjoyable job situation that comes closest to play, but with awesome responsibility and grave consequences for mistakes. If you achieve that, I will be extremely happy for you.

There are many definitions of success, and finding success can involve a variety of career paths. According to Lauren Stiller Rikleen in her book *Ending the Gauntlet: Removing Barriers to Women's Success in the Law* (Thomson Legalworks, 2006), it is time to redefine what it means to be successful in the legal profession. She offers hope that the legal profession will eventually allow the opportunity for all lawyers to succeed within the context of serving clients, raising healthy children, caring for elderly parents, and participating in communities. These are admirable goals, and I, too, hope that they can be achieved. However, to accomplish this end result of recognizing different models of success and allowing for professionals to flourish under those new models, the retention rates for women, especially, will have to improve. It is a bit like the chicken and the egg. The retention rates cannot improve until the work-life issues are effectively addressed, and the work-life issues cannot be effectively addressed until there are enough women remaining in the profession to help bring about the changes.

There are many models of success, and success must be viewed on a continuum. What is successful in one setting might not be successful in another. Success always should be viewed subjectively and in terms of the difficulty presented by a set of circumstances. You can find success as a part-time lawyer as easily as you can find success as a full-time lawyer. You also can find success by leaving the practice altogether. The definition of success will depend on the definition of your needs. Only you can define those. Settling for less when the circumstances require it does not reduce our effectiveness and should not reduce our pride. Sometimes, just surviving is the definition of success.

It is interesting to note what some of my contributors consider to be their greatest accomplishments. It represents a broad definition of success, and you might be able to find your goals and objectives somewhere in the particular examples.

One contributor, a judge, says that her greatest accomplishment is having a positive effect on society through her decisions and adjudications. Another private practitioner says that her greatest accomplishment was a successful pro bono representation of a Somalian woman who was seeking political asylum. Similarly, a partner in a worldwide law firm, with many significant cases and victories, cites her successful pro bono representation of the female employees of a correctional institute in a class action sexual harassment lawsuit. She spent more than a year working on the case and was one of the lead trial attorneys in a five-week jury trial in federal court. She recalls that the working conditions for those women were terrible and that she had a unique opportunity to make a difference in their lives.

A young contributor cites a successful negotiation of a real estate deal, explaining the documents to older male partners of a big firm and getting a congratulatory call from the client as a great accomplishment. The greatest accomplishment for another is being a successful sole practitioner for 16 years, and yet another partner with three children cites becoming a partner in her firm as her greatest accomplishment. She says that it was extraordinarily difficult and that she wasn't sure that she could do it once she realized the personal discipline and commitment that it would require. Another contributor cites the "big" government settlement that is still referred to as "her case," and still another found great satisfaction in not allowing others to define success for her or to limit what she thought she could accomplish. Others cite their persistence in reentering the profession, in some cases more than once, after leaving for personal and family responsibilities as noteworthy accomplishments. It appears that just being able to say that they "hung in" under difficult circumstances and cared enough to try again means more to them than the big case or the impressive title. Another contributor cites the 14-month trial in which she was lead counsel and successfully defended the United States government against a claim of between $150 million and $200 million in damages. The case was affirmed on appeal. Her efforts were featured in a cover story in the *ABA Journal* in 1989 and continue to represent state-of-the-art use of technology two decades later.

These are all noteworthy successes and are very diverse in their focus and appeal. Some contributors have told me that it was the hardest question to answer because there are so many definitions of accomplishment and success. Others have said that it was easy to identify the simplest thing that brought them the most pride. The answer really does not matter. It is the process of looking back on a career and examining what it has meant to you. Hopefully, one day, you, too, will experience that satisfaction and great feeling of accomplishment in the legal profession. If you pay attention to the lessons in this book, my money is on you.

The Economy Matters—A Lot

How does a bad economy affect lawyers and law firms? Let me count the ways! It is a trickle-down theory, from the impact of a bad economy on clients, to the impact of a bad economy on lawyers and law firms, to the impact of a bad economy on law students. It all came crashing down in the fall of 2008, after a decade of a strong economy that had seen unprecedented profits in business and resulted in a stock market continually on the rise and profits and salaries for partners in big law firms at levels at one time unimaginable. Law firms were experiencing tremendous growth and previously undocumented demand for services. In 1985, there were approximately 40,000 lawyers in the *National Law Journal*'s list of the 250 largest U.S. firms (the NLJ 250), and 20 years later, in 2005, there were nearly 117,000 lawyers in these firms. In 1987, the average size of an NLJ 250 law firm was 194; 20 years later, the average was 513 lawyers. The traditional gap between law firm starting salaries and government and public interest jobs became a chasm, and first-year salaries at top firms across the country went above $160,000, compared with $48,000 to start for state and local prosecutors and $40,000 for legal services lawyers. New associates were outearning the judges they appeared before ("With the Downturn, It's Time to Rethink the Legal Profession," *The New York Times*, April 2, 2009).

The economy was a burgeoning bubble, and it burst. The reasons for the imploding of the economy are not critical to this discussion and will be debated and refined for many years to come. The important fact for the purposes of this book is that it happened, and the impact on the profession of law was, in some cases, alarming. In a Bureau of National Affairs, Inc. (BNA) *Corporate Counsel Weekly*, December 31, 2008, interview with Jacquelyn Finn and Paula Campbell Millian of Finn and Associates, LLC, a legal search firm in the Washington, DC area, Finn observed that, after 30 years in the business, she has never seen a job market as bad as the one that began in the fall of 2008 and continued into 2009. As you will see, however, it is not all bad news. Difficult and challenging times also present opportunities for positive change.

As this book goes to press, the economy continues to be weak, and law firms and lawyers are being impacted in a big way. This dose of harsh reality and a downward spiraling economy must be addressed early on because it affects so many decisions and so much of what is discussed later in the book. In a good economy, much is possible. In a bad economy, opportunities can be limited. Many of the options addressed in the first chapters of this book will depend on a healthy economy. For example, how much leverage you have in negotiating the terms of an employment contract will be very much affected by the economy and the laws of supply and demand. How much confidence you will feel about job locations will also be affected, as will your choice of specialty and practice venue. It could be a difficult couple of years before the economy starts rolling again and knowing what to expect is helpful.

You also should be aware that many of the observations included in this section are unique to large firm practice and that the effect on smaller firms may not be as significant. After all, what happens to a large law firm in New York City, Washington, DC, Chicago, or Los Angeles during difficult economic times might be very different than what happens to a smaller firm located in a more remote area of the country. This, then, is the "view from the top," although I do try to provide insight into the effects around the country whenever possible. However, how the bad economy affects smaller law firms with differing structural frameworks and business demands remains to be seen. You also need to keep in mind that this information only applies to law firm practices and that there are many opportunities in the law beyond the law firm, as you will read in Chapter 4. Please keep those things in mind as you read on.

Law firms are changing as the result of the economic downturn, and layoffs and reductions in forces are reported on a daily basis. It is not your father's law firm any more, or even your mother's, for that matter. There is a paradigm shift under way, and firms are rethinking the traditional practice. They are rethinking how they pay employees and partners and how they bill—including alternative fee arrangements, lower per unit and per project costs, and entertaining client requests for proposals (RFPs) for law firm services. They are also rethinking whether they can absorb hiring associates at past rates, whether they should increase lateral attorney hiring (hiring lawyers with experience in areas where the firm wants to expand the practice), and, in some cases, whether they should reduce health and disability benefits, passing those costs on to the lawyers. Some contributors report that large law firms are changing from the triangular model, where partners leverage off the work of junior lawyers, who bill out at reduced rates, to a more quadrangle model, where there are a variety of ways of measuring competency and fee arrangements beyond the billable hour. Those same commentators say that this is an ideal time for law firms to change—because they can. There is less pressure on law firms today to stay the way they are and have been for so many years because the legal job market is much less dynamic than in the past and lawyers typically are not leaving to join the competition for reasons of better compensation and benefits. Lawyers are staying put in this economy and hoping for the best. As a result, law firms have the opportunity to focus on investing in the trust that has been broken over time between the firm and its clients and between the firm and its lawyers. The reasons for the broken trust might stem from lack of appreciation for legal talent and for the value of clients in a burgeoning economy that produced false security and false expectations. Whatever the reason, most commentors agree that it might be a good time for law firms to assess and reassess.

Under the pressure of the downturn in the economy, law firms are not experiencing the same need for client services as in the past, and they are responding to budget constraints. Clients are not able to borrow money and obtain credit as in the past, and business activities in many areas have ground to a near halt. Correspondingly, layoffs in law firms are at an unprecedented level as revenue pressures lead to operational improvements to preserve profitability. In April 2009, more than 3,000 lawyers had lost their jobs across the country since the first of that year—3,000 lawyers in four months. It happened at all levels of practice, but it hit large law firms particularly hard. As a result of a combination of factors, several of the largest law firms in the nation went out of business, including Heller Ehrman, a venerable 500-plus-lawyer firm founded in 1890. Others merged or were acquired just before the bank called the loans and effectively locked the doors to the firms. Firms that had participated in the merger and acquisition mania of the last decade—the mania that drove big firms to become bigger, drove up salaries and fees, and resulted in huge overhead and loss of flexibility from locked-in expenditures—suddenly had to pay the piper, which meant employee layoffs, salary reductions (in many cases based on numbers of billable hours), reduced bonuses, pay freezes, increased cash contributions for both equity and nonequity partners (which sometimes eliminated nonequity partners entirely), and a host of other painful measures. In addition, collections became very slow and, as corporate clients went out of business, unpaid law firm receivables were assigned positions in bankruptcy proceedings. Firms needed to shift gears from a growth model to one of increased efficiency and cost-effectiveness.

The news from the fall of 2008 to the spring of 2009 was grim, and the daily accounts on legal tabloids like *www.abovethelaw.com* and Web sites like *www.Americanlawyer.com* were depressing. (These sources can be very useful in keeping the pulse of the legal profession in such challenging times, and a lot of what is published there was under the surface in the past. In general, this is probably a positive development, and it certainly is a useful research tool. Other good sources are "Churn" at AMLAW DAILY on the American Lawyer Web site and the Wall Street Journal blog at *blogs.wsj.com*.) These sources reported fear at every level of law practice as lawyers tried to tighten belts at firms to save the business, tighten belts at home, where budgets were being impacted by reduced salaries and partner draws, or, worse yet, job loss. Although these sources rarely report on issues that do not affect large law firms, colleagues across the country report changes to practices in small communities and in remote areas, as well. One commentator, who practices in a small community in the West, states that, although the bad economy has not yet impacted his small personal injury practice, he thinks that it is highly possible that his entire geographic area lags as much as two years behind the rest of the nation and that firms like his will feel the effects in the future. He further adds that his area never really sees the "great" times and that the hope is that they will not experience the "horrible" times either. He does note, however, that firms of between 10 and 15 lawyers in the larger communities in his state are feeling the effects of the economic downturn, especially those that have done a lot of construction and real estate and development law in the past. Another sole practitioner in the West bluntly states that, "There is no business coming through the door, and the practice of law in rural America is at an absolute standstill. The only attorneys I know who seem to be making a living are the litigators and plaintiff's counsel dealing with insurance companies that are trying to low-ball settlements. It is definitely time to go fishing." Another commentator in a small to medium-size Midwest firm says that billings have been flat and that the only reason collectibles have increased is that the firm made the decision to accept credit card payments. He said that the litigation group at his firm has been "slow" and that this has been a surprise because bad economic times generally result in increased litigation. However, the litigation practice of his firm centers around workers' compensation claims, and he said that employees seem reluctant to report injuries because they do not want to draw attention to themselves in case there is a mass layoff in the future. He said that the business and transactional practice in his firm has shifted from mergers and acquisitions to collections and foreclosures, not surprisingly. He further reported that, although his firm will hire the summer associates from the summer of 2008, they likely will not interview summer associates for the summer of 2010 because they see the opportunity for picking up lateral hires instead. They also have frozen hourly rates, as a marketing tool, and he notes that historically his firm has always tried to "bill for value," which has usually meant cutting bills to reflect the real value of the work. Interestingly, he added that this practice has resulted in the ability of the lawyers to make a decent living, but "none of us are planning to move to Palm Beach or Palm Springs any time soon."

The news is not very different from the South. One commentator reports that, in the areas where development and land use was booming some short years ago, the volume of legal work related to these projects is "way down." It is also reported that the general practice firms in these areas are struggling. Bank-related practices are finding that the foreclosure work that is related to the economic downturn is not going to the local firms as much as it used to. The megabanks now use megafirms, and the local attorneys—many of whom have been on the board of directors of regional banks for years—no longer get the work. This commentator also reports that the family law practice is down because unhappily married people can't afford lawyers and are stuck in homes they can't afford to sell at current market value. Another commentator in a larger firm in the South reports that the reduction in state spending has impacted practices across the area. The uncertainty about the use of federal stimulus money has impacted school projects and economic development projects, including bond work, to name just a few. Even public defenders are at risk in terms of the public funds available to pay those attorneys. As you can see, this economic downturn has a long reach.

Additional transformational changes are looming on the horizon, and it will be a "wait and see" exercise to see how deep firms go in reconciling the bottom line during tough times. For instance, will there be an end to paying all attorneys at the same experience level equally? It might be that firms will change the approach to a combination of salary, variations in billable hour rates, and bonuses. There could be different expectations with different results.

The impact on recent law graduates and particularly the 3Ls and 2Ls has been significant. The 3Ls, who had accepted job offers, were suddenly confronted with changed promises. Firms realized that they were not able to add additional overhead from associate salaries and benefits, and "creative" associate programs started popping up. At first, it was only from a few firms, then it took over as the norm. It was a new reality that toppled the expectations of law students across the country. The programs had different names, but there was a consistent theme. Whether they were called sidebar programs, furlough programs, or paid leaves of absence, (all euphemisms for "we don't want you now"), the message was the same: If you will just go away for a while and not drag down our bottom line—and we don't have work for you anyway—we will see you in six months or a year when we hope things are better. Some of these programs reached beyond incoming associates to more senior associates who might be interested in alternative venues for a while. Most of these programs had financial incentives, some as high as $45,000 to $75,000 for those associates deferred to September 2010, and included reimbursement for the costs of bar review courses and bar entrance fees. Some of them also included assistance from the law firm in finding positions in pro bono and public service jobs during the interim period and included substantial monthly payment from the law firm for those involved in approved programs. So, associate lawyers and new graduates were looking at a defined amount of downtime in exchange for reduced pay. For some it was a welcomed respite of reduced stress time, but, for many others, it was a problem because the student loans were lurking, and their parents' 401K or other retirement program had been wiped out by a "bear of all bears" stock market that seemed to plummet lower on a daily basis. The legal tabloids and blogs were full of depressing stories about out-of-work lawyers and disenchanted law students.

In case you think that this only affected law students at the 3L level, think again. As the 3Ls, who were graduating in May 2009, were being deferred to law firm start dates in January 2010 or even later into the fall of 2010, the 2Ls were beginning to get the dismal picture. It was now a competition between 3Ls and 2Ls for jobs. If the 3Ls were deferred a year, it meant that those jobs would not be available to 2Ls after graduation. At the 2009 annual NALP conference, Frank Kimball, former hiring partner of McDermott, Will & Emory and founder of Kimball Professional Management, opined that the tactic of deferring incoming associates, either for a few months or for a year, "has the potential to be a mess" because it is not certain whether firms will have the capacity to absorb when two classes show up at once. Law schools have responded to the deferral problem in a variety of ways. Some schools established master's programs for deferral victims to concentrate on the practical skills that those lawyers would have gained in their first year of law practice. Other law schools started programs to employ deferred associates as mentors or assistants at the law school. In some cases, these programs might qualify for the stipend programs that law firms were supporting for deferred associates who chose public interest jobs, and, at best, it is likely to be a case-by-case evaluation. Law schools also started to reach out to alumni and faculty in a much greater way to assist graduates and deferred associates in finding positions.

Now that you understand the new economic realism, what does this mean to you? Here I am reminded of a cartoon that appeared in the *Parade Magazine* section of Sunday newspapers all over the county in the spring of 2009. In the cartoon, two caterpillars are head-to-head on a leaf, and one says to the other, "If this downward trend continues, we may have to cancel our plan to turn into butterflies." For the caterpillars, that would be a radical and life-altering event. However, you do not have to make such rash decisions. Rather, you should consider the consequences of the economy and make informed choices.

For starters, a down economy means that you as law students, recent law graduates, and associate lawyers do not have the leverage that similarly situated job seekers have had in the past. According to one of my contributors, the days of "I do not do windows" (associates complaining about the quality of the work and the failure to meet expectations) are over. It is a buyer's market now more than ever. You either want a job or you do not. No one is taking the time to try to convince you or woo you. It is a new definition of tough love, and you might not end up where you expected to be. In this market, you will have to do whatever it takes to create and protect job security. Use this time to gain experience in a variety of practice areas, even if it means that you have to work on things that do not interest you as much. If you want to be considered to be a "player" in the firm at a later date, after you have gained more experience and a little gray hair, be a team player from the beginning. (The importance of being a team player is discussed further in Chapter 4.)

As a result, many of you will have to determine how to deal with the sidebar and furlough programs or other leave of absence programs that will be offered to you by firms deferring your start date after law school graduation. You will have to decide whether you take the minimum compensation and head for Tahiti for six months to a year or whether you take the maximum compensation and head to a pro bono or public service position. It might be tempting to take a rest when you did not expect it or might not get it again for many years, but you need to remember that actions have consequences. Consider all of the options and make the right choice.

Law students and 3Ls interviewing for jobs also will have to consider the current economy in assuring top grades and in demonstrating commitment. Firms are hiring fewer associates in this economic climate, and the competition for the top jobs is heightened. It is the classic example of separating the wheat from the chaff in the big law firm setting. Opportunities to demonstrate your talents might be affected. Some law firms are shortening summer associate programs and substituting more "content-focused" experiences for the past experiences of over-the-top sporting events and cocktail parties in lavish settings. Firms are paring back these things and trimming the price tags. In the long run, this might be a good thing because it will provide a more realistic view of law firm life.

The few firms that provide any summer associate experience for 1Ls might be cutting those programs entirely or not calling those students back for the critical 2L summer experience so that they can get a look at more students before the hiring decisions.

Law students and law graduates will also have to consider the economic environment in choosing the practice specialties they wish to pursue. Many of these specialties have been impacted by the economy, and it will be important to be flexible. Bruce MacEwen, founder of the online legal and economic newsletter *Adam Smith, Esq.*, has stated that practices like corporate transactions and mergers and acquisitions are not activity centers at the moment (Georgetown Law, *Res Ipsa Loquitor*, "The State of the Legal Profession," Spring/Summer 2009). The NALP's 2009 Annual Conference addressed this issue. The managing director of Hildebrandt International, a leading consultant to law firm management, reported that activity in the bankruptcy practices for large law firms was up for 2008, which was no surprise in the current economic times, and that the securities regulation practice also was on the rise. Although he also reported that the litigation practices for these firms had fallen off, generally speaking, most of the commentators and contributors agree that litigation will remain in a growth mode. Law school career counselors and lawyer placement specialists also report that other kinds of regulatory practices are up, including health care, Food and Drug Administration, and banking, and that work related to corporate investigations and bailout monitoring will be on the rise. They also report that there could be more work in the labor, environmental, and energy areas, particularly where those practices are affected by federal stimulus money and the projects supported by those funds. (For more information, see Interview with Finn and Associates, LLC in BNA, *Corporate Counsel Weekly*, December 31, 2008.)

Prospective law students also will be impacted. Because the economy is also impacting hiring for college graduates, many of them will apply to law schools and business schools as a "safe haven" to wait out the economic downturn in the atmosphere of academic incubation. With an increased number of applications, competition for admission to these graduate programs will become even more intense than in the past. It has been reported that both Yale Law School and the University of Texas School of Law are experiencing an 8 percent increase in applications ("Best Defense? Seeking a Haven in Law School," *www.wsj.com*, March 19, 2009).

The past is the past. Now let's look at the future. What can we expect for the legal industry in the near future? Most commentators expect that it will not be pretty and that there will be no quick turnaround for the legal business. It is predicted that there may be some "uptick" possible in certain practice areas like bankruptcy, labor and employment, regulatory, and infrastructure and stimulus-related legal work. As a result, you might want to make a note to yourself to follow the federal stimulus money that was allocated by Congress in the early months of 2009. Jobs are likely to be created in those areas of discipline. However, even if there is an improvement in the short run, this is not likely to help law firms as much as you might think. The law firm receipts of 2009 are not likely to have much impact on law firm operations until 2010. The demand for legal services is also predicted to be flat for at least 2009. Even though there might be some modest increase, it likely will be offset by the discounting of fees to assure competitiveness. More layoffs are predicted, as well as other cost-cutting measures. All of these things have dire consequences for jobs and profitability.

So, there you have the stark reality of the recession that began in the fall of 2008. By now you must be ready for some good news. The good news, if there is any, is that this economic environment could create opportunities for women. After all, according to the panelists at the WomenLegal conference in New York City in April 2009 (presented by Ark Group/WomenLegal Magazine), the change revolution started with women who forced firms to address a different way of doing business and flexible work arrangements. Now, the revolution has spread to more of the fundamental elements that law firms and lawyers have accepted as the norm for too long. The end result might be a very different legal environment than we ever expected or contemplated a few short years ago. As law firms take steps to reduce occupancy costs and create options for doing work from a variety of settings, it is possible that part-time, flex-time and "virtual" employees who are working from remote sites could benefit in terms of flexible work schedules. There also is a great opportunity for women attorneys in full-time practices to step up and contribute to management, and women should be raising their hands to volunteer. It is clearly time for law firms to give up on stale ideas, and women can help lead the way. They are good managers and excellent relationship builders, and both will be critical to winding out of the morass of the economic downturn. Justice Sandra Day O'Connor was quoted as saying that she did not always agree with Justice Thurgood Marshall, but having him in the room made her look at things differently on issues of discrimination and race. Similarly, just having a woman in the room with fellow decision makers can make others think about the problems from a different perspective.

Women might also benefit from other structural and transformational changes. Some of the changes will involve alternative fee arrangements that will require more efficiency and will not be dependent on the billable hour. Women typically have developed high efficiency levels in response to work-life demands, and their relationship-building skills will be key to the new fee structures and arrangements with clients. Women's participation on legal teams also is being viewed very critically by corporations and other clients where women have risen to high levels of management and power. Many women in-house lawyers and managers expect diversity on their outside legal teams, and diversity surveys are being required by these clients. Surveys are now requiring disclosure of which lawyers worked on a representation and how many hours each lawyer worked. Gone are the days of putting a woman lawyer or a minority attorney on a project only to create the perception of diversity. It is now important to the client to see the actual participation, and what is important to the client must be important to the law firm. According to Marc Gary, executive vice president and general counsel of Fidelity Investments, as many as 500 corporate counsel have issued statements, in both 1999 and 2004, pledging to consider law firm diversity as a factor in hiring outside counsel (Georgetown Law, *Res Ipsa Loquitor*, Spring/Summer 2009, p. 26).

In this new law firm environment, women have the opportunity to exercise their competency and their imaginations to take on issues and to show management that they are loyal members of the team. Women lawyers should become more proactive and address issues in an institutional way. They should challenge themselves to come up with programs that will put the firm in a good light with clients, and they should volunteer to put a team together to address the issues. It will provide value to the firm, and it will showcase women's leadership skills. There are many opportunities for leadership in these challenging economic times, and women should pursue quality leadership roles and shy away from the traditional roles that have been available to them in the past. It will not be easy, but it will be wise. Throughout the process, you will have to remember that first and foremost, you must keep up your billable hours to have influence and credibility. After all, it is a business, as you will discover in Chapter 4.

There also might be another silver lining to the economic cloud of doom, and it will affect both male and female lawyers. As pointed out by Deborah Epstein Henry, founder of Flex-Time Lawyers LLC, at the 2009 NALP Annual Conference, an enhanced work-life balance could be one of the results of this law firm restructuring. Now that the economy is down, there is a new emphasis on value. It might be that legal employers no longer need to pay all lawyers the same amount of money for the same amount of required work. Instead, we could see lawyers selecting lower hourly targets and receiving compensation that reflects their reduced workload. Programs like this can be a great benefit to an associate with extensive commitments outside work for family and other responsibilities.

I would like to think that you feel better now. More than that, I would like to think that many of these problems related to the economy will be over and old news by the time that you read this book. That would be the best result *if*, in the process, law firms and lawyers changed the way that they do business to benefit not only the clients but also the law firms as institutions. That might include lower pay for lawyers, but is that necessarily a bad thing? It might mean that associates will not need to work the grueling hours that many have encountered, and it might also mean less pressure to go into private practice for law graduates who want to do something more personally fulfilling. It also could have a beneficial effect on law school tuition and keep other costs controlled so that students do not graduate with such enormous amounts of unmanageable debt. More schools might go the way of Northwestern Law School, which recently became the first top-tier law school to reduce the law program to two years. In doing that, it is possible that law schools also will have to put a greater emphasis on practical skills to get the most benefit from the reduced course load. These results will pay homage to the old adage that a financial crisis is a terrible thing to waste.

Enough about the dismal and disturbing economy. It is time to move on. However, please remember that the economy and its effects must be one of the filters through which you view the advice and lessons of this book. It will be your responsibility as the reader to make certain adjustments where the economy plays an important role in terms of opportunities and options. Good luck.

3

Women today can have it all—family, children, a profession, whatever they want. They are smart and accomplished like men and nothing can hold them back.
—Enthusiastic but Naive Young Woman

Be Realistic About Your Expectations

The issues discussed in this chapter can be very weighty and difficult to resolve. They involve personal philosophies and strategies, and it might take several attempts to arrive at a satisfactory solution. You likely will have many stops and starts, but, after reading what follows, you will be better equipped to address the issues.

Being realistic about your expectations is, perhaps, the most bitter pill for many women attorneys and women law students to swallow: You are not a man, and many of you will have to adjust your expectations accordingly. No matter how you view it, the law is still a male-dominated profession, and the norm is full-time practice. Realistically, in the private sector, full-time practice can be at least six days a week, ten hours a day. As a result, your experiences as a woman in the profession are going to be different than the experiences of an equally talented man in the profession, if, in addition to a career as an attorney, you also want a home, a successful marriage, and happy, well-adjusted children. Contrary to what was told to women in the 1960s, who flocked to law schools in large numbers during the women's liberation movement and who worshiped Betty Freidan and Gloria Steinem, you cannot have it all. You can have all of it some of the time, you can have some of it all of the time, but you cannot have all of it all of the time. You will have to be flexible and adjust your expectations to have most of it most of the time.

Although it is difficult for a law student to predict the circumstances in any particular work environment prior to becoming an employee there, thinking about the flexibility that you might need in the future should start long before the employment commitment. It is difficult to determine the balance that will work best for you at specific times of your professional life, but the inquiry should become part of your self-assessment if you think that you will need flexibility in the future. This is an ongoing dialogue for most young women, and the truth is that the specific terms of employment will have to be negotiated between an employer and an employee to meet mutual needs. The more you know about the issues and the way they are being handled in the workplace, the better.

The "Having It All" Debate

The "having it all" issue has been vigorously debated for the last 40 years, and that debate is likely to continue far into the future. Women lawyers, especially, tend to be smart and competent and they instinctively want the same opportunities as men. The general discussion took an interesting turn during the 2008 presidential campaign when Senator John McCain, the Republican candidate for president, chose Governor Sarah Palin of Alaska as his running mate and vice presidential candidate. At 44 years of age, Governor Palin had five children, including a baby with Down syndrome and a pregnant and unmarried teenager, and she claimed to have an effective work-life balance that would allow her to successfully carry out the responsibilities of vice president and to assume the responsibilities of president if the need arose. The debate was especially important because, at 72 years of age, Senator McCain would have been the oldest president elected in U.S. history, and concerns about his health and the possibility of the vice president having to step up to assume the responsibilities of the president were real. Governor Palin was photographed often surrounded by her family and holding her newborn. She offered information during interviews that included her habit of breastfeeding the baby in the governor's office and the inconvenience of a breast pump. For many Americans, it was too much information, but it certainly put the issue front and center. The debate was viewed by most people as fair and square because Governor Palin had injected motherhood into the campaign from her first speech at the Republican National Convention when she identified herself as a "hockey mom" and she surrounded herself with her husband and children on the campaign trail.

At first, the American people, especially those from hard-working middle America, relished the image of Sarah Palin as Superwoman, and I can recall at least one half-page colored image of Governor Palin in the *Washington Post* depicting her as Rosie the Riveter of World War II fame, with biceps flexed and the slogan "We Can Do It" above her head. These were heady times for many American women who identified with Governor Palin and her middle America lifestyle. These women were empowered by the thought that someone like them could become vice president, and perhaps president, of the United States. However, with time, the blush was off the rose as many of these same supporters started to see her less as their ideal but more as "like them," and they realized that they, as mothers of young children, especially children with disabilities, were not capable of taking over the reins of government at the national level. As the failing economy in the fall of 2008 took over the campaign spotlight, however, the "having it all" debate fell to a secondary position. At that point, women worried less about having it all and more about putting food on the table for their families.

The debate has not died, however, and that is a good thing. The same *Washington Post* article that included the image of Governor Palin as the Rosie the Riveter look-alike stated:

> Palin has reignited the never-resolved mommy wars—not the old ones between mothers who stay home and those who work, but the ones inside every mother who has a choice. Should a woman nourish her personal ambitions to succeed at her career while trying to raise a family? Was it selfish or superhuman of Palin to go back to work almost immediately after her son's birth? Was it fair to her constituents, the residents of Alaska? After all, most mothers remember barely functioning from lack of sleep when they had new babies. Is it anybody's business? (*Washington Post,* Style, September 12, 2008)

These are core issues, and I suspect our granddaughters and their granddaughters will be grappling with them for a very long time.

Would the work-life balance have worked out for Sarah Plain if Republicans had won? Perhaps it works for the Governor of Alaska, and perhaps it does not. Interestingly, as this book goes to press, Govenor Palin has announced her intention not to run for a second term as governor of Alaska for personal reasons. Whether the work-life balance "works" is completely subjective and depends on how satisfied the woman is with the result. It is not what the woman says in speeches or the appeal of photo ops with children and family. Many women seemingly can do it all, but doing it is not the same as doing it to the woman's own satisfaction. Trying to do it all under the circumstances of work-life and family constraints can lead to a great deal of guilt for some women. On the other hand, achieving career excellence and recognition in the profession is so satisfying for other women that they are willing to reduce expectations on the family side.

For some interesting reading on this subject, I recommend *How Can I Get Through to You? Closing the Intimacy Gap Between Men and Women* by Terrance Real (Scribner 2002) for the proposition that historically men have not had to change to accommodate family considerations and that, by contrast, everything has been expected of the women to make the work-life-family scenario work. This book proposes that women should not be expected to change any longer. As long as women do everything, men will let them. It is really up to women to end this pattern and to demand equality in this situation.

This work-life discussion might sound old-fashioned to you, and it is understandable that you might think that nothing will ever deter you from your chosen career of the law. I respect that perspective, and I remember it well. However, many of you will find that the defining moment for you and your professional aspirations will be the first time you lay eyes on your newborn baby. That moment is likely to give way to a cosmic shift, and the earth will move while you fall in love all over again, as overly sentimental as that might sound. With that one exception, you might be just like your male colleagues and able to attain the same professional results without interrupting or reshaping your career. For many of you, though, having a family life and becoming a mother will change things, and you might find the need to redefine your priorities. This approach might feed into time-honored female stereotypes, but it can be argued that there is merit in accepting certain stereotypes when those stereotypes reflect a reality that is not likely to change. Author Leo Tolstoy reflected on motherhood in his novella *Family Happiness*. Although written more than a century ago, it remains apropos today: "A new feeling of love for my children and the father of my children laid the foundation of a new life and a quite different happiness."

The example of former Justice Sandra Day O'Connor is worthy of consideration in this context. In her book, *Sandra Day O'Connor: How the First Woman on the Supreme Court Became Its Most Influential Justice*, (2005, Ecco), author Joan Biskupic chronicles a life that should be very instructive to all women lawyers on the work-life issue and for its examples of perseverance and resolve. The author portrays Justice O'Connor as a feminist who made the decision to work from within a male-dominated system rather than to rebel against it—and she succeeded. Quoting Justice O'Connor's brother Alan, the author paints a picture of a little girl who was never afraid of work and never afraid of a challenge—one who led by her performance and her comments, not by her complaints (Biskupic at 53). She had gone through life allowing challenges to shape her and to take her places where other people would not go (Biskupic at 19).

Sandra Day graduated from Stanford University Law School in 1952, in the top 10 percent of her class and with membership on the board of editors of the *Stanford Law Review*. Even with those accomplishments, she did not receive any offers from the law firms where she had applied for jobs; rather, she was offered a position as a legal secretary by a large California law firm. She declined that offer and eventually took a position in California local government as a deputy county attorney with San Mateo County. After her third son was born in 1962, she spoke at Arizona State University and addressed the work-life issue as follows: "Do marriage, families, and careers for women mix? It depends, of course, on the personalities of the husband and the wife and the special needs of the children. For me, the answer has been emphatically 'Yes.' The ultimate happiness to me is the feeling of fulfillment which comes from doing constructive work for the good of society and mankind" (Biskupic at 31).

In addition to intellectual acumen, sustainable drive, and an engaging and likeable personality, the key to the success of Justice O'Connor in achieving such extraordinary heights within the context of work, life, and family was her remarkable ability to focus on her professional work in spite of personal issues like childrearing and illness. She had achieved the right "mix" for herself, and it allowed her to have a career that included private practitioner, state legislator, appeals court judge, and associate justice on the United States Supreme Court, where she became the swing vote on some of the most important cases to come before the Court during her tenure. In fact, in the last years that she was on the bench and when Justice Rehnquist was the Chief Justice, the Court was often referred to as the O'Connor Court.

So, when Justice O'Connor announced her plans to retire from the Supreme Court in July 2005, at a time when her influence was at its greatest, some women reacted harshly and contended that she was betraying the feminist cause. For O'Connor, who had once stated that working women should put their families first (Biskupic at 336), it should not have been a surprise to anyone. Her husband, John, was suffering from Alzheimer's disease, and she felt that he needed her. That was that.

Justice O'Connor's story is very important, especially for its demonstration of the tension between love of home life and family and the desire to indulge in important and satisfying professional work. It should stand to remind us that there are many things that cannot be predicted in life and that all we can expect of ourselves is to try to remain true to objectives and do the best we can under the circumstances.

Biskupic's book also presents a different and contrasting female role model. In describing United States Supreme Court Justice Ruth Bader Ginsburg and comparing her to O'Connor, the author describes how O'Connor and Ginsburg differed on the work-life issues. Ginsburg, the mother of two children, also had challenged female stereotypes. She did not cook, for instance, and she recalled reprimanding the principal of her son's school for telephoning her whenever the boy was in trouble. "This child has two parents," she told the principal. "Please alternate calls for conferences." She believed that women would not be liberated until men took equal care of children. She is quoted as saying, "If I had an affirmative action program to design, it would be to give men every incentive to be concerned about the rearing of children" (Biskupic at 260).

There you have it: two contrasting role models and two remarkable results. Both women found the mix that was most comfortable and achieved to great heights within that context. You, too, will have to find the mix that works for you.

For women who want to have children, when to start a family is a great concern, and young women lawyers are no exception. Often-asked questions include whether it is better for the woman attorney to "get it over with" during the last boring semester of law school and while studying for the bar exam or whether it is better to wait until later once the woman has established a practice. I heard from a young woman at one law school that the number of pregnant third-year students was on the rise to get pregnancy and delivery over with early and hit the ground running at the first job after graduation. There are other women lawyers who are very glad that they got the first challenging years of their practice behind them without concern for child care and that they waited to have children a little later in their careers. This is a very difficult decision and it will depend on the particular circumstances that you share with your partner and the goals that you set for your family life. No matter what route you choose, or if you come up with some kind of a compromise, it will be a very demanding time in your life.

However, ask most attorney-mothers and you are likely to hear that the decision to have a child was very rewarding, in spite of the fact that it complicated things on the professional end. In fact, it appears that the delayed professional ascent for women because of child care responsibilities renders the advancement of women all the more remarkable. You are also likely to hear that, regardless of the age of the mother when her baby is born or the professional circumstances of that time in her life, a woman's ambitions and priorities generally change after she becomes a mother and she views her "contribution" to the world more in terms of family than self. This often presents significant dilemmas for women because, typically, they do not compartmentalize like men do. Most men can separate office from home much more easily than most women can. Women are typically the CEOs of their families, and that is not likely to change.

Once you have made the decision to start a family and have survived the difficult issues of childbirth and maternity leave, while keeping aspirations of professional life alive, you will be faced with one of the most difficult decisions you will ever make. That decision centers around when—and if—you go back to work after the baby is born, how much you will work, and who will care for your child while you are pursuing your profession. There are many excellent models of success that I could share with you, but, in the end, it is all too personal to make any of them particularly instructive. Success in this context is all about what works for you and your partner, if appropriate, and you might not get it right the first time around. Keep trying, however. It will be worth it.

When that time comes, there is every possibility that you will decide that you can work and have a family, too. That is admirable because it gives real meaning to the personal value of what you do professionally. However, you will be surprised at how a baby changes your life and your dreams. At some point, you might decide that your main focus, if not your exclusive focus, must be your family. It might happen the first time you see your newborn baby or it might happen when you arrive late once again at the sports event and miss your child's first hit or goal or other great play. Or it might not happen at all. It is different for every woman, and the important thing is to try to protect yourself and your family so that you have choices about the appropriate mix of your professional and family life.

Your choices will start early, much earlier than the time when your first baby actually arrives. In this analysis, I make a reasonable assumption. Most likely you, as a young woman lawyer, will choose a partner who also is capable of producing a large salary. The combination of two high-level salaries will give you and your partner an opportunity to "live large," and it is very difficult to resist that temptation. After all, you have suffered through years of higher education, you are working very hard, and you might feel that you deserve the payoff of spending. Be careful with that kind of thinking. It can be the road to big debt. A habit of living large will work only if both salaries continue at high levels. Of course, that is the expectation, but there is potential for your life to take another course. One of the things that often affects that expectation is the desire to have and care for your children. You will want to have the flexibility to make a difficult decision, if necessary or desirable, to cut back on your practice for a while. If you have developed a lifestyle that requires the salaries of both you and your partner to support it, your choices either will be limited or you will find yourself borrowing to live. This is never a good idea.

You might say that this will not happen to you because you will not be the primary caretaker of your children and you will always be able to work full time. Good luck with that analysis. Unless you have been ignoring life and society around you, you must know that the likelihood of that being the case is slim. Women will always be the primary caretakers, with relatively few exceptions, and, quite honestly, most women prefer it that way. That does not mean that the primary caretaker cannot work, however. What it means is that, even as a working mother, you will be the primary caretaker for your children, the one who makes the decisions for their day-to-day care and the one who bears the greatest responsibility for their day-to-day well-being. Yes, your spouse or mate might help you, but keep that in perspective and recognize that some men are much better at this than others. Consider some of the humorous stories that you hear colleagues and friends share about male caretaking experiences, whether it is for children or aging relatives. As funny as these vignettes might be over a glass of wine or a cup of coffee, it ceases to be funny when it happens to you and your precious child. My contributors report this over and over, and I doubt that this age-old reality is going to change at any time during your professional life. Although it might be difficult for you to imagine yourself, a brilliant young woman attorney, cooing over a baby and obsessing about every burp and sniffle, it is most likely in your future if you are going to have children. Be prepared for it, and do not limit your choices by giving into your imprudent desires for "living large" as you climb the professional ladder.

If you choose to go back to work while your child or children are young, there are many satisfactory options for child care, including family members, nannies, and babysitters. Literally hundreds of thousands of women have used one of more of these options, and their children have flourished. However, you should anticipate that having your children cared for by others, even family members, is rarely a totally satisfactory arrangement for the mother. For most women, caring for children is intuitive, and there is a need to nurture. Many women instinctively feel that they can provide the caretaking most effectively, and they find it hard to delegate something so personal. Those women usually do not have confidence that the job will be done by others to the woman's satisfaction. You should also anticipate the "mommy leaving baby" scenario, which can be heartbreaking but is not life-altering for either you or your child if you have quality child care or school arrangements. These quality arrangements are not always easy to find, however, and every woman lawyer-parent that I know has her own horror story. The problems do not stop with young children, either. Older children and teenagers can be equally demanding, with sports and other extracurricular commitments, performances, and help with homework. You simply exchange one set of demands for another.

There is also the matter of elder care. With seniors living so much longer today, many children find themselves responsible for their parents as they age. Most often, these responsibilities fall to a daughter rather than a son, and these care responsibilities also affect a woman's career path. Very often these parental responsibilities coincide in time with the child care responsibilities, and this can make the situation even more difficult as it relates to a woman's career. These women are known as the "sandwich generation" for very good reason.

Either way, if you want a full-time law practice and have the primary responsibility for child care or elder care, you must anticipate adjusting your expectations for the office or for the home. Housekeepers, nannies, and stay-at-home husbands or mates can fill this role. Nontraditional families have become more popular in recent years, and we are seeing more men assume the primary caretaker and homemaker roles and, in some cases, there is a successful sharing of these roles by the couple. This arrangement most often works when the husband or mate is not a full-time lawyer or in another equally demanding business. So, you see, satisfaction in your law practice might depend on who you marry and the expectations of your mate. Really, the earlier you think about these things, the better. You cannot expect to be a full-time attorney, perfect mate, ideal mother, and excellent homemaker at the same time. Let's face it, there is only one of you. The best that you can hope for, in that situation, is to find a model that works for you and that delivers most of what you want. Remember, you cannot have it all all of the time.

One of my contributors reminds me, however, that some work-life balance issues cannot be anticipated and must be experienced to determine how to handle them and what works best for the individual. The most thorough planning might not be effective without on-the-job training. Another contributor emphasizes that, as a practical matter, work-life really means working the children around the work environment that you choose, not the other way around. However, that same contributor holds out some hope that work-life issues will improve in the workplace simply because men are also beginning to demand change for their own lives. She points out that, in the past, firms have had work-life policies, but most of those policies did not work because the male attorneys at the decision-making level could not relate to the problems women were experiencing as primary caregivers. In effect, the men just did not "get it." However, as men become more interested in flexible time for themselves, my contributor believes that the workplace environment might begin to change around the needs of the individual lawyers, and that will benefit women. She believes that the work-life challenges will not be resolved until enough women are in partnership positions to force the structural shift that is necessary.

A full-time law practice as an attorney-mother presents many challenges. On the one hand, some partners and supervising lawyers might try to lighten the load on working mothers as a form of protection that generally translates to less attractive and less interesting work assignments. As a result, that protection can become limiting to the working mother who wants the opportunity for good and meaningful work and believes that it is her place, not the firm's, to determine whether she is up to the challenge. Another downside is that it might create resentment among the women lawyers who do not have children and are expected to do all of the really challenging work that is not offered to the mothers. In this context, the instinct to protect could work to actually harm the young woman associate-mother in the firm.

Most women lawyers want high-quality work and meaningful access to clients, not just the work-life-family balance. They particularly resent an appearance of "dumbing down" associated with some accommodations. One of my contributors, a male managing partner, believes that the young female associates who make a conscious decision to remain full time after the birth of a child do so to get their careers off on the right track. For most of them, productivity and production matter and are always on display to the firm's partners and shareholders. These women associates want to be outstanding and to have the numbers to prove it.

According to a September 25, 2008 article in *Working Mother* magazine, the law firms that provided the best conditions for working mothers offered the following amenities: an on-site child-care center that is open evenings and weekends; flexible schedules and telecommuting options; a 24-week leave to care for ailing family members; and an 18-week maternity leave policy, which extends to adoption leave in at least one of the firms. Other benefits that were particularly appealing to working mothers are a month's sabbatical after five years of service, an expanded child-care program, lunchtime mentoring, a program for women of color, private nursing rooms for breastfeeding mothers, and personal leaves of absence for up to five years. To respond to the need for quality work, at least one firm provided major assignments for lawyers with reduced schedules.

For those who do not want to keep a full-time law firm schedule and successfully balance work and family, there are excellent options in government, corporate, or academic worlds and public interest and nonprofit practices where the full-time work might allow more time for personal life and family. These jobs tend to have friendly environments, provide excellent opportunities for advancement, and better accommodate the work-life issues. However, the key is how to get those jobs when the need arises. The best advice is to keep your eye on these opportunities among your professional colleagues and the clients of your firm and to have an exit plan that might include going to an in-house corporate practice. You should also get involved in bar association committees and industry associations early in your practice to take advantage of networking that could lead to a satisfactory result.

For those who prefer to stay in a law firm at a less than full-time schedule, there are also many options. The subjects of flexible work arrangements and alternative schedules are discussed later in this chapter in "The Quest for Flex."

Maternity Leave

Chances are that you are not in the market for this information yet. It seems so far off, and you have other critical issues to focus on now. That will be true of many of you, but a book addressing issues relevant to women in the law would hardly be complete without a discussion of maternity leave. So, take it for what it is worth at this time in your life, and file it away. For most of you, it will come in handy in the future.

Fortunately, the days when firms and employers dictated the terms of maternity leave, or chose to allow it at all, are long gone. There is now a minimum threshold under the Family and Medical Leave Act (FMLA), which was enacted in 1993. The FMLA requires employers with more than 50 employees to provide three months of unpaid leave for an individual who has been employed at the business for over 12 months for the birth or adoption of a child or to care for an ill family member. The terms that you are able to negotiate with your firm will vary, however, and you might be able to go beyond those threshold requirements. For instance, some employers will allow additional leave time without pay, and some employers will count sick leave and vacation time toward the total of three months leave.

Although there were some advantages to negotiating maternity leave on an ad hoc basis before the law was enacted—particularly for women who had proven themselves to be very valuable to an employer—the minimum threshold is a guarantee that was hard-fought and is very important to safeguarding women's rights. In addition, most firms have policies in place that reflect this entitlement but also address issues of flexible work hours, telecommuting, part-time hours and compensation, and requirements for advancement. You should be asking about how those matters are addressed in your firm, most advisedly after an offer has been extended to you. However, you can certainly do informal background research before that time. In addition to determining if there is a written policy and the content of the policy, you also will want to know whether the policy is made public, whether some decisions are made on a case-by-case basis, and, if so, the criteria for those decisions. It also will be valuable for you to know how many employees have taken advantage of those options in the recent past, and how many of those employees have been promoted. These questions and related issues are addressed in a variety of publications and Internet resources, including the Center for Work Life Law (*www.worklifelaw.org*), Project for Attorney Retention (*www.pardc.org*), Center for Work-Life Policy (*www.worklifepolicy.org*), and Families and Work Institute (*www.familiesandwork.org*). At some point, it will be worth your while to check out one or more of these resources.

Women of my generation applaud the FMLA, although many of us do not think that it goes far enough in providing benefits to young and struggling working mothers. However, our memory of the time when we were at the mercy of employers on this issue does not make us yearn for the "good old days." Those were tough discussions, not only because there was no baseline—or if there was, it was bad—but also because the male partners and law firm managers were very uncomfortable with the entire subject matter. Being pregnant in and of itself was not seen as "normal" for a professional woman, and men hardly knew how to talk about the subject. I recall being told by a named partner in my firm that I had "shot myself in the foot" by getting pregnant just when my partnership was being discussed. Yes, "shot myself in the foot." Hard to believe. The men also did not know how to act around pregnant working women then, and I always knew that many of the pretenses at concern for my health and well-being were somehow mixed up with the men's own fears that my water would break on the job! You can only imagine their consternation when I asked to move to a much smaller office in the final months of my pregnancy because it was closer to the ladies' room. The only thing that finally made sense to them was that I was not losing as many billable minutes on the long walk to and from the bathroom. We have indeed come a long way, but there is still a long way to go.

One of my concerns when I was negotiating maternity leave with my firm in 1984 was for the women attorneys who would follow. Although the firm members were very supportive of me and were trying to do the right thing for the first woman litigator in their firm—not to mention the first pregnant woman litigator in their firm—their concerns were obviously very different from mine. They encouraged me to negotiate maternity leave on an ad hoc basis because, according to them, I would get a better deal that way, based on my past contribution to the firm and future expectations for my practice. By contrast, I was interested in establishing a policy that would benefit other women who would face the same issues in future years. So, I successfully pushed for a formal written policy, which was very generous in its terms. I was able to negotiate up to a year's leave for maternity, benefits to continue for the first six months, and retention of my office for the entire leave period. The last one was of great importance to me. Losing my office was like losing my identity as a professional, and I will always be grateful to my firm for allowing me that benefit. I was proud of the policy that I had negotiated, and I saw it work to the benefit of other young attorney-mothers who came after me. As it turned out, it was the most liberal policy of the Washington firms that I researched during my negotiations, and it was much more expansive than what was later provided under the FMLA. However, I was playing from a position of strength, a theme that you will hear over and over in this book. First build a strong case for your value, then negotiate.

One of my contributors, a male managing partner, cautions about a pitfall related to the issue of maternity leave. His firm is generous in providing maternity leave and covers the practice of the departed lawyer with other lawyers during the leave period and allows a gradual reentry at the conclusion of the leave. Although those provisions typically are somewhat unproductive and result in a loss of profit to the firm, they are viewed as an investment in the returning lawyer. The problem arises, however, when, after all of this accommodation and cost to the firm, the lawyer on maternity leave informs the firm at the last minute that she will not be returning. This is very poor form and creates a feeling of ill will and lack of good faith. Although the decision not to return to work is understandable, the timing of the disclosure is not. This is to be avoided at all cost. If you have any reason to believe that you will not be returning to work after maternity leave, you should discuss this with the firm at the earliest possible time. What goes around comes around, and the legal community tends to be very small. You always want to operate in good faith and preserve your options.

Today, there are many different models for maternity and family leave policies. Talk to women in the firm and to your colleagues at other firms. The local women's bar association will likely have resources and programs that address these issues. It is always possible to negotiate on the terms that go beyond the threshold of the FMLA, but you will have to do that from a position of strength that typically involves other women in your firm. Learn to work with them to present a united front. There is no room for prima donnas in this scenario. Take care of yourself, but think of the other women around you and the women to follow. It will generate benefits, and it will make you proud.

The Quest for Flex

If full-time employment does not work for you, you might want to address flexible hours or alternative work arrangements. Working mothers continue to have a keen interest in flexible schedules and alternative work arrangements to balance family and work responsibilities. However, the quest for flexible time has changed in recent years and is not exclusive to working mothers. Today, both male and female attorneys are expressing a need for flexibility as a counterweight to the demands of practice, particularly the big law practice, and the interest is not limited to attorneys with children or families. Very often these days, professionals also are desirous of having more time to pursue avocations and to enjoy their youth without giving up their profession. The need for flexibility is not necessarily age-related, however, and older lawyers who are experiencing burnout are finding that they desire flexible schedules as well. A recent *ABA Journal* online article points out that 31 percent of the 300 lawyers surveyed in large law firms and corporate practices said that they wanted a less stressful work life, and another 30 percent wanted to work fewer hours or increase their personal time. Only 2 percent said that they wanted to make more money (*ABA Journal—Law News Now,* "Lawyers Want More Time, Less Stress, Not More Money," October 7, 2008). According to another online article entitled "Law Firms Offering More Flexible Schedules" (*Law 360,* August 22, 2008), with billable-hour pressures at an all-time high and an increase in the number of attorneys concerned about their work-life balance, law firms have slowly begun to offer more flexible schedules. As a reflection of this debate and the possibility of cultural change, at least one major law school offers a program on work-life issues and does not limit the discussion to the female experience. As a result of these recent developments, you should anticipate the possibility of some resistance from your male colleagues, who, arguably, would benefit from the same degree of flexibility that you might be requesting. For them, the writing career that needs attention or the sabbatical to Kenya could be as important as child care is to you. Those issues, like many, will be worked out in the societal debate, but you need to be aware that they could affect your choices.

You should also be aware that some male lawyers will inevitably be pulled into the discussion as gay marriage becomes a reality and paternity leave for gay couples and related issues will have to be addressed. This is the next horizon for work-life, and it will challenge law firms to expand the work-life discussion and to stretch the typical law firm model. It will be interesting to watch this evolve, especially because the subject matter will be uncomfortable to many among the law firm establishment. In fact it is likely to be much more uncomfortable for them than the discussions surrounding women's issues have been. Imagine that!

One of my contributors, a law school career counselor, makes a very strong case that work-life is not relevant to the discussion as a "woman's" issue. She points out that it is an issue for men, also, and that it really only becomes relevant as a woman's issue within the context of becoming a partner on flex time. Although I agree with that proposition, I am not willing to exclude a discussion that will bear so heavily on many of you and will require some of the hardest choices that you will ever have to make.

For many women, who are experiencing personal and professional responsibilities on a collision course, full-time work in any setting simply is not an option. Those women typically contemplate whether to leave the practice altogether or whether to seek an alternative work schedule, usually part-time, job sharing, teleworking, or another flexible work arrangement. One of my contributors describes a pattern of the 26- to 27-year-old female associate, who, faced with issues of family and children, leaves her practice "temporarily" to reassess her career rather than sticking with the practice and persevering under some model of flexibility. The reality is that, once removed from the practice, many of these young women do not return to their profession. This contributor believes that the key to staying in the practice is a combination of commitment and perseverance by the female attorney and the quality of support for an alternative schedule that is offered by the supervising attorneys.

Leaving practice altogether is a difficult decision for many women lawyers. In that decision, the operative question becomes this: If you leave your practice, will it make you happier and a better spouse and mother? For many, the answer is no. If you are one of those and continuing your practice on an alternative schedule is what you choose, you will have to negotiate carefully and be prepared to work more hours than you are paid for. Practically speaking, part-time law practice means 40 hours a week, and it might include a reduction in benefits, limited opportunities for advancement, and a reduced perception of your commitment by colleagues. If these things are not insurmountable problems for you, part-time practice might be a suitable solution. If so, gain the support of your colleagues, and avoid overreaching or promising too much. Make alliances and friendships first, establish your role as a valuable team player, and then negotiate from a position of strength. In other words, prove yourself before you ask for accommodations, and remember that proving yourself is about more than writing a good memo. It is also about how you present yourself in the law firm environment and how you gain the support of senior members of the firm. "Face time" with key members of the firm is very important so that they get to know you and your value to the firm early on. This will take some effort. It was easier in "the old days" when you actually had to walk down the hall to the partner's office to present the completed work product. Today, most supervisors prefer to get things by e-mail so that they can access them in a variety of settings, and you simply click Send to advance an attachment via e-mail. There is no face time involved in that. Technology is not always a positive thing, and you will have to work harder at face time in the current setting.

The "prove yourself first and ask for accommodations later" approach worked for Justice Sandra Day O'Connor. In her book, Joan Biskupic quotes Justice O'Connor: "I did the best I could in order that they [the employers] would feel that I was indispensable. Then when I told them that I very much needed to work only part-time and asked them if they wouldn't work out an arrangement for me, they then agreed to do it because, by then, they decided that they needed me even on my terms" (Biskupic at 34). This is consistent with Justice O'Connor's definition of power: "The ability to do. For both men and women, the first step in getting power is to become visible to others—and then to put on an impressive show" (Biskupic at 36). This is pretty good advice from a very credible source.

Part-time or flexible hours are different models for addressing the needs of employees who cannot work full time and need an adjustment of schedule to deal with family or personal issues. Part-time practice generally involves fewer hours of work per week, whereas flexible time can be a rearrangement of daily schedule in the office or reduced hours to respond to family needs. Job sharing might also be an option. Another option described as "balanced hours" is getting a lot of attention these days. According to the Project for Attorney Retention, an initiative of The Center for WorkLife Law of the University of California Hastings College of Law, "balanced hours programs, unlike traditional part-time programs, allow attorneys to work individually tailored reduced schedules that are designed to meet the firm's business needs while maintaining the attorney's ability to work and to develop professionally without stigma. Balanced hours programs involve active management of workloads in proportion to reduced hours, emphasize client service, and promote the values of the firm" (*www.parc.org*). This sounds like a combination of flexibility and part-time schedule that better addresses the needs of both the attorney and the law firm than the traditional models. You will find that law firms and other employers call programs by a variety of names, but the underlying objective for all of these programs is flexibility of schedule.

These alternative work models might be attractive for many women because they can provide a greater connection to home and family. Many private firms and public-sector offices are making flexible time accommodations, and it has worked for thousands of women lawyers. According to statistics, 34 percent of women attorneys work part time at some time during their careers (Creating Pathways to Success, Advancing and Retaining Women in Today's Law Firms, Women's Bar Association of the District of Columbia Initiative on Advancement and Retention of Women), and teleworking has helped to make these options even more successful.

From the law firm perspective, making accommodations in terms of alternative work schedules makes enormous business sense. According to one of my contributors, a managing partner in a very large law firm, there is a great opportunity for a law firm to find a good balance on the issue of flexibility and to meet the needs of employees in the work-life dilemma. All firms want to have successful women lawyers to improve the quality of service to clients and to enhance the attractiveness of the firm. This contributor believes that the merger and acquisition activity of the new millennium is producing larger firms that have an increased ability to be more flexible and to pilot new ideas. The larger firms have greater operating leverage and are not as resource-constrained as smaller firms, according to this contributor. As a result, the good news is that women might find more opportunities for satisfactory accommodations on the work-life issue as time goes on. This could be dependent, however, on the economy and the profitability of the firm. In a bad economy, where overhead concerns become heightened, the desire to provide flexibility might be chilled.

On the other hand, flexibility might have a special appeal to employers in a down economy because of the salary reductions that accompany certain types of flexibility. It is an interesting trade-off. The effects of a downward spiraling economy on law firms and lawyers were explored earlier in Chapter 2, and I refer you back to that discussion.

Regardless of the surrounding economic circumstances, it is always important to ask for flexibility in the right manner. One of my contributors says that many women and other special interest groups approach the request for flexibility and the need for change as an entitlement and in the wrong manner. He offers the following advice: If you encounter something unexpected that is an issue for you that requires some flexibility from your employer, be constructive in the way that you approach management. Address issues of concern in an appropriate manner and do not wait for the issue to become a problem that you then complain about to the irritation of management.

According to another contributing managing partner, the correct approach in requesting accommodations is to go to management with a long-range plan that goes something like this: "When my kids are in pre-school, I will work X percentage of time. When my kids are in elementary school, I will work Y percentage of time, and when my kids are in secondary and high schools, I will work Z percentage of time. These are the clients that I think this schedule will work for, and I will continue to service those clients and build a stronger relationship with them. I cannot make any promises, but this is my plan." My contributor believes that the firm will respect you for having a serious plan that includes the needs of the firm and that it will go a long way toward cementing your positive future in the firm.

The success of the pursuit for flexibility will often turn on the law firm structure. Law firms are still structured around the male professional model of full-time practice, and this expectation actually can become a de facto requirement for partnership. A cartoon presented at the Project for Attorney Retention (PAR) First Annual Conference in Washington, DC in May 2008 demonstrates this result. The cartoon depicted an older male attorney on the speaker phone to his secretary: "Miss Gaines, send in someone who reminds me of myself as a lad." The message is that men want lawyers in their same image. However, women still do the lion's share of the child care in this country, and most women lawyers cannot fit into that model. In addition, the results of an MIT study cited at the PAR conference showed that 78 percent of law firm partners are married to women who do not contribute to the family income, and this, very often, is the model that law firm partners prefer.

Most law firms are controlled by partners like Miss Gaines's boss, and alternative schedules for lawyers pose a huge challenge to these law firm managers. However, most firms today have taken up that challenge. One of my contributors tells a very positive story about the evolution of part-time lawyers in his firm:

> The first alternative schedule for us was in the 1980s and was not granted for the typical home and family reasons. In that case, a very talented single female lawyer requested an alternative schedule because she was certain that she would not find a mate working a full-time schedule at a national law firm. She was very convincing and able to push back the opposition to convince the law firm of her proposal. She took herself off partnership track, an absolute requirement in those days, worked part time, found her mate, and eventually married and had three children. She is still part time today, working as an administrative assistant to the chairman of the firm. The early 1990s saw the first part-time partner in our firm, and she worked 85 percent of the time, with one day a week off. Today, the firm has a number of part-time female partners, who typically work the bare minimum of full time (approximately 1,900 hours per year) and are evaluated on the quality of the work not the number of hours worked.

It might not surprise you that this firm is one of the best firms for women lawyers raising children, according to the list compiled by Deborah Epstein Henry and published in *Working Mother Magazine*. Other firms also have found part-time associates to be a win-win situation. A recent article in *Working Mother Magazine* includes many examples of successful part-time work arrangements and includes the following remarks from a male partner who became a believer in the part-time concept. He now says that

71

The payoff [from allowing part-time schedules] is tangible, with talented attorneys staying on staff and talented attorneys joining the firm. I learned this personally when I tried to recruit an associate from another firm, but she and I could not agree on her schedule. She wanted part-time, and I needed full-time. I did not hire her, but I soon found out that I had made a big mistake and that not hiring her was the worst option. I was better with her three days a week than zero. So I called her back to tell her that she won and that I needed her—part-time. (*Working Mother Magazine,* Focus on the Best Law Firms—Part-Time Partners, November 16, 2008)

Many of you will find yourself in the throes of part-time or flexible practice at some time in your careers, and I hope that you will find a situation that works as well as what was just described. However, although it appears to be a suitable solution to the work-life problems, many women lawyers report that this type of practice option can be a double-edged sword, and they find the option to be the worst of all worlds. I have heard women say that it really boils down to "Which nobody do I want to be?" They report that anything less than full-time practice can make you feel like a nobody lawyer and a nobody caretaker in your personal life and that these issues of dissatisfaction in your personal life can become very burdensome. My own experiences are instructive.

As a part-time lawyer with a significant amount of litigation responsibility, I employed a part-time nanny for my two young children. I worked at the office three days a week, and was home with my children the other two days of the work week. Nanny did not come on those two days when I was not supposed to be working because arguably I did not need her then. Right! Tell that to the judge or the client or the managing partner who needed me now.

Some of my most vivid memories include the telephonic motion with a federal judge while my children, having discovered the box of imported, hand-blown glass Christmas ornaments, proceeded to destroy those ornaments one by one. I tried desperately to concentrate on my arguments while Santa went by without a head, the wingless angel passed by . . . you get the picture. Then there was the time I negotiated a large commercial lease for two hours by telephone while my children destroyed the house around me. These were hair-raising experiences, and I was completely exhausted after each one, but you can bet that these types of things are going to happen. Winning the motion and successfully negotiating the lease provided some cause for celebration, but it was short lived. It is very hard to schedule around part-time hours, and it becomes an issue with most full-time lawyers who share your matters and do not want to pinch hit for you on your days off.

One of my contributors practiced with a woman attorney who was working part time and had two small children. On the days when the part-time lawyer was not scheduled to be in the office, she often found it necessary to be there. On those occasions, she brought her children with her. The other attorneys and staff were annoyed by this and considered it part of her responsibility to arrange for child care in those situations. Her attitude was that she was not being paid for overtime and that she could not afford to hire a babysitter. This was the wrong response and did not gain the support of her colleagues. Many of the secretaries drove long distances twice daily to deliver and retrieve children from quality day care. They did not want to babysit other people's children or have them interfere with the office routine, and in most situations, they were being paid less than the offending part-time attorney. Keep your mommy profile and problems with kids out of the office as much as possible. Full-time lawyers and staff members often have children but do not have the option of working part time; they do not want to hear you complain. The truth is that you still might have to employ an army of helpers, such as child care providers, housekeepers, yard workers, and miscellaneous others to be successful in a part-time practice. In fact, maintaining that army of helpers could take all or most of your part-time salary.

Another of my contributors, a managing partner, points out that there are only two appropriate responses to a request for an alternative schedule—either "yes" or "goodbye." If the female attorney is worth keeping, the answer has to be "yes" because a negative response eventually will drive the attorney from the firm. If, on the other hand, the attorney is not highly valued, the answer should be to say goodbye and let her leave for a place where she can be more successful. The firm calculates the cost of attrition in this analysis and tries to avoid these costs wherever possible if the attorney is highly valued. If it is handled correctly, the job satisfaction among part-time attorneys is high, and the talent is retained.

According to this same contributor, the key to successful flexible job arrangements of lawyers is whether the job gets done in a satisfactory manner, not the number of hours the attorney works. However, he qualifies this by saying that alternative schedules work better when the part-time lawyer is junior and that flexible schedules do not work as well when the part-time lawyer is a more senior lawyer or a manager. There is constant demand for decision making from senior lawyers and managers that interferes with the success of part-time schedules at those levels. This particular contributor is the beneficiary of alternative scheduling and has an entire team of part-time women attorneys working in his high-visibility antitrust practice. They work on different days so that there is always coverage in the office, and they work as a team and alter their schedules, if necessary, to accommodate deadlines. The work gets done, the part-time lawyers have the flexibility they need, and the manager tries very hard to make it work for all of them.

All part-time experiences are not this ideal, however. To realistically address the part-time or reduced hours options, you will need to deal with some harsh realities. You need to be aware that these options can result in less prestigious work assignments and lack of respect from those who do not view part-timers as "serious" about their careers. The flexibility of these options is often viewed as preferential treatment for women and is resented by full-time colleagues.

In the April 2004 edition of *ABA Journal-Law News Now* (*www. abajournal.com*), author Stephanie Francis Ward describes the satisfactory arrangement of a part-time law firm associate and asks the question, "So, why aren't more associates leading the call for reduced work hours?" and answers it as follows:

> Experts say it boils down to fear. There's a stigma attached to part-time work, says Joan Williams, co-director of the Center for WorkLife Law at

the University of California Hastings College of Law. Sexism only contributes to this stigma, she says, because many lawyers seeking part-time situations are women with child care concerns. She also cites the fear of getting bad cases, bad office space and being excluded from important meetings. . . . Resentment is another frequently mentioned concern. No one wants full-time colleagues to complain about having to work nights and weekends because part-timers bailed early. Likewise, if part-time lawyers are kept on the partnership track, it can raise eyebrows among the full-time set.

These are important things to think about.

You also should be aware that, according to the November 2007 National Association of Women Lawyers (NAWL) Survey on Retention and Promotion of Women in Law Firms, questions about level of commitment might cause firms to limit their investment in women who are working part-time schedules. The study concludes that if part-time work is not to become a dead end for junior women attorneys, firms need to change their policies to recognize part-time work as a temporary stage within an individual's legal career. Making mentoring and professional development activities available to those part-time attorneys evidences an investment by the firm and will help the part-time attorney to return to full-time practice at an appropriate time down the road. However, the existing low retention rates and failure of attorney-mothers to return to practice after their "temporary" departures will continue to have a chilling effect on how employers view the wisdom of expenditures on these programs. It is possible that some of the attorney-mothers will have to make certain sacrifices to return to work to dispel these perceptions and assist in gaining greater ground in the future. It is the pioneers that open the road for those to follow, but the pioneer road can be very rocky.

As a result of some of the pitfalls of part-time lawyering, women need to be prepared to defend their commitment to the profession while working part time. Borrowing from another professional experience, I was impressed when I heard the following. A woman partner at a national accounting firm put it this way. "I am not a part-time partner. I am a partner with fewer clients or matters. I am 100% committed to the clients that I have; I just have fewer than others" (Remarks of A. Economos, Partner, Ernst & Young, LLP, as reported at the Project for Attorney Retention (PAR) First Annual Conference, Washington, DC, May 2008). Some firms have balanced hour coordinators who can be very helpful in this situation. The balanced hour coordinator typically communicates the business imperative to associates and partners and plans a process and a schedule geared to success for all the participants. I recommend the Project for Attorney Retention publications *Solving the Part-Time Puzzle: The Law Firm's Guide to Balanced Hour Programs* (2004) and *Balanced Hours: Effective Part-Time Programs for Washington Law Firms* (2001) for more on this subject. If you are considering this option, you should also talk to women in the firm who work less than full time and are considered successful. Very often these women are "under the radar" because they are trying not to call attention to their unique situations. Seek them out.

Even with the limitations and challenges just discussed, it is clear that part-time or flexible time practice can be a successful interim or permanent career strategy. It keeps you in the profession and satisfies your intellectual needs, even if you are running on no sleep and eating at your desk. The alternative is opting out of the profession in these difficult years, and reentering the profession at a later date might turn out to be more difficult than you think. For those of you who ultimately choose the part-time option, I wish you good luck. There are plenty of women who have made it a success, and I hope you join their ranks. Again, the key is anticipating the problems and finding workable solutions.

Whether you are returning to law practice on a flexible schedule after starting a family or are seeking flexible time for another reason, you most likely will revisit the decision from time to time or revise the plan to fit new circumstances, and these additional resources on the subject will come in handy. I recommend the following to you: *Balancing Work and Personal Life—Developing Flexible Work Options for Lawyers* (*www.wisbarlorg/.AM/ Template*), and *Juggling It All: Exploring Lawyers' Work, Home and Family Demands and Coping Strategies* (GULC EBW Library).

The Off-Ramp Dilemma

The concepts of "off-ramp" and "on-ramp" were first introduced by author Sylvia Ann Hewlett in *Off-ramps and On-ramps: Keeping Talented Women on the Road to Success* (Harvard Business School Press, 2007). In her book, the term *off-ramp* refers to a career path detour, typically for family reasons. According to the author, traditionally, the 60 percent of women throughout industries who have taken this path are welcomed back with unemployment or underemployment. Hewlett chronicles the reasons for what she calls nonlinear discontinuous careers (mostly for motherhood or elderly care demands) and, among other recommendations, makes the case for flexible work arrangements that can be successful for the employer and for the employee. She argues convincingly that it should be in the interest of businesses to be flexible enough to retain or rehire the talented women who also want to be married and have children. Other recommended reading on the subject includes *Back on the Career Track: A Guide for Stay-at-Home Moms Who Want to Return to Work* by Carol Fishman Cohen and Vivian Stein Rabin (Business Plus, 2007) and *The Comeback: Seven Stories of Women Who Went from Career to Family and Back Again* by Emma Gilbey Keller (Bloomsbury USA, 2008).

Although temporary interruption from practice is problematic enough for a woman attorney with cases and clients, extended off-ramp can have other significant challenges. Leaving the practice of law altogether for any significant period of time can often be very dissatisfying for women attorneys for a variety of reasons, including lack of mental stimulation, loss of interaction with colleagues, and loss of dignity. Another important consideration is the reduction in income that women face when they take time off from practice. For women who are used to making their own money, this can be a problem, regardless of whether the husband or partner provides adequately for the family. Professional women, like professional men, tend to measure their value in terms of income and what a client is willing to pay for their services. The adjustment to other measures of value, like the rewards of motherhood and satisfactory performance as CEO of the family, is often a hard one to make. Additionally, as Betty Freidan points out in her feminist tome, *The Feminine Mystique* (W.W. Norton & Company, 1963) the risks of being financially dependent on a partner can be extreme. These are huge problems to address and can seem overwhelming. However, extended off-ramp is necessary for some women for a variety of personal reasons, and it needs to be handled wisely and well if the woman wants to position herself for reentry into practice at a later time.

In her biography of Justice O'Connor, author Joan Biskupic quotes Justice O'Connor on this subject. Justice O'Connor explained that, after staying home for a period of time to care for her young children, she went back to work to avoid what had become full-time volunteerism. "Really, I needed to go back to work, because I had gotten so busy in civic and community affairs that I was desperate to go back to work so I wouldn't have so much to do and I'd have a good excuse [for declining volunteer requests]" (Biskupic, at 34). My own experiences with working part time and taking time off from practice to address family needs are consistent with the experiences described by Justice O'Connor, but the value of those volunteer and community activities cannot be overlooked. Very often, those experiences will forge relationships and open up opportunities that might become valuable to you in the future when you need flexibility in your practice or work life. These experiences can create very important alternatives to private practice during the challenging childrearing years.

Fortunately, the subject of off-ramp and reentry into the workforce is finally starting to get the attention that it deserves in the legal profession. Law schools are beginning to recognize the need to inform their students about the issue, and at least one law school is offering a program for lawyers addressing reentry issues. American University's Washington College of Law program, entitled "Reconnect, Refocus, and Reclaim Your Legal Career," is on the cutting edge and was introduced in the fall of 2008, cosponsored by the Women's Bar Association of DC, the National Association of Women Lawyers, and the DC Volunteer Lawyers Project. The program includes instruction by Washington College of Law faculty, facilitation by leaders in the field of career and professional development, interactive and practical sessions, one-on-one professional coaching, creation of an individual action plan for reentry, and opportunities to connect with peers who share similar backgrounds and work-life challenges. It is not surprising that a program like this would spring up at the Washington College of Law, which, similar to New England Law|Boston, was founded more than 100 years ago by two pioneering women at a time when women were generally excluded from the legal profession. The founders fostered a tradition of providing opportunities for women, and, according to the promotional materials for the program, "their extraordinary foresight and perseverance form the foundation of [the] school." This specialized program, for lawyers who have temporarily put their careers on hold and are considering reentry to law practice, provides a gateway for women and men alike to reclaim their legal careers and contribute to the profession. In addition to law faculty members, the program features the contributions of practicing attorneys and career and professional development experts.

I was fortunate to be a panelist for this program in November 2008, and I witnessed the need for this kind of instruction and dialogue. Most of the attendees at the program were women, and their frustrations and disappointments were apparent. Some had been out of practice for many years, and the challenges of reentry were daunting. Of all of the individual stories, however, the one that concerned me the most involved a woman who had taken off four years to raise her children. In response to the panelists' recommendations that the attendees take a very close look at what they had done during the time that they were not practicing to explain that absence and to apply any skills gained during that time to the current job market, this woman claimed that she had done nothing but child care during that four-year period, a situation that clearly was regrettable for her. Although the panelists tried to encourage her to be candid with prospective employers about that period of time, those responses were unsatisfactory for her, and I felt at a loss to help her. As a result, I again encourage you to make the most of your off-ramp experiences in view of the future and to keep yourself involved and current in your profession.

The reality is that many women simply like to work, and they like to work in the profession that they have chosen. They like to be productive and enterprising, and they find professional life to be stimulating and particularly rewarding. For those women, it might be imperative to continue to work, whether from within or from outside the profession of law. For them, taking time off from practice might only be acceptable if they are fully engaged during that time, whether for pay or as a volunteer. It will keep them interested and mentally engaged, and it will feed their self-esteem. The option, for them, would be to hide a light under a barrel, with the risk that the light would go from dim to out.

The Gender Divide

Although many of the legal barriers that historically prevented women from entering the legal profession have been removed, informal and structural impediments to women's full participation within the legal profession still exist. A recent 2007 NALP survey on retention and promotion of women in law firms found that there is a growing income gap between men and women lawyers as they move up the partnership ranks, that the large majority of women who start as associates in firms are not promoted to equity positions or leadership roles in the firms, and that law firm management is overwhelmingly male. The survey is the only national study of the nation's 200 largest law firms, which annually tracks the progress of women lawyers and collects data from entire firms rather than from a selection of individuals within those firms.

Specifically, the 2007 survey shows continuing gender imbalance at upper levels of law firms, including the following findings.

- At each level of promotion, male lawyers earn more than females. Male of-counsels earn roughly $20,000 more than females, male nonequity partners earn approximately $27,000 more than females, and male equity partners earn almost $90,000 more than female equity partners. In addition, at firms with exceptionally high hour requirements, male equity partners earn $140,000 more than women in the same position. The conclusion is that hard work pays off much more "handsomely" for men than for women.

- The representation of women at the level of equity partnership (those who share in the profits) is approximately only one woman to every five men at large firms. As a result, the survey also shows a continuing lack of progress in moving women lawyers into more senior positions.

- Women comprise only 15 percent of the members of law firms' highest governing committees and fewer than 10 percent of managing partners. A remarkable 15 percent of large firms have no women lawyers on their highest governing committee.

A comparison of the weekly salaries of men and women shows the following:

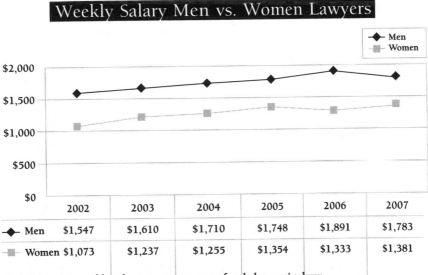

Weekly Salary Men vs. Women Lawyers

	2002	2003	2004	2005	2006	2007
◆ Men	$1,547	$1,610	$1,710	$1,748	$1,891	$1,783
▪ Women	$1,073	$1,237	$1,255	$1,354	$1,333	$1,381

Women lawyers' weekly salary as a percentage of male lawyers' salary:

69.4%	76.8%	73.4%	77.5%	70.5%	77.5%

Bureau of Labor Statistics, "Median weekly earnings of full-time wage and salary workers by selected characteristics," for 2006 and previous years. http://www.bls.gov/cps/cpsaat39.pdf

These are grim statistics, and it is better that you know them at the outset and are not surprised by them later. Unfortunately, there will have to be a critical mass of women who stay in the law and sacrifice to climb the partnership ladder to make much of a change in this result. However, the advent of part-time partnership and other responses to the work-life challenge might allow women to have greater representation in the boardroom and make greater strides in salary equity over time.

There also are inherent gender differences that work to curtail some opportunities for women. One of my contributors tells this story. She joined a conservative insurance defense firm after graduating from law school. All of the partners were men, except one. The partners had a regular practice of playing handball and squash at the all-male University Club, where most of the firm's partners belonged. The partners would often invite the male associates for a quick game of squash or handball and lunch. Of course, the women associates were never invited. Although the partners would have defended the practice on the rules of the club, it effectively meant that young female associates did not have the same face time with the senior partners and, therefore, developing the same rapport and connections with the partners as the male associates were able to do was much more difficult. It turned out to be very career inhibiting for young women. This contributor believes that such behavior is never appro-priate and that law firms need to be cognizant of the messages that are sent and the opportunities that are affected by these practices. If law firms want to leverage the immense talent of women lawyers, they need to provide women an equal opportunity to connect with experienced senior members of the firm, both inside and outside the office.

Another of my contributors says that it was often difficult for her to feel part of the law firm because of these same types of curtailed opportunities. The male attorneys often golfed together, went out for drinks after work, played tennis together, and participated in other sports activities together. The female attorneys were not included in these social and recreational settings. These types of experiences foster collegiality among the participants, and, when women cannot participate, they lose out on opportunities for getting to know senior attorneys in an informal setting. Women also complain that the male associates who participate in these activities are typically the first ones to come to mind when a more senior participating male attorney needs an associate to work on a case. The same social and recreational settings are also the ones that offer client development and rainmaking and, as a result, women are often excluded from the very events that could lead to promotion and partnership. As my Constitutional Law professor used to say, "What is sauce for the goose is sauce for the gander." The law professionals should strive for equal opportunity and treatment for all.

4

Always be in charge of your own career. It is extraordinarily unusual that any other attorney in your organization will take the time to express enough interest in your career to help you soar to the top. Unlike most experiences that you have had to date, there is no road map, no blueprint guiding you to success as a lawyer. There is no recipe which guarantees achievement of your goals. Hard work is only one of the factors of success, and you should not leave your future to fate.

—60-Something Woman Partner

Legal Imperatives

By contrast to the weighty themes of the last chapter, the following two chapters are designed to address more practical issues like choice of practice specialty, choice of practice setting, and the obstacles inherent in a daily law practice that can derail a career before it gets started. Avoiding these obstacles will make addressing the other important issues much easier. This information is presented in the following format: Lesson Presented, Discussion, and Examples. The examples are appropriately captioned "Case in Point." If you do not see yourself in some of these examples, you are either very lucky or very naive.

Some of the anecdotal material presented here is included to demonstrate how far the profession has come in the last 30 years and to give hope to aspiring young women attorneys. It is a credit to the profession and to lawmakers that certain behaviors were identified as inappropriate and unfair. Although women lawyers still face unique challenges, for the most part, those offensive behaviors have been eliminated.

Although this book is not intended as a male-bashing instrument, it should come as no surprise that many of the subjects addressed below involve the male-female relationship in the workplace. Women attorneys, who are actively involved in the practice and in leadership roles, are in the minority in the legal profession, and, as a result, women lawyers are required to fit into a distinctly male structure. Because men and women are very different in emotional makeup and behavior (or are "wired differently" according to one of my contributors), this presents certain challenges for both the male and female attorneys. Although I acknowledge the other side of these issues, it is not my intent to address each issue from the male perspective. However, I am joined by a respected colleague in the Epilogue in an attempt to present that valuable perspective to you.

I also recognize that some of the pitfalls identified here are not unique to women lawyers. Some of the issues can present problems for male lawyers as well. Treating support staff well, controlling your temper, and learning to gain and retain clients, for example, can apply to both male and female attorneys. To the extent that these discussions will benefit male readers, I am enthusiastic about that result. For those men who read the book, it might serve as an assist in accomplishing my objective. I welcome their participation and hope that it will cause them to be more prepared for and more enthusiastic about keeping talented women on the job and enhancing the reputation of the legal profession. Not a bad trade-off.

You should start putting the lessons of this book into practice as early as possible. If you do, you will hit the ground running at your first job.

Choose Your Specialty Well

Choosing the right specialty is key, and it should start in law school. If you are a woman who wants it all—marriage, family, career—you need to be very careful how you plan your legal career. The business world in general has become very specialized, and the field of law is no exception. Your choice of specialty could affect the rest of your life. Although it is possible to change specialties during the course of your career, that is not the preferred route. Rather, you should want to choose well and take the best advantage of accumulated experience throughout your career.

One of the most important questions to ask is this: "Why did I go to law school in the first place?" In the law review article entitled "Letter to a Law Student Interested in Social Justice" by William P. Quigley, professor of law at Loyola University New Orleans College of Law (*DePaul Journal for Social Justice*, Volume 1, Number 1, Fall 2007), Professor Quigley ponders the often heard sentiment from a law student, "The first thing I lost in law school was the reason that I came." Unfortunately, this is much too often the case. Although the dilemma is presented within the context of public interest law, the discussion seems to hold true in a wider context. Professor Quigley writes:

> It pains me to say it, but justice is a counter-cultural value in our legal profession. Because of that, you cannot be afraid to be different than others in law school or the profession—for unless you are, you cannot be a social justice lawyer. Those who practice social justice law are essentially swimming upstream while others are on their way down. Unless you are serious about your direction and the choices you make and the need for assistance, team-work and renewal, you will likely grow tired and start floating along and end up going downstream with the rest. We all grow tired at points and lose our direction. The goal is to try to structure our lives and relationships in such a way that we can recognize when we get lost and be ready to try to reorient ourselves and start over. (10-11)

Holding to dreams can be difficult, but it is particularly important when your career is on the line. The millenial generation and the current economic downturn might be contributing to the balance that has been sought by lawyers for a very long time, and that new balance might eventually define the practice of law and provide more opportunities and flexibility. Big law, and the dot-com and financial services industries, which have dominated for so long, have not set good examples for the value of personal time, and it is a credit to this new generation of lawyers that they are asking some important questions in planning their careers.

The Litigation Specialty

Although "litigation"—trying cases before courts or other adjudicatory bodies—is technically a practice and not a specialty, it bears discussion here, especially because so many lawyers are engaged in this practice. It is unusual today to find a large law firm without a substantial litigation practice because the United States has become a very litigious society, and many disputes end up in the courts or before other adjudicatory bodies to determine the rights of the parties. In litigation, trial practice skills are applied to many specialties, or subject areas, within the large body of law. There is employment litigation, personal injury litigation, contract litigation, estates and trusts litigation, civil rights litigation, and myriad other types of trial practice. These same specialty areas can also be practiced in nonlitigation settings, as discussed later in this section. Think of it this way. A lawyer, in a contract specialty practice, can draft a contract for his or her client. That lawyer can negotiate the contract and continue to advise the client about the client's rights and obligations under the contract and the rights and obligations of the other party or parties to the contract. However, if the parties to the contract end up in a dispute over contract performance, that same lawyer might not be the appropriate attorney to represent the client in the courtroom. It might take a litigator with years of trial experience and a different set of legal skills to take on the representation at that point.

Litigation is very exciting and includes the thrill of appearing before judges and juries and engaging in the type of combat that has dominated the silver screen and television for decades. Think Spencer Tracy and Katherine Hepburn in the silver screen classic *Adam's Rib* and the popular television series *LA Law* and *Boston Legal*, depending on your age or passion for old movies and reruns. Toting your briefcase and your boxes of "smoking gun" documents into an imposing and stately courthouse can be a real high. Watching seasoned litigators demonstrate their skills in a court of law is an exciting pastime, in and of itself, and it is no wonder that litigation attracts so many young law graduates.

In addition to the thrills, however, litigation can be a very demanding practice, and it also can be less compatible than others with the desire for an enriched home and family experience. Many in my generation of women lawyers did not pay adequate attention to this. Most of us were in law school during the Watergate days, and we were caught up in the excitement of litigation. We flocked to televisions in the law school lounges during class breaks to hang on the words of the Watergate prosecutors. Some of us were lucky enough to have professors like Sam Dash, famed Watergate prosecutor, grace our law schools. We made certain that we had adequate credentials to be attractive to litigation firms, and we joined the ranks with great expectations. Our experience was good, for a while. The late nights and weekends at the office, the constant travel, the unending demands from a combination of senior attorneys, clients, opposing counsel, and judges were tolerable as long as we were solo acts. Then came the marriages, the kids, and the resulting personal conflicts, followed by the corresponding lack of flexibility from law firm management. We had to choose, and we did not always make the right choices to advance our personal and professional lives.

Some of these litigators stayed in the practice but went on the "mommy track," forfeiting expectations of advancement and partnership, and some abandoned their legal careers entirely. This often led to disillusionment and resentment and interfered with relationships in the workplace and at home. For those who chose professions over personal lives, there was a great price to pay, which often resulted in unsatisfactory personal lives and inexperienced and unsatisfactory nannies raising kids. In most cases, neither choice was a satisfactory result. Some, like me, who chose the personal over the professional during those critical childrearing years, ended up with what appear to be fractured résumés as we went from place to place looking for "workable" situations. In my case, I was lucky to find some very satisfying compromises, but many other women lawyers were not that fortunate. Choosing your specialty well and avoiding the problem at the outset is the key.

Litigation is still a very exciting field. Pick up the front page of any major newspaper in this country, and you are likely to find at least a few articles dealing with lawsuits and related issues. As a result, litigation continues to attract some of the brightest minds in the legal field, women and men alike. However, give it plenty of thought. Although you studied Civil Procedure and Evidence, and probably did a trial practice clinic in law school, that does not mean that litigation is the only practice field that you should consider. You would not choose a car with so little thought!

Certain litigation experiences also wear you out over time. One of my contributors has been prosecuting drug dealers and rapists for most of her career. She reports that this work takes an incredible emotional toll over the years, as you might expect. What is exciting when you are young and energetic might become very difficult in the later years of practice. Although this is true of many types of practices, it is particularly true in criminal prosecution and defense.

You might also find that you will have to break through the stereotypes to be successful in litigation. This sounds easy, but, in reality, it could be very difficult. In a January 1, 2007 article in *The America Lawyer* entitled "Obstacle Course," author Amy Kolz concludes that to make it in the male-dominated world of litigation, women have to break through old stereotypes to build top-tier practices. For example, Kolz describes a top litigator at a prestigious big law firm, who also was the only female attorney in court representing a major Fortune 500 client. She successfully broke the pattern of assuming the snack duty for the trial team (as the "woman" team member) but still ended up getting coffee for the lawyers. "Patterns are hard to change," said the lawyer.

According to Kolz, even after women lawyers have proven themselves at all levels of the practice, female litigators are still struggling with the old stereotypes. More than 30 years after women first entered the profession in large numbers and have climbed to impressive positions of power and control in every aspect of the legal business, Kolz provides many additional examples of women litigators today being asked to get sandwiches and perform other tasks that smack of more subtle gender expectations. Cultural and societal biases still run rampant and render less aggressive female styles tempting in order to just "get along" in the profession. Women attorneys find themselves ratcheting it down in the courtroom, where a male colleague would not make the same decision, and choosing not to cross their arms for fear of conveying negative body language.

As observed by Kolz:

> They're expected to attend to all of the details of running a case; and yet, to advance their careers, they must resist becoming the stereotype of the "pleasing" female. They're expected to be tough advocates for their clients, but not too tough, lest judges or opposing counsel call them the dreaded b-word. Many balance the long and unpredictable hours of litigation with family responsibilities, but many also feel they must work harder than men to prove that they are serious about getting the good assignments, and eventually the prize of partnership. They must consider the implication of every gesture, from bringing coffee to mentioning child care problems.

Kolz contrasts this experience to that of the men, who simply have to be lawyers, not male lawyers.

This balancing act also carries over to the work-life discussion, and, as Kolz points out, women find themselves working a full-time schedule to be given the privilege of working "part time" to respond to family needs. Women litigators find the part-time or flexible schedule especially hard to keep. Even though male litigators, who are fathers, also struggle with finding the work-life balance, the burden of family still lands disproportionately on women, particularly during their childbearing years as women try to climb the firm ladder to partnership.

The result of this untenable balancing act, as described by Kolz, is that many successful women litigators keep "superhuman schedules" and have to battle traditional stereotypes about the "mommy track." Women described the need to prove devotion to their legal careers and the further need to work harder than male colleagues to demonstrate that devotion.

Although many women, admirably, make it to partnership and levels of management in top national litigation firms while also meeting requirements for generating new clients and new matters, the bar is extremely high. For those who do, they present valuable role models, mentors, and advocates for women junior to them.

If litigation is your choice and you also can anticipate a time when you will need flexibility for personal reasons, think about developing a secondary specialty that will help you transition to that practice at some time in the future when personal considerations might require it. Transitioning might be difficult, and you need to hold the firm or department management to their promises. If you make decisions based on a promise of transition, make them keep their word and be very careful of the exceptions. "Just a little litigation" is like "just a little pregnant." There is no such thing.

Job sharing or the team approach might also allow you to work part time and continue in the litigation field. I have heard successful accounts of part-time women lawyers sharing litigation responsibilities to assure that one of them is in the office and "on the case" at all times. It takes excellent organizational and management skills to make this work, but women are up to the challenge. We are women, after all.

Another logical transition from litigation is a legislative practice in the public sector, either on the staff of an elected official or within one of the many committees of government, or in the private sector in a lobby practice representing clients who want to have an effect on pending legislation. Litigation skills translate very well to these administrative practice settings, and it can be very rewarding work. This was one of my stops along the way during a litigation career. When the demands of raising two small children became incompatible with the combination of my litigation practice and the litigation practice of my husband, I opted for a position as chief of staff for an elected official. This job took advantage of the skills I had developed in persuasive writing, strategic planning, and the challenges of an administrative process. It turned out to be one of the most interesting and satisfying jobs of my career.

A judicial clerkship is another logical transition for someone trained in litigation. Even though the traditional career path might include clerking for a judge immediately after law school, this strict model seems to be changing.

Case in Point

"I wanted to stay in litigation after the birth of my first child, so I left my firm to become a clerk to a federal judge. Today many judges are increasingly more interested in clerks with experience in the practice, and this was a very satisfactory transition for me and one that opened up many opportunities when I left the court. I worked full-time and still had the flexibility I needed for family and children. Two other of my fellow women clerks at the court proposed a job sharing arrangement to a judge and prevailed. It is all about creativity and making the sell. A lot depends on how you package things."

—Julie, 40-Something

Another contributor is a "career law clerk" to a federal judge, and this position allows her the flexibility that is necessary to attend to the needs of her three small children. Although she works full time and is married to an attorney in private practice, she is able to have more predictable hours than she experienced in private practice. According to her, most of the judges in her district have career clerks because the case load and the complexity of cases has increased to the extent that turning all law clerks over on an annual basis can affect a smooth transition of case responsibility. As a career law clerk, she has all of the same responsibilities and quality of work as an annual law clerk, but she also has some management responsibilities with clerks and interns.

In addition to litigation, there are other specialties that seem uniquely unsuited to a healthy balance of personal and professional lives. Merger and acquisition work (buying and selling companies and creating corporate conglomerates) is another good example. However, it is not my intention to make a list that risks painting with too broad a brush and fails to recognize that there are always exceptions. It is more important to have each woman lawyer carefully examine specialties of interest to her with realism and great scrutiny. An early evaluation of this kind will help to avoid imprudent decisions that could have adverse consequences in the future.

Beyond Litigation

If litigation and the other demanding practices already discussed are not for you, consider the alternatives. There are many, and you might be surprised to discover how interesting those practices can be. Remember that these practices are based on the same bodies of law and subject areas discussed earlier, but they simply approach the subject area from a non-litigation perspective. These practices tend to be more regulatory and transactional, and they can be extremely interesting and satisfying. Some of the most successful stories that I hear come from women who chose nonlitigation specialties like intellectual property, health care, financial and investment services, real estate, bank regulation, elderly law, estates and trusts, tax, ERISA, and adoption and family law. Most of those women are still practicing, and they have been able to manage their law firm and public-sector practices in addition to having satisfactory personal lives. For those who desired more autonomous routes, they were able to segue into solo practice without too much difficulty. These women are fulfilled at their practices and continue to make very significant contributions to the profession. Some of them have practiced for more than 30 years and, in semiretirement, still maintain a few clients to keep themselves active. It is a great result, and they did not experience the disillusionment and disappointment of choosing between all and nothing.

Nonprofit, public interest, and government practices also are extremely rewarding and uniquely relevant to improving society. The opportunities in these general categories are replete and are explored further in the next section, "Choose Your Employer Well."

It needs to be acknowledged here that there also are compelling practical restrictions that come into play when choosing a practice specialty. Foremost among them are considerations of repaying student loans. In that situation, it is not only the job that is best suited for you but also the job that will help to pay back the school loans in the shortest period of time. This is understood, and it leads to some very difficult balancing of interests.

For a good book on the various specialties within the broad field of the law, I recommend *Guerilla Tactics—Legal Jobs of Your Dreams* by Kimm Alayne Walton, JD (Gilbert Law Publishing, Thomson West, 2008), which presents a thorough overview of the practice choices. You might also wish to consult the NALP publication *Jobs and JDs*, which addresses the types of jobs that most women pursue. However, try not to embrace the time-worn perceptions at the expense of avoiding the realities for yourself. Do sufficient homework on the job that you are interviewing for and avoid gravitating to "softer" practices like nonprofits and certain government positions simply because they appear to be more woman-friendly. One of my young women contributors describes these as "pink practices" and warns against choosing them to the exclusion of other more high-profile practices that might interest you more. Although the reality is that some practice specialties, as a general rule, might be better for women in terms of the work-life issues, you should not preclude other opportunities without proper investigation.

In other words, you should not self-select out of litigation just because it is litigation. Women are well-equipped to handle the intellectual and practice challenges of litigation, even in big law firms, but they might be more comfortable in alternative settings. On the other hand, you might find that things are not what they seem and be positively surprised that a particular practice that you would have ruled out could present a practical and valuable career path for you. Give every opportunity a chance by being well prepared and asking good questions. As a lawyer, you are trained in fact finding, so get the facts and make an informed decision about your future.

Doing an internship at a law firm or nonprofit or the government before you commit to a full-time job after graduation is a good way to get the information you need. However, you should be aware that the traditional law firm summer associate experience is often very different from what you will experience as an associate after law school. The purpose of the summer associate program is to woo you, to create excitement about the firm, and to make you want to get an offer. The parties, sports activities, and other events that you will experience during the summer are not representative of the type of attention and camaraderie that you will find when you become an associate. One law school career counselor describes a conversation that she had with a student who was very positive and particularly excited about the summer experience. The female student described softball games and bowling events and other outings that she found especially enjoyable, and she said that she could tell that the associates enjoyed the events as well. The counselor told me that she felt compelled to point out to the student that, although the student went home after those events, in most cases the associates returned to the office for two or three more hours of work before calling it a day.

Choosing a specialty and developing a career plan is most valuable if that plan anticipates change and takes you through the various phases of your career. The best model for work-life will be founded on a love for the work that you do. One of my contributors emphasizes that finding satisfaction in your work and making the money that you need to live can result in a great adventure. She says that we do not talk enough about what we love when evaluating work and professional experiences.

Women should use their natural skills to figure out what is best for them. It should be viewed as a worthwhile mental exercise, not as a burden. Women must dedicate the skills of creativity, reality recognition, and bridging, to name a few, to determine what is appropriate for them in current circumstances. Women are natural "fixers of problems" in most settings, and this is no place to overlook that natural skill. The analysis must be done strategically, yet casually, to avoid excessive stress. Problems arise when women do not take this on as a challenge that will positively affect their futures. That is when they derail, and, once derailed, they very often do not return to the practice. For many, this was not the desired result.

So, do your homework and choose well. Talk to your law professors and interview women in the profession. For those of you who are practitioners, talk to other women attorneys with experience in a variety of specialties. Try to be realistic and propel yourself five to ten years into the future and imagine the consequences of your choice. It will be time and effort well spent. Also, avoid being influenced by your colleagues. You are unique, and you are the product of your experiences and personal needs. If you value home and family, be honest about it. If you are prepared to sacrifice those things because other things are more important to you, be honest about that, too. The only correct answer comes from you, and finding the right fit will help you avoid unnecessary surprises later. There is plenty of diversity in the profession to respond to a variety of needs. Check it out, and be prepared.

Choose Your Employer Well

Selecting your first employer is one of the most important decisions that you will ever make. It will be your first experience in your chosen profession, and you should want it to be as good and satisfying as possible. It is not a time to act impulsively or to let others make the decision for you. On the other hand, one of my contributors, a male managing partner, sees this somewhat differently, and he takes issue with the priority that I have given to choosing your employer well. He points out that lawyers change jobs much more often today, and he thinks that the type of work that you choose to do is far more important to your future job satisfaction than where you choose to do it. I value his opinion, and I recognize the importance of doing work that is interesting and satisfying. However, I also think that most lawyers, especially women, desire a professional home where they can stay as long as possible. Unlike men, women with families have many other responsibilities outside of work, and the security of work venues compatible with their needs can assume very high priorities in their lives.

In your search for a suitable employer, first consider which employers have opportunities in your chosen specialty, what geographic area you want to live in, and where you will take the bar exam. According to law school career counselors, women law students tend to start with a more definitive idea about their career paths than their male counterparts. Women approach it as an ends-to-means analysis and a way to further themselves as professionals and individuals, and they tend to focus on the specifics of their futures. This is a good thing, and it will be very valuable as long as women stick to the plan, make good decisions on detours, and continually reevaluate. However, according to law school career counselors, for a woman, determining where to live and where to write the bar exam might become a decision based on a current romantic relationship or "the love of her life," and that can get tricky. It is especially problematic as the age of entering first-year law students goes up, and young women find themselves in serious romantic relationships at the same time that they are making critical career decisions. Beware of the limitations of taking a job to follow a mate. Evaluate the relationship to determine if it will last and whether there are other options, such as the mate relocating. Career counselors report cringing a bit when they have conversations with female law students that begin with "my boyfriend. . . ." These should be head decisions, not heart decisions—to the extent possible.

In making this important decision, take full advantage of your law school career counseling office. Many law schools make appointments with the career counselors mandatory for first-year students, including counseling on résumé and cover letter preparation and focusing on goals and aspirations. Do not stop there, though. Continue to consult the career counselors throughout your time in law school and get as much good information and assistance as possible. However, be aware that there is an inherent conflict between the role of the law school career counselor in advising young law students and lawyers. The career counselor has a duty to provide good information but also must keep good relations with employers to safeguard the ability to place students in the future and to protect relationships with contributors to the school. It can be a fine line.

You will see from the List of Contributors and the profiles of my contributors in Chapter 6 that they include women from both private and public-sector employment. The diversity of their practice experiences is broad, and you should read the profiles carefully in the hope that you will find yourself in one of those descriptions. These women have not sugar-coated the challenges in their choice of practice and employer, but one constant theme comes through with ringing clarity. They all have enjoyed their professional experiences, and I hope that you will be able to say that for yourself when you look back on your own career. Now let's look at some of the different types of employment settings that young lawyers will consider.

Traditional Large Law Firm Practice

If the large law firm setting is what you choose, be prepared for the reality. Life as an associate in the very large or "mega" law firms, referred to today as Big Law, is often described to me as "brutal." Associates report being on call, and they say that working for a partner who does not have family responsibilities is especially difficult. Those partners are most often workaholics and contact the associate day and night through an assortment of phone, e-mail, and text messages. This technology trap virtually puts the associate in the office 24/7. The billable hour requirements are very high, and the opportunities for a personal life are restricted by those circumstances. The atmosphere is often like that of a pressure cooker, and there can be very low career satisfaction. On the other hand, the experience gained in a large firm setting can be invaluable, and young attorneys often are able to handle the chaos. It is a serious trade-off of experience for lifestyle, but it is the preferred strategy for many young attorneys. Many decide to work in this environment for a few years, pay off their school debts, and then move to a practice that allows more flexibility for personal life issues. Others learn to love the quality and excitement of the work or develop lifestyles that require high salaries and limit their choices for career change—what one of my contributors refers to as the "golden handcuffs" of great money and reduced options. It is not one size fits all, and predicting your response to the large firm environment is not always easy. There are no right or wrong answers, just the ones right for you.

History shows that young women lawyers are very attracted to large firm practice. Since 1985, 40 percent of the law graduates have been women, and 70 percent of those joined private practice firms out of law school (*Creating Pathways to Success: Retaining Women in Today's Law Firms*, Women's Bar Association of the District of Columbia Initiative on Advancement and Retention of Women, May 2006). In many cases, these women took jobs in Big Law. This is predictable because, in law school, you often hear the large firm experience described as the "plum," the one that everyone wants. It is very high-visibility, and it often hoards the limelight. However, it is only one of many employment choices, and you need to at least consider the others.

One of my contributors stresses that you must not only know the facts about any firm you are considering, but you also must be honest with yourself. According to him, lawyers coming to work in a big firm setting must understand what they are signing up for and must want to do that job. Many associates do not last in Big Law because they were not honest with themselves or they did not take the time and effort to be informed about what it would take to be successful in the large firm setting.

100

He points out that law firms require time and effort from their lawyers, which is converted to revenue. The better the lawyer is, the greater the demand for that lawyer's skills, the higher the rates that can be charged, and the more revenue that is produced. It is a business, and decisions are made consistent with the business model. You will read more on this in "Remember That Law Is a Business" later in this chapter.

The reality of large law firm practice creates a revolving door that can be very unfortunate for the profession. According to a law school career counselor, acceptance of the status quo by the Big Law firms raises concerns that the firms do not value the contribution of bright, experienced young lawyers as they should and do not view them as long-range assets to the business. The firm leverages off the associates for years until they are burned out and leave, well before the firm has to consider them for partnership and equity positions.

However, there is a lot of money to be made during the first years of practice at big law firms. Women law graduates, like their male counterparts, often go for the money and do not look beyond the five-year window that it will take to pay back their law school loans. Most midlevel associates surveyed by *The American Lawyer* and reported in the August 1, 2008 edition of the *ABA Journal*, plan to stay at their law firms for the short term, but few have aspirations of being there for the long term. The statistics quoted in the article also reflect the likelihood of layoffs and cutbacks in the current economic downturn and the fact that those considerations factor into the decisions about how long associates can see themselves staying at their firms. Associates recognize that the times of making partner when you "sat back and rode the gravy train" are long gone, and they have reservations about making partner and working long hours and having primary responsibility for developing clients. By contrast, the article discusses smaller firm practices where job satisfaction ratings were higher.

Other young lawyers, who are not as strategic, simply ignore the issue of the revolving door and tell themselves that they will address the problems later. They typically address the issue when the loans are paid off and when they are thinking about starting a family. Many of the women will find a way to stay through one pregnancy and one baby but will leave after the second child comes along. The deciding factor for many of them at that time is whether they can afford to leave the Big Law environment and the money. Those that can afford to leave the big firm, because they have kept their lifestyles in check in terms of spending, often do. Those who have not paid attention to those issues might not have the flexibility to leave and settle for less income.

One law school career counselor reports that "the hiring philosophy in Big Law is broken." She says that the "chew them up and spit them out" experience for associates is standard, and she faults the employers for the fact that most young lawyers last only five to seven years at Big Law. She describes conversations with former law students who are disappointed in the high pressure environment of Big Law that leaves no room for a personal life. The young lawyers report that they do not have time to meet people socially and to find a life partner. They work hard toward acceptance on the partnership track and then, one day, they look up and realize that they have no life and no options—no mate, no kids, and living alone. Panic sets in, and this is especially true of women, who also have ticking biological clocks to worry about. When this counselor asks the employers if they explained the reality of a Big Law commitment to the students, she gets answers like "No. They would not accept the offers if we told them that." Beware of this pitfall. Remember that law firm hiring partners want to be able to present the very best entering class to the firm. It is not necessarily in their best interest to watch out for you. You must watch out for you.

You need to understand that the downsides of Big Law are not just the result of the inflexibility and insensitivity of large law firm management. They are also driven by the level of service that clients demand and pay for and the resulting fee structures and required billable hours that are necessary to provide the service. Remember that the primary competition is not for good lawyers—there are plenty of those to go around. Rather, the most important competition is for clients, and the way to gain and keep clients is to meet their demands and exceed their expectations. That is where the 24/7 comes in, and there is no other proven way of achieving that goal.

Although it is very important to choose a firm that meets your financial and practice needs and provides you with compatible colleagues, it is also important for you to look at the firm structure. If partnership is your goal, take a look at the partner/associate ratio and determine the potential for partnership. Look at the percentage of partners who are women, and calculate your opportunities for advancement. Look at the partnership scheme. Are there various classes of partners? What does that mean for advancement opportunities? Some firms have only equity partners, who share in the profits of the firm, and some firms have two levels of partnership, typically income partners and equity partners. Income partners are paid a guaranteed salary but do not share in the profits of the firm. As a result, if the firm has a banner year, the income partners will not share in the phenomenal profits. However, income partners also do not share in the losses. If there are two levels of partnership, inquire about the time line and criteria for promotion from income partner to equity partner. You want to avoid a situation where you will be stuck at income partner with very little possibility for promotion to the equity partnership you might desire.

The First Annual Conference of the Project for Attorney Retention (an initiative of the Center for WorkLife Law (*www.worklifelaw.org*) at the University of California Hastings College of the Law) in May 2008, entitled "Positioning Law Firms for Long-Term Success: New Strategies for Advancing Women Lawyers," included interesting material on what women should look for in firms. Ida Abbott of Ida Abbott Consulting, LLC, outlined the following points, which I think are particularly instructive:

- Look for firms where promoting women into key leadership roles and client relationships is a firm policy—a law firm culture that ensures that women are considered, groomed, and promoted at the same rate as men. You want a firm that sets goals for women in these positions and holds supervising attorneys and the firm leadership responsible for reaching these goals.

103

- Do not trust the information on the firm Web site or at firm retreats. That information might include meaningless programs that are put in place as a quick fix. You should be looking for an institutionalized program that represents a culture shift for the law firm in the direction of helping women succeed in their profession.
- Ask the questions and expect the firm to have answers. Ask both male and female attorneys, and listen very closely to what the men say. Ask your questions from the perspective of a woman who wants to know how she is any different from the many women attorneys who were not advanced. Look for a firm that gives supervising attorneys a stake in the success of women attorneys. Some firms give monetary rewards to supervising attorneys and take feedback from junior lawyers about their supervisors.

To assist you in identifying the right issues and asking the right questions, I recommend the *Cheat Sheet* guide (*www.flextimelawyers.com*), by Deborah Epstein Henry, the founder of Flex-Time Lawyer LLC, in cooperation with the New York City Bar Association. It is a list of in-depth questions women need to ask to discover a firm's commitment to retention and advancement and focuses on areas that, historically, have been stumbling blocks for women. Some of these include mentoring, workplace flexibility, and partnership advancement.

One of my contributors, a law firm managing partner, urges young lawyers to take control of their careers from the beginning of their practice. He encourages you to view a law firm with a critical eye and determine which practices within the firm are the most successful—which practices have the most resources allocated to them, which have the most influential partners, and which are recognized the most in defining the success of the firm. In his estimation, your greatest chances of success lie in those practices, and you want to be in a practice that will make it easier rather than harder for you to succeed.

Satellite offices of a large firm are also options. Satellite offices of large firms can be attractive because they typically are smaller and often present greater opportunities for young lawyers to gain early responsibility and valuable experience. It can mean meeting with clients, making court appearances, and taking other significant practice responsibilities earlier in your career. However, there also can be problems with a satellite office. The home office often does not have an adequate marketing strategy for the satellite office and might not provide resources for the greatest success of the office. The home office might also present valuable programs and educational opportunities that are not available to attorneys in satellite offices. These situations are to be distinguished from the multiple offices of the typical big law firm. In those situations, the various offices around the country and the world are often as large as the home office and present multiple large firm settings within the same firm.

If practice in a small firm, as further discussed later in this chapter, is attractive to you, you need to be aware that mergers and acquisitions can transform a small firm into a larger firm in very short order. The law business today is very dynamic in terms of mergers and acquisitions, and firms are merging and acquiring other practices for a variety of reasons, including eliminating competition, adding critical practices, and dealing with economic constraints. During economic uncertainty, mergers and acquisitions are driven as much by survival mechanisms as by the traditional business motivations. Most of this merger exploration and activity is reported in periodicals like *Legal Times* and the legal tabloids and Web sites, and you should pay close attention to those sources. You also should ask questions of your law school career counselors who will likely be "wired into" the most current information.

Mergers and acquisitions change the firm structure, both positively and negatively. It is important that you anticipate these changes and that you position yourself to have choices. You might have chosen a small firm for a reason, and you might, via merger action, be facing life in a much larger organization. The degree of your choices will depend on how aware you are of what is going on in your firm. Keep your eyes and ears open, and get as close to the "heartbeat" of the firm as possible for a young attorney. One way to do this is to get on committees where some of this might be discussed. You will have to take time away from the billable hour to volunteer for these committees, however, and this is not necessarily attractive to women. Women, typically, are "doers," and they very often avoid environments that are structured on consensus of committee members and emphasize sitting, listening, and scheduling the next meeting. Women often view these types of experiences as a waste of time. One of my contributors recalls her frustration with her male colleagues who sat around during settlement talks exploring every small possibility. She was interested in devising a plan of action, and executing on the plan. Men and women very often approach problem solving differently.

You might share some of these same frustrations, but do not let it stand in the way of opportunity. Get on committees, keep your antennae up, and talk to persons in the power circle who you can trust. It will pay dividends in the end when you are able to use this information to protect your ability to make choices. If you know that the firm is headed in a direction that will not be comfortable for you, you can use that information to pursue your options. On the other hand, if you are too buried in the billable hour to take notice of important signs of change, you might be blind-sided and have forfeited some of your options.

Becoming active in the firm committee structure is important for other reasons, as well. You want to understand how business decisions are made and the results and repercussions of those decisions. Understanding how business is done at your firm or organization will reduce your anxieties about others controlling your future. It also will benefit you if you ever become a solo practitioner or set up a small partnership. In those settings, you will be a businesswoman as well as an attorney because the economic realities of a small practice often preclude hiring office staff and consultants to run the business end of the practice. In addition, committee involvement might also assist you in creating alliances and familiarity with important firm members and partners who can become very valuable to you in other ways. Partners often will look to associates who they like and feel comfortable with when assigning work. That is a trickle-down effect that can benefit you and help you in building your practice.

Your salary needs likely will play a big part in your decision on where to start your practice. Let's return to the NALP graph of salaries, discussed in Chapter 2, as you determine your salary needs after graduation from law school. If you need an annual salary of $70,000 to meet your debt load and living expenses, you might conclude that your needs fall somewhere between the high and the low and that there will be plenty of opportunities to find a job to meet your needs. However, the information and the graph can be deceptive. Although the high end of $160,000 represents a solid number and can be substantiated through research of the top-tier law firm compensation levels, the median of $40,000 is simply what is in the middle of $160,000 and all of the salaries on the low end. In reality there is much on the low side of $40,000 but little on the high side of $60,000. As a result, your need level of $70,000 might preclude you from considering certain types of jobs. For a more expanded discussion of starting salaries and how they are affected by demographics, see *Starting Salaries: What New Law Graduates Earn—Class of 2007* (NALP 2008) and *Jobs JD's, Employment and Salaries of New Law Graduates, Class of 2007* (NALP 2008).

Learn to love to negotiate. Think of Denny Crane, the colorful character on *Boston Legal* played by William Shatner, and the Price Point television commercials featuring his character and the mantra, "Don't you just *love* to negotiate?" The answer very decidedly should be "yes." Be prepared to negotiate on a variety of things with a prospective employer, especially salary. According to the law school career counselors, women are more reluctant to do this than men. It might have something to do with the historic societal taboo about women discussing money or asking for it. Get over that—it is so yesterday—in fact, it is many yesterdays ago. Get comfortable discussing money. A career in the law is all about money. How will you advocate for the most money for your client if you cannot do it for yourself? Go to the follow-up interview armed with the most current salary information and advocate from a position of strength. Be polite, but firm. Be honest about your salary requirements based on real obligations (school loans, car payments, etc.). This is a "value" issue, and women need to value themselves in this discussion, just like men do.

On the subject of negotiations, I recommend the following books to you: *Women Don't Ask: The High Cost of Avoiding Negotiation and Positive Strategies for Change* by Linda Babcock and Sara Laschever (Bantam, 2007), *The Power of Nice: How to Negotiate So Everyone Wins—Especially You!* by Ronald M. Shapiro and Mark A. Jankowski (John Wiley and Sons, 2001), and *Her Place at the Table* by Deborah M. Kolb, PhD, Judith Willams, PhD, and Carol Frohlinger, JD.

For those who choose Big Law, the career counselors advise that you constantly assess the benefits of the firm versus the detriments of hard work and untenable hours. The benefits might include the learning and practice area opportunities, the pro bono and professional development opportunities, the mentoring opportunities, and compensation and benefits such as health care. The most positive benefits analysis will include a high level of autonomy in the work, a high quality of interesting work, supportive and interesting colleagues, and an acceptable work-life balance. This benefits analysis should be done on a yearly basis and should also include the qualities of the annual reviews that most associates receive at law firms. Young lawyers should take full advantage of all opportunities for growth and should take a candid look at the work-life balance to determine whether the large firm practice environment will help them achieve the lives they desire.

Career counselors report that many students just have to *try* Big Law and that they cannot resist the temptation. Positive summer associate experiences often affect the decision to join big law firms. Law career counselors report that the students come back from the second summer associate experiences raving about their experiences. The lure of the wining and dining is just too great. If you choose this path, and many of you will, good luck. The fact that Big Law has chosen you speaks volumes about your talents and capabilities. Use them well and wisely.

Before we leave the subject of Big Law, you need to note again that large law practices are undergoing structural reorganizations and strategy revisions in response to the economic recession that began in the fall of 2008. I refer you back to Chapter 2 for a discussion of the economic impact on law firms and lawyers, and I urge you to keep this information in mind as you choose your practice setting.

The Alternatives to Large Law Firm Practice

Although Big Law and medium to large-size law firms are very popular among law school graduates today, that practice might not be for you. If you are a woman who will not react well to huge amounts of pressure and the billable hour requirements or who does not want the personal life sacrifices that define large firm practice, it is a good idea to look at the options to a large national practice.

Smaller firms and firms located in more remote geographic areas might be better for you. You should not shy away from these options. There are many styles of practicing law, and they are all rewarding in their own ways. Just because you might not be designed for the pressures and demands of large law firm practice does not make you any less of an attorney. Some of the most professionally satisfied lawyers I know are practicing in small firms and small communities throughout America. My brother, for example, practices in a small town in Montana. He lives on a beautiful ranch with views of three distinct mountain ranges and watches deer, elk, great blue herons, sandhill cranes, bald eagles, and an occasional panther along his stretch of a superb trout stream every morning. He has a pretty good life from my perspective—and from his, I know. Another family member practices at the foot of the Rocky Mountains and often bird hunts with his dogs in the morning before he leaves for the office. My father practiced in a small town in Wisconsin for 50 years and had an exceptionally rewarding career. At his funeral, I was moved to tears by the wonderful stories that his clients shared with our family. When I asked one elderly woman to explain how she knew my father, she said, "My dear, he was our lawyer, and he saved our farm—more than once. He took care of us." On hearing this, my husband and I stood in amazement as we contemplated our experiences in big-city national practices. We knew that such a thing would never be said about us by our clients. Our clients are more likely to be talking about the outrageous size of the legal bills when we are dead and gone.

There is a great variety of work in these smaller practices, and it keeps the attorneys very interested and interesting. As one of them pointed out to me, "The actual practice of law is not much different [than a large city practice]. It is just that I don't have to drive hours or leave on weekends to do the outdoor activities that I enjoy." These attorneys develop relationships with their clients, many of whom are also their friends and neighbors, and these attorneys gain a great deal of satisfaction from helping their clients make decisions that improve the lives of those clients and benefit the communities as well. Most often, they also have very desirable work-life balances and qualities of life. Solo practice within these settings can also be attractive in terms of autonomy and personal reward. However, you need to consider the possibility that you might have to work years without turning a profit before you establish a successful business. If you are the only breadwinner, this can be a problem.

Those who do not want to pursue private practice at all will choose to pursue alternatives, and it is important to know what some of those alternatives might be. Options in public service (including government, the judiciary, public interest, and nonprofit practice), nongovernment organizations (NGOs), trade associations, and alternative dispute resolution entities might be more interesting to those women. These options present completely different practice models, including the possibility of more flexible schedules and the availability of management positions earlier in a career, and some of these opportunities might include guaranteed income, generous benefits, reasonable hours, earlier opportunities for advancement, excellent retirement programs and other lifestyle considerations. One of my contributors points out that, although the hours and dedication are not necessarily less in these practices, the rewards are very different. First Lady Michelle Obama addressed the rewards of public service in her address to the Democratic National Convention on August 25, 2008: "In my own small way, I have tried to give back to this country that has given me so much. . . . that's why I left a job at a big law firm for a career in public service."

The opportunities in government run the gamut from local government to the federal government. Government attorney positions at the city or county level can be very interesting because of the breadth of issues and the opportunity to see a more immediate effect from efforts than at the higher levels of government. I worked as chief of staff to an elected official on the county level for eight years of my career. The county was one of the largest in the country, and that job was extremely interesting and professionally satisfying because of the variety of issues encountered. Most chief of staff and administrative aide positions on the state and federal level require a law degree, and it was particularly helpful on the local level, as well. In that job, I worked with lawyers in the Office of the County Attorney, and I enjoyed interfacing with them on a daily basis. They were excellent lawyers, and several of them are contributors to this book.

State government jobs can be very interesting as well, and the opportunities at the federal level are even more varied and specialized. Although the U.S. Department of Justice and the state counterparts are the agencies with the greatest concentration of lawyers, almost every agency of government has its own office of counsel, and you should not overlook those opportunities. There are also opportunities in the various administrative law bodies throughout the state and federal government and as legislative and administrative aides in congressional offices and the offices of state legislators. The judiciary is another career path that offers interesting and rewarding job experience from local courts to state courts to federal courts. Many of these positions are political, and membership and activity in local bar associations are recommended for lawyers interested in ascending to the bench. Jobs in the related fields of mediation and arbitration and other alternative dispute resolution programs are also worth exploring. Other interesting settings within government include offices of prosecutors (who represent the interests of the public in the prosecution of the accused in a criminal case), public defenders (who represent those accused of crimes), and legal services for indigent persons.

The experience of one of my very successful contributors comes to mind. She and I graduated from law school at about the same time. Instead of pursuing litigation in the private sector and following the money trail, she chose an agency of the federal government. She has been there for almost 30 years, has advanced to assistant department head, has had the advantage of flexibility to deal with some significant family health issues, and has a great retirement program and benefits in her future. In addition, she has had a very fulfilling career in an exciting field of the law, and she was a woman pioneer in her field. I often contemplate why more women of my generation did not go this route at a time when there was a government mandate to hire women and taking that route might have made many of the difficult work-life choices easier. My best guess is that it had something to do with failing to define ourselves.

In addition to government practice, public interest, and not-for-profit practices can be very professionally rewarding and address issues that are uniquely relevant to society. Generally speaking, public interest law addresses gaining justice for disadvantaged and underserved individuals or communities; promoting the interests of the public through the protections of the agencies of government; protecting and preserving the world's health and resources for the public good; and preserving, protecting, and defending human rights, civil rights, and civil liberties. Public interest law can be practiced in government agencies or in public interest organizations, usually nonprofits, and public interest law firms, which are generally smaller firms that focus on individual plaintiffs or class actions and policy that impacts litigation. Not-for-profit organizations include nongovernmental organizations (NGOs) and charities. The role of a lawyer in a charity includes reviewing the laws of each jurisdiction where the charitable organization solicits contributions and advising on compliance responsibilities; overseeing preparation of all applications, forms, and reports for timely filing with government organizations; assisting with annual reports; and monitoring government regulations and laws affecting the organization. (For more information, see *The Law of Fundraising*, 3rd edition, by Bruce R. Hopkins (John Wiley & Sons, 2008.)) There are certain law schools in the country, like Seattle University School of Law, that emphasize public interest practices in their curriculum. If you are interested in these practices, you should research these schools and communicate with the administration and professors about the programs.

Ada Shen-Jaffe, Distinguished Practitioner in Residence on the Seattle University School of Law Web site explains the attraction of a public interest practice as follows:

> People commit to public interest work for many different reasons: it is part of their core identity, it gives greater meaning and significance to their lives in a way that capitalizes on their professional skills, they want to make a real difference in someone's life by reducing human suffering, righting a wrong, stopping an unfair practice, or ensuring that justice is not just for some but for all. In addition to any of these motivations, public interest law demands a higher level of creativity, hard work and devotion than any other professional undertaking, and can provide the greatest professional and personal satisfaction and rewards you will ever know. Add to this the privilege of working with social justice-motivated colleagues with whom you will share a treasured bond, and you have a winning combination of factors leading to a lifelong commitment to public interest law no matter where your legal career may take you. There is always a contribution you can make, a role you can play in the furtherance of justice.

There are recent reports that increased financial pressures brought on by higher law school tuition and resulting larger student loans are making it harder to attract young lawyers into public service and to keep them there. The NALP survey, released in September 2008, found that pay scales for public lawyers in the Northeastern region—New Jersey, New York, Pennsylvania, and six New England states—are generally higher than the national average, with New Jersey leading that list, but that the figures still lag considerably behind the private practice earning levels. In that context, it is worth considering new federal legislation, the College Cost Reduction Act of 2009, which addresses the cost of higher education and repayment of student loans. This program provides repayment assistance and loan forgiveness in certain circumstances, including public service, and is very worthy of your attention.

Practically speaking, it might be a good idea to try your hand at public interest work while in law school to gain invaluable experience and practical legal skills and to develop professional contacts. Justice Sandra Day O'Connor put it very well: "In engaging in public service, law students are awakened to the sense of personal satisfaction that comes from helping people, a feeling they are not likely to experience in their other classes." Here are some job resources to consult in exploring the various areas of public service law:

For Non-Profits: Idealist.org; Equal Justice Works; The Public Interest Law Initiative; PSLawNet.org; and National Legal Aid & Defender Association (NLADA) Job Opportunities

For Public Interest Law Firms: The National Association for Law Placement (NALP) Directory of Legal Employers; Yale Law School's guide to public interest law firms; and Harvard Law School's guide to public interest law firms

For Government: *www.USAJobs.com* (the Web page for all federal government job openings) and the Web sites for state and local government offices

Another option for public-interest-minded law students is teaching at a law school. Although positions in academia are very competitive and typically require experience in practice, some students might consider this as a future career option. The Society of American Law Teachers Web site (*www.saltlaw.org*) will be helpful in gaining information about this option. You also should be aware that globalization has created fascinating opportunities in emerging economies outside of the United States. Although many of these opportunities are in the large law firm setting (in the last 20 years the number of lawyers working overseas for the NLJ 250 firms has grown at a rate of more than ten times the number of lawyers working in the U.S. offices of these firms), there are also opportunities in smaller firms and in myriad settings throughout the world. Your law school career services offices should be able to provide information and advice on those opportunities.

As you can see, there are many alternatives to the traditional large law firm practices that tend to dominate the landscape in the discussion of law in the media. There are often no partners to deal with in these settings, there is more flexibility and fair treatment in response to individual needs, and the subject matter is intellectually challenging. The trade-off is financial, in most circumstances, and you must decide if that is a trade-off that works for you. It might be that salary is not the most important consideration for you, and, if so, you should not overlook these opportunities. I know many small firm practice and public service attorneys who have had fascinating careers with a choice of flexible schedules to address the needs of family and personal life.

Although the world of the in-house business lawyer is not a subject of in-depth discussion in this book, I feel compelled to mention that practice setting as another viable option to be explored. One of my contributors left private practice to work part time as in-house counsel at a high-tech firm. It was a very positive change for her, and she found that the company truly valued her advice, considered her an integral part of the company, and relied on her in decision making. The company president was particularly supportive of family needs for all of his employees, not just the women. Another contributor works in private wealth management, a specialty that she recommends because it attracts many women and is a particularly good working environment for them.

That brings me to a very important question: What makes a good working environment for women? My contributors offer the following guidelines on that issue. Factors that make a good working environment for women include a preponderance of women attorneys; positive role models for women attorneys, including successful examples of flexibility in terms of work-life issues; a compensation system that rewards teamwork over individual achievement and changes the behavior of all employees for the better; and challenging work and promotion consistent with performance. One of my contributors sums it up very well: "Where you find collegiality you will also find an environment that is good for women."

Another of my contributors describes the following positive working environment.

Case
in
Point

"My law firm practice manager is a mother of three school-aged children, including a baby that she adopted recently. The manager brought the baby to work for the first few months after the adoption so that she could 'bond' with her new child. In turn, the manager has been supportive of several female associates in our practice group who wanted to return to work part time after having babies. The manager's leadership in the office sets a positive tone that contributes to the very positive working environment. I had problems during my first pregnancy and was confined to bed for a ten-week period. When I returned to work, the manager rallied support for me and eventually recommended me for partnership."

—Linda, 30-Something

One of my contributors describes her most favorable and positive work environments as women-owned businesses. In her experience, women owners tend to be tough but ferociously loyal and fair, as well as much more flexible when it comes to competing family responsibilities. This makes me think that it would be a good idea for you to keep in touch with your female college friends who are pursuing MBAs, as they could provide just that kind of client environment for you one day.

Whatever specialty or employment environment you choose, make sure that your choice includes a positive relationship with your colleagues and a good working environment for women. During the interview process, ask members of the firm to lunch or out for a drink after work to get to know them while you are making your decision. Although we might think that personalities should not be that important, we all know that they are. Seek out your comfort level, do your homework, and listen to your gut.

For more on this subject, I recommend *Beyond the Big Firm—Profiles of Lawyers Who Want Something More* by Alan B. Morrison and Diane T. Chin (Aspen Publishers, Wolters Kluwer Law & Business, 2007).

Be an Excellent Lawyer

Above everything else, whatever your specialty or wherever you decide to practice, you must be an excellent lawyer. Being an excellent lawyer means more than just working hard, staying abreast of recent developments in your specialty that will benefit your clients, and providing excellent client service. In addition to working hard, being an excellent lawyer also means working smart. Most everything that you will want in your practice, in terms of flexibility, accommodations, and special considerations will depend on whether you are an excellent lawyer who is valued by your employer. It is key. One of my contributors puts it this way: "There is no free lunch, and you will pay a very high price for lack of preparation and dedication."

For women, especially, working harder and being better in what is still a male-dominated profession is very important. However, this should not be difficult. Women are at the top of most law school graduating classes today. Women lawyers are smart, and they recognize that there is no substitute for hard work and persistence. Keep your eye on the prize and do not allow yourself to get derailed by the pitfalls. Be aware, however, that, according to the November 2007 NAWL National Survey on Retention and Promotion of Women in Law Firms, even this will not entirely level the playing field. Information gathered in that survey indicates that hard work pays off for men much more than for women. The ABA Commission on Women in the Profession report, *A Current Glance at Women in the Law 2007*, found that female lawyers earned only 70.5 percent of the weekly salary of their male colleagues (as you might recall from the chart in Chapter 3). Paying close attention to the lessons addressed in this book, however, might help to give you a leg up in this fight. And it is a fight. Make no mistake about that. Most law students and lawyers are familiar with the Latin phrase *Illegitimi non Carborundum*, which translates as "Don't let the bastards get you down." Women aren't even an afterthought!

To "keep up with the boys"—or to surpass them—women lawyers must learn to ask for work. Women lawyers need to get comfortable asking managers for projects and making the case for why they are the best choice for the work. Women must be willing to ask and volunteer and embrace risk. If women lawyers do not learn to ask, they will forego valuable and meaningful work and might become disillusioned and resentful. This could lead to an unfortunate decision to resign and should be avoided at all costs.

Asking for projects might be more difficult for women. Women are reared to think that it is not good manners to say "I want" and to promote themselves. Promotion of this kind is often referred to as "constructive engagement" or raising issues with people who have greater power. The key to this type of dialogue is conducting yourself in a professional manner while being firm and persuasive. This same problem arises in the context of promoting work and getting new clients, which is addressed in "Find a Comfort Zone for Promoting Work" later in this chapter.

You also should not hesitate to speak up when you perceive a problem. In most cases, the problem is not going to go away, and you are better advised to meet it straight on and try to work with your supervisor on a mutually acceptable solution. Very often, the partner or supervisor will be much more receptive than you might expect. Similarly, conducting yourself appropriately sometimes means pushing back. Don't be afraid to do this. Men do it all the time, and they expect you to do it. The key to both of these situations is how you conduct yourself. Pay close attention to your delivery, and make it work for you.

Being a woman can work to your advantage in becoming an excellent lawyer, and you should use it that way. Do not hide it, but do not flaunt it either. Hiding your femininity and your unique skills as a woman is a waste of natural resources. Keep it subtle, however. Many women, for example, can be very effective at negotiation and consensus building because of their natural charm, and they can easily gain concessions based on their appeal. Women should not be afraid to use those talents and to maximize on them. Overdo the feminine approach, however, whether by appearance or demeanor, and it will gain you a negative reputation that only a huge rainmaker can survive. Knowing the difference is critical.

Women seem to be particularly skilled in the areas of organization, communication, dispute resolution, and other "people" issues. These skills can become especially valuable to a supervising male attorney, who might be classically disorganized and detest personnel issues. Offering assistance with these thorny issues and tapping into your unique experiences and talents as a woman can work to your advantage in these situations. Women also tend to be more empathetic and compassionate than men, and they often are very tuned into societal problems. Because the practice of law is the reflection of societal problems, these attributes can be very helpful and valuable. Women need to use their strengths to their best advantage.

Being an excellent lawyer also means that you must be taken seriously. You might be attractive and appealing, but you are also a law student or lawyer and deserve to be treated like a professional. Some men in the legal profession find it difficult to take female colleagues seriously, and some even like to see their female counterparts fail. I know it sounds harsh, but it is true. A suggestion by a woman might be ignored or dismissed, whereas that same suggestion from a male colleague is treated as worthy of consideration. Male attorneys often hold female colleagues to a different standard, and they throw up roadblocks and indulge in stereotypes. They also can use women's inherently helpful nature to demean them and relegate them to inappropriate supporting positions. This is not as true as it used to be, but it still occurs in subtle ways, and you should be aware of the pitfall. You must demand to be taken seriously, and, once you are, you will be in a position to influence the way you and other women colleagues are perceived and treated. Here are some examples of the obstacles that male colleagues can intentionally throw up as challenges that are inappropriate.

Case
in
Point

"Early in my practice, I was co-counsel with a young male attorney in an out-of-town trial that lasted a week. At the conclusion of the trial and upon return to the office, the senior partners and supervising attorneys gathered in an office to be debriefed by the male colleague on the events of the trial. I was not invited to the debriefing, even though I had responsibility for half the issues at trial. Later, when the decision came down from the judge, again I was not included in the discussion, even though I had been equally as successful in the outcome of the trial as my male colleague. I felt excluded and embarrassed at the treatment by my male colleagues, and I stewed about it in both instances. I knew that this "boys club" behavior was wrong, and I should have walked right in and joined the discussion. Step up and take your rightful place and make your male colleagues take you seriously."

—Jenna, 60-Something

Male judges can be even more challenging and can present impossible dilemmas. I have personal experience with this.

Case
in
Point

"The year was approximately 1981, and I was arguing a motion in federal court before a notorious judge. This judge was consistently voted one of the most irascible federal judges in the nation, and he was becoming old and, reportedly, a bit senile. At the outset of the argument, the judge admonished me with these words, 'Girl, woman, whatever you people like to be called today, I want you to know something about my courtroom. I expect you to try your cases like a man, cite your authority like a man, and take everything that I have to give you from this bench like a man. Do you understand?' As I nodded in agreement, the judge bellowed, 'Because we do not discriminate in this courtroom, missy.' I was astonished, and those present in the courtroom exploded with laughter. Is this what I had gone to law school for? Of course the behavior was outrageous, but I had no recourse. I took my licks and lived to have many other similar encounters with this same judge, including the following remark by the judge when he had no choice but to rule in my favor, 'What have we come to in this profession when we let women speak so freely?' "

—Susan, 60-Something

I also recall a male state circuit court judge, who failed to address me by name during a five-day trial, even though he called my male colleagues by their names and referred to them as "counsel." The best he could do for me was "she" and "her" when directing comments to me or about me. I was later told that I was the first woman attorney to appear in his courtroom, and I guess it was challenging for him as well. The year was 1981. In approximately that same year, one of my contributors reports being addressed by a local judge as "Honey Child" when she presented an order for his signature: "Yes, Honey Child, I will be happy to sign that order."

Fortunately, the profession has evolved over the past 30 years, and the acceptance of women is not the problem it once was. Some of this progress might be due to the fact that older male lawyers now have daughters in the profession, and they have a much closer view of the resolve and determination that it takes for most women attorneys to succeed. Although things have changed for the better today, proving worth and gaining respect continue to be high hurdles for women lawyers.

Stand up for yourself and be sure that you are taken seriously. Above all, be an excellent lawyer. It cannot be said too many times.

121

Do Not Tolerate Gender Bias

Treat your male colleagues with respect and expect equally good behavior from the men in your practice. Never let a male colleague use your gender or your feminine appeal against you to deny you job opportunities. Again, these types of things are much rarer than they were in the days when I started practicing law because of federal protection prohibiting such inappropriate behavior. However, subtle versions still exist today, and you should always be on the lookout for these pitfalls. Never countenance sexual harassment, stereotyping, and discrimination that can be used to deny women equal pay, equal work, and safe working environments.

In addition to gender discrimination, you also need to be aware of discrimination based on your family responsibilities. The Center for Work-Life Law at the University of California Hastings College of the Law includes a definition of family responsibilities discrimination that I include for your future reference:

> Family Responsibilities Discrimination is unlawful employment discrimination against workers who have family responsibilities. Pregnant women, mothers and fathers of young children, and employees with aging parents or sick spouses/partners may find themselves discriminated against. They may be rejected for employment, demoted, harassed, passed over for promotion, or terminated—despite good performance evaluations—simply because their employers make personnel decisions based on stereotypical notions of how they will or should act.

Here are some examples of family responsibilities discrimination:

- Firing pregnant employees or telling them to get an abortion if they wish to remain employed
- Giving promotions to less qualified men or women without children rather than to highly qualified mothers
- Developing hiring profiles that expressly exclude women with young children

- Terminating employees without a valid business reason when they return from maternity or paternity leave
- Giving parents work schedules that they cannot meet for child care reasons while giving nonparents different work schedules
- Fabricating work infractions or performance deficiencies to justify dismissal of employees with family responsibilities

All of these things are against the law, and if you believe that you are falling victim to these practices, you should consult an employment attorney. Although it is the 21st century, it might not be your imagination. There are still some uneducated and untrainable people in the workplace.

One of my contributors makes the following observations. In the beginning of her practice in 1979, there were many gender bias incidents. The one that mattered the most to her was being passed over for partnership for a male colleague who was the department head's "pet." She also recalls incidents when she was overlooked for staffing on major pieces of litigation because the male partners who were heading up the litigation did not like to travel with a female associate. She observes that she never was sure how much of that attitude was driven by the attitudes of their spouses. Other of my contributors had similar experiences.

Case in Point

"I began practice in the late 1970s and quickly rose to the top of my class of associates. I was assigned to excellent cases and was gaining extraordinary experience. After my second year of practice, I was assigned to the trial team for a very large litigation that involved considerable travel with my supervising male attorney. In the days before leaving for the trial, I began to have difficult conversations and unanticipated conflict with the supervising attorney over what appeared to be small and inconsequential issues. I had no choice but to confront the supervising attorney to discuss the reason for his behavior. After

123

avoiding answering the question several times, he finally admitted the reason for his discontent. He told me that he did not feel comfortable traveling with me because I was a 'temptation' to him and that he preferred to travel with a male colleague who could join him for a game of hoops at the health club gym. Amazing, but true."

—**Donna, 60-Something**

It is interesting to note that an episode of the television series from the late 1980s, *LA Law*, dealt with a similar situation. A young woman attorney was passed over for excellent work that she was entitled to because a male attorney found her attractive and could not deal professionally with his attraction. As it turns out, there were many episodes of that television series that highlighted real issues of conflict between men and women in the legal workplace. The viewing public, as a rule, thought it was great fiction, and it was a very popular show. Those women, like many of my contributors, who were living it daily, knew that it was anything but fiction.

Another contributor, a litigator, recollects this from her experiences in the early 1980s.

Case in Point

"I was involved in a settlement conference with five male attorneys, and the judge greeted each male and shook each male's hand at the start of the meeting. When I extended my hand, the judge intentionally withdrew his hand, in a very public snub. It seemed clear to me that the judge was signaling the male attorneys that 'this woman will not be taken seriously in this courtroom and you men have nothing to worry about.' This particular judge had a reputation for not wanting women in his courtroom, and many years later he was forced to resign from the bench in disgrace after a number of claims of sexual harassment were brought

against him. When I returned to my office after the settlement conference and informed one of the senior partners in my firm about this
outrageous event, the male partners seemed shocked and supportive but
commented, 'Well, I guess we can't send you to any more conferences
with Judge X if he has a problem with women.'"

—Jill, 40-Something

There is no excuse for this kind of behavior today, and there wasn't
much excuse for it 30 years ago. Men know the rules and must pay the
price if they break those rules. You cannot be denied work that you are
qualified to do because of your gender. Do not allow this to happen. Bring
it to the attention of the appropriate law firm committee chair and nip it in
the bud. Bad behavior does not get better with age.

Another of my contributors describes her first years in government
practice during the 1970s as tough because many of the clients (other
government employees) were men who were not used to dealing with
women professionals. She describes unfortunate episodes where men
propositioned her and made crude remarks to her with impunity.
However, during the 1980s, when women were more prevalent in the
workplace, conditions improved, although she was still subjected to back-
handed compliments like commenting on a job well done "for a girl"—not
only from clients but from opposing counsel and judges!

Not all gender bias is overt, and you must also be on the alert for more
subtle forms of gender bias like patronization. If a male colleague or a client
is not contacting you directly because of some perceived bias, talk to your
managing lawyer and expect him or her to remedy the situation. One of my
contributors describes an example of this when a mediator did not want to
deal with her and virtually "talked to her" through her male co-counsel.
Similarly, do not allow a male supervisor to relay messages to you through
a male colleague or to allow a male colleague to parcel out assignments for
the supervisor. Very often this will result in the loss of opportunities for

good work as the male colleague cherry picks the best cases before making assignments to you. This is effective discrimination that can seriously impact your career in a negative way. You should complain to the supervising attorney as soon as this happens. If it persists, you must take it to another level and make your career choices based on how satisfactorily it is resolved.

One of my contributors, a partner in a midsized law firm, has this to say on the subject of gender bias:

> The gender bias that is really dangerous is the kind that you don't see or recognize. My law school class in 1979 was 30 percent women, and I would not have believed it then if you had told me that, in 2009, on average, only 17 percent of law firm partners would be women and that women would still be earning substantially less than men. The cumulative effect of the loss of so many women over time is dramatic, and the loss to the profession of all that talent and creativity is enormous. Although I practice with a lot of wonderful men, it just isn't the same as having fellow women in the practice. I think that it is particularly difficult now because the men are just as worn down and frustrated as the women by the departure of so many women. Unfortunately, however, I sense that the men see the departures of women as evidence that there is something wrong with women rather than something wrong with the practice.

Another of my contributors, a partner in a large international firm, regrets that she did not stand up to gender bias when it first occurred.

Case in Point

"It was not until late in my career that I experienced gender bias, specifically when I moved into positions of leadership in my firms. I think that there is still a huge bias against women in leadership positions, in part because there are so few of us. I did not handle the discrimination very well. Instead of calling my male colleagues on it when it happened, I laughed it off and tried to 'fit in.' That was a mistake and part of the reason for the failure of my previous firm was that I did not push hard enough or build the alliances with men that I should have to take a stand on things I knew were wrong. I truly regret that."

—Trudey, 50-Something

A contributor, a partner in a midsized national firm, points out that most of the gender bias that she has experienced has come from clients. She believes that the bias is twofold: Either women are not perceived as tough enough to "fight the fight" or they are perceived as being too tough because they choose to work, particularly if they also are mothers. She identifies it as an "old conundrum" for women and part of the balancing act that they struggle with both externally and internally. She also observes that this leads many young women to adopt different personas to try to give the clients what they want or think they want. This, unfortunately, makes the job more difficult and less satisfying. She recommends learning how to be yourself as early as possible to avoid this result and she also recommends that you do not to try to act like a man. Another contributor, a specialist in a sales environment, also has experienced clients who do not want to deal with a woman. Her experience has mostly been with older clients who are not used to women, and her advice is to try to find some common ground. If the client is a man, talk about a local sports team. If the client is a woman, ask about children or grandchildren. Men do it, and so can you. This is not acting like a man as much as acting like a clever attorney.

Also remember that questions about whether you intend to have children are not fair game today. One of my contributors, who began practice in the 1970s, recalls inquiries like "Who will care for your children if you have a late jury trial?" and "Why shouldn't we give this job to a male applicant who needs it to support his family?" Although we had to tolerate this years ago, employers are prohibited by law from making such inquiries.

Here are some more examples of gender bias from the past. It is important that I include this material. On its face, it might indicate that there is no longer an issue and that it is old news. However, unless the young women read about the past and the issues that older women in the profession have had to endure, there is a risk that the young women will not understand the nature of their responsibility. Past as prologue, which you already know I consider to be very important.

One of my contributors, a member of the judiciary, tells this ironic story.

Case in Point

"I was lead counsel and the only woman member of a trial and appellate team that was successful at an appeal, and we were at a hearing to schedule the retrial. The male administrative judge accommodated all of the requests for scheduling from counsel, for reasons including vacations, until he got to me. When I requested that the trial not be scheduled for the first week of school so that I could get my young children settled in a new school, the judge immediately set the trial for that very week. I was outraged by the obvious gender bias but controlled my anger. I would handle it differently today. Such behavior should be brought to the attention of the bar association or chief judge."

—Janice, 50-Something

I agree with this contributor. The behavior is outrageous and should not be tolerated. However, I offer this further advice. Challenging the behavior of a judge should not be taken lightly. Attorneys must do what is right for their clients, and they must factor that into all decisions. Annoying a judge who could have influence on your case might not be in the best interests of your client. Some things cannot be overlooked, however. This same contributor describes being physically attacked by opposing counsel. During a sidebar conference, a male lawyer took a swing at her in front of the judge and other attorneys! She was furious, but it did not seem to have much effect on the other mostly male attorneys or the judge. It makes me wonder what those same lawyers do today when they are scheduled in her court!

A different twist on this is what I like to call avoiding the carrot that becomes a stick. Women are typically generous and helpful and view their role as making life easier for others. These traits can be used against you, however, if you are not careful. Another of my contributors tells a story about a woman attorney who, to her detriment, was willing to help out with a personal favor for a male colleague.

Case in Point

"This happened to me when I was a new associate at a law firm. A male colleague was going on a business trip and did not have time to pick up dry cleaning that he needed for the trip. He asked me if I would pick the clothes up for him when I was out of the office getting lunch. I was able to help him out and agreed to do it. As it turned out, I was very sorry for my kind and generous nature. The male colleague was involved in a wager with other male attorneys in the firm about whether they could get me, a woman attorney, to do 'domestic' tasks. They used this information in a way that demeaned me and attacked my professionalism. According to them, it was all in 'good fun,' but it did not feel that way to me."

—Phyllis, 60-Something

Gender bias like this should not be tolerated. However, you must be careful to distinguish generational bias from professional gender bias and resist overreacting on feminist issues. I am not suggesting that you tolerate genuine insult and ridicule based on your gender. You are smart enough to know what is intended as a slur and what is driven by something much less insidious. In some cases, the male offender might be from a different generation and does not understand the offense or intend his words to be offensive. Maintaining a sense of humor in those situations can be very important to your professional future. There are many good examples of this, but my favorite of the anecdotes contributed for this book is one about a female associate preparing for her first trial.

Case in Point

"Prior to leaving for the trial, I was called into the office of a named partner in the firm who was the responsible partner on the case. The conversation went something like this. 'Now, Ms. X, you know that you are the first woman to go to trial in this firm. You are expected to try this case like a man. By that I do not mean that you should curse like a truck driver or roll up a pack of cigarettes in your shirtsleeve. However, I never want it to be said that you lost the case because you were in the ladies' room doing your hair.'

"The year was 1981, and this is a true story. I was stunned and reacted by assuring the male partner that I intended to conduct myself with all appropriateness during the trial. I was very controlled and polite, but, as I left his office, I grabbed a candy bar from the 'honor snack' display in the corridor, failed to deposit the requisite 25 cents, and headed for the ladies' room—but not to do my hair. I unwrapped the candy bar and smeared the chocolate all over the mirror in perfect concentric circles that reminded me of the partner's face. I did this over and over again until I calmed down, and then I started out the door of the bathroom before I remembered that a woman cleaned that room at night. I went back into the bathroom and cleaned the mirror until it shined again. He was not going to ruin her day, too.

"I thought about it for the rest of the day, still angry but also a little confused. I knew how inappropriate his words had been, but I also knew that he was older and a bit out of touch with the new female professional scene. He loved and respected his wife and daughter, he had always supported my career, and he had provided me with great opportunities and had been complimentary of my work. The bottom line was that he just did not know any better, and there was no real harm done. Sometimes you just have to decide to take a pass."

—Virginia, 60-Something

As previously pointed out, most of these are tales from yesteryear. However, one of my contributors, a young woman lawyer, recalls being patronized by statements like, "Little Lady, you don't mind if I smoke do ya?" and "Does the Mrs. consent [to the order]?" You see, it is not all in the past.

One of my contributors, a member of the judiciary, has this to say about gender bias in the practice of law today:

Men still demonstrate great gender bias, although it is often more subtle. This is true of clients, lawyers, and judges. Some are very nasty toward women, perhaps in an effort to intimidate. Many are misogynistic; many are paternalistic, not recognizing that paternalism is a form of gender discrimination. They simply think that they are being nice to the "ladies," and I am not talking about holding the door open. I am talking about the belief that women should be the primary caregivers for children and family and that men do not have an equal responsibility to care for home and hearth.

Another of my contributors, a young woman partner, takes particular offense not only with gender bias but also with the related male chauvinism. She states,

It is disheartening when a male colleague mistakenly assumes that a female colleague cannot handle a particular project because she is a woman or because she is not tough enough to handle a complex matter. In truth, women are a lot stronger emotionally, mentally and physically than men, and we can make the tough decisions. And, do not even talk to a man about childbirth!

Another young woman partner states,

Quite frankly, the practice of law and politics is not for the faint at heart. I try to keep in mind that the problem is with the person who holds the bias and not with me. It typically is evidence of great insecurity on their part. Stepping toward higher ground in my own thinking and goal formulation consistently has helped to neutralize any negative impact associated with such biases. The reality is that I have little control over how people think; however, I do have the ability to influence the way they behave around me. In extreme instances, I have sought the counsel of colleagues.

I was particularly pleased to read the response from one of my young contributors. She describes a career where gender issues have been few and transparent. However, she also cites the following incident.

Case in Point

"An older male partner in my practice group remarked about my long hair and said that I resembled a flight attendant more than a lawyer. I always dressed appropriately for the office, and on that day I was dressed very appropriately in business casual attire. My response to him was to the point. I told him that there are all sorts of women in the profession these days and that he had better get used to it and that even women with long hair have brains. I also reported the conversation to my supervising attorney, a woman, and the supervisor made certain that the male partner was reprimanded."

—Ellen, 30-Something

This same woman attorney describes an incident when she was putting lengthy objections on a deposition record, and the much older male opposing counsel stated, "Don't threaten me, young lady." She responded,

"Don't patronize me." I was proud of her that she did not add "old man," although I could tell that she wanted to!

So, here you have a 30-something female lawyer who starts out by saying that she has not encountered gender bias and then goes on to describe some fairly significant examples of it. She is a fiery young woman, very passionate, and an excellent lawyer, who refuses to get bogged down on the subject of gender bias but who also takes a strong stance against it. I think that this might be the new model and that today's young women attorneys know how to deal with it. I hope that is the case because it appears that gender bias, however subtle, has not disappeared from law practice.

Focusing on the positive is the right approach to this subject. One of my contributors sums it up well: "We should not dwell on the past. The answer is to get into the position of power so that women can start writing the rules." Another of my contributors has learned how to turn the tables on this subtle discrimination. After she had her child, senior men in her practice would assume that she was not as committed to her practice as the women attorneys without children. She would be asked to attend meetings at 5:00 in the afternoon, for instance, "if you are still around then." Her response was exactly what she would recommend today. If she was not available at 5:00 p.m., she would offer to meet at 7:30 p.m. or at 6:30 a.m. the next day. She says that is effective in diffusing the inappropriate mentality.

Fortunately, there is some good news. Strangely, there are times when overt sexism can benefit you. One of the outstanding trial experiences of my career involved a plaintiff who had suffered from toxic shock syndrome allegedly caused by a product manufactured by our client. I was a second-year associate, but I was given first-seat experience taking depositions, arguing motions, and preparing witnesses for trial in federal court. Why? Because the case manager needed a woman attorney to depose the plaintiff and her mother and examine them at trial to avoid the perception of a male "beating up on" these key female witnesses. I learned more on that one case than I had learned in the prior two years of my practice. Sometimes gender issues can work to your advantage. Do not miss those opportunities because you are indulging in a knee-jerk reaction to what you perceive to be sexist.

Be a Team Player

Just as you must be an excellent lawyer, you also must be a team player in most work environments, with the possible exception of solo practice. Being a team player is a very important concept and one that is stressed by the managing partners of law firms who contributed to this book. One of my contributors states that women are naturally equipped to be team players with abilities to bring about consensus and to build a true sense of legal community. You will read more about this later in this chapter in the section "Remember That Law Is a Business."

Embracing the team concept is sometimes harder for women, who might not have extensive backgrounds in team athletics and military training. Those experiences not only toughen up the men on the field and in preparation for combat, but they also prepare young men for the team play that most law practices require. Fortunately, for the past several generations, there has been a greater opportunity in competitive athletics for women in schools and colleges, but the experiences for women and men still are not equal. Although it is true that today women are excelling in more athletic endeavors, many of those endeavors do not depend on the team concept. Consider, for instance, the sports of swimming, horseback riding, and gymnastics that have attracted many young women on the national and international stages but are not typical team sports. Other women's sports, however, like softball, basketball, soccer, and lacrosse, offer greater possibilities for team play, but the number of women who engage in those sports is relatively small. In addition, the team concepts that are taught in the military do not affect most women. The number of women in the military is still small by comparison to men, and most of the readers of this book will not have that background.

My own story helps to demonstrate the point.

Case in Point

"My husband and I attended law school together. He started first, and I followed two years later. We were both successful law students, but our experiences were very different. My husband had played on sports teams all of his life, had been on a NCAA championship team during college, and had been a fighter pilot during the Vietnam War. The hazing that most often accompanies that kind of training and the necessity for teamwork to survive the competition were a strong foil for the intimidating and cut-throat law school environment with its emphasis on the Socratic method and competition. Without those types of unique male experiences in my background, I had to work harder to navigate some very unfamiliar waters. Even today, although embracing the team concept is not an insurmountable hurdle for women, I think that it often does not come as naturally to women as it does to men."

—Susan, 60-Something

The team concept is very important to success in a law firm. Based on their backgrounds and experiences, many men evaluate success in terms of the team experience, and they will jump on any indication that a woman is not a team player. That weakness, perceived or real, can become the justification for decisions against the best professional interests of those women. Be careful and do not let this happen to you. Embrace the team concept and make it work for you. Be an invaluable member of the team and a helpmate for those teammates who are floundering. Eventually, you will become the team leader because of your talent and work ethic. At that point, you can direct the team, which is what you wanted in the first place!

Fortunately, there are many more opportunities for team experiences in the curriculum at most levels of education today. Educational institutions, in general, seem to be following the example of business and business schools where the team approach has been embraced and has been very successful. This can only work to benefit women.

One of my contributors, a law firm managing partner, has other excellent advice on this subject. "Whatever you do, never turn down work." The work is going to come to you no matter what; you might as well look happy about it. The perception of being a team player and a willingness to get the job done will go a long way in establishing you as a valuable member of the firm or organization.

However, by contrast, one of my young women contributors cautions you on this subject:

> In an effort to be perceived as a team player, I often accepted the less desirable legal projects that my male colleagues had declined in favor of high-profile work. Looking back, I should have been more aggressive in pursuing the legal work that I wanted instead of what was offered to me and asked of me. I discovered that the firm did not value some of these projects, and my male colleagues were receiving better training and more interesting work that ultimately helped them advance faster.

I can identify with her remarks, and I can relate them to my own experience at one time. Perception of the value of work to a firm is very important, and you will do well to pay close attention and keep your ears open for what contributions are valued above others.

Your choice of how to be a team player and the wisdom of doing that in a particular situation will very often turn on the facts. Evaluate each situation in terms of the benefits to you as well as the benefits to the employer, and you will usually make the right decision.

Be Prepared to Reinvent Yourself

Once you have become an excellent lawyer and a team player, do not get too comfortable with yourself. It might become necessary for you to reinvent yourself. Women encounter this much more often than men because of work-life issues, and you should anticipate it. It might discourage you at first because of the energy and long hours that you put into "getting it right." However, it might become necessary, and you should keep in mind that reinventing yourself is a very positive response to changed circumstances. You might end up with a somewhat "fractured" résumé, but, if you do it right, you will not have to totally abandon your education and training.

Do not be afraid of change. It is a good thing. It makes you examine who and what you really are and what you want to be. Reinventing is no substitute for good planning, but good planning cannot defend against unanticipated circumstances. Keep loose, be creative, and play the hand that's dealt you.

You should be aware that some legal specialties are harder to transition from and within than others. For example, transitioning to part time in a litigation practice can be especially challenging. As discussed earlier in this book, litigation is especially unsuited to a part-time schedule because of court-imposed deadlines and unanticipated response dates. However, some litigators have been able to make the transition successfully, with the support of outstanding staff and colleagues and the team approach. If you do not anticipate such a smooth transition to a more flexible schedule, you should always consider alternative practice venues. Don't give up on a career without first trying to make it work.

I have to look in the mirror at this point. My experience is so relevant here that I cannot duck it. On the one hand, my résumé looks a bit like someone used it for target practice. It is full of holes that cry out the names of my beloved children and the needs of my family. On the other hand, it shows resolve to remain in my profession, in one manner or another, and I am very proud of that.

I began my career as a litigator, and that was an exciting and very fulfilling pursuit for almost five years. However, after my first child was born and I determined that I needed to work part-time to satisfy the needs of my family, I transitioned to more of a general practice, which included a combination of business practice and charitable pursuits of my law firm. It was not very satisfactory and did not challenge me professionally, but it kept me in the practice and at a law firm that had become like family to me. After my second child was born, less than two years later, the opportunities for part-time practice had all but disappeared under new leadership at the firm, and I was forced to find another law firm where those opportunities were purported to exist. The second firm promised a part-time general business practice as of counsel with minimal travel that would get me through the critical family years. It sounded good, and I jumped at the chance to make some sense out of a hectic life, as I clung to the desire to continue in my profession. The promise, however, did not meet the reality, and I found myself pulled into federal court litigation very soon after joining the firm because my practice background matched the need. That was followed by one litigation after another, and I ended up leaving the firm. What followed was an important hiatus from my professional life.

Case in Point

"I was tired and discouraged from fending off what seemed to be the inevitable, and I became a stay-at-home mother for eight years. However, the important thing is not that I left my profession for a period of time, but, rather, what I did during that time period to keep up my contacts and to build a bridge toward my future. I stayed very active in civic activities and in charities. I was elected to a local civic board of directors where I addressed issues of land use and zoning. This was a new area of interest for me, but it included a structure of administrative review that was very similar to litigation. In this work, I testified before government committees and boards and interacted with local elected officials.

I gained a reputation in that field and in the area of local government, and that experience served me very well as a way back into my profession. At the end of the eight years as a stay-at-home mother, I was recruited to work for a newly elected local official, and I served as his chief of staff for almost eight years. After that experience, I was teed up to reenter my profession as a partner in a land use and zoning practice."

—Susan, 60-Something

Mine was not a simple career path, and the "off-ramp" experience was difficult for me. I did not handle all of it as well as I could have, and I now wish that I had swallowed my pride at certain junctures and just thrown myself on the mercy of the law firm to help me find a solution and to make them live up to their representations and promises. It was difficult because there were no guidelines for part-time practice in those days. However, although I should have taken the longer view, some of what I did was very successful, and it all had a satisfactory ending. In this context, it is important to note that I had no women role models at my firm to give me guidance on these issues. It was a lonely road, and I am heartened to know that young women today have many more resources and, hopefully, will use those resources to make good decisions. That, of course, is why I have written this book and have put all of this collective experience at your fingertips.

Seek Out Women's Practice Initiatives

Do not try to go it alone. Many of the issues concerning women in the practice of law are still evolving, and women's forums and women's practice initiatives are very helpful. Take advantage of them.

Women's practice initiatives are typically programs directed specifically at women lawyers and law students and include professional development activities, social networking events and formal mentoring programs. There seems to be increased interest in the profession for making these initiatives available to prepare law students and young women lawyers for leadership roles and to improve retention rates. Look for these opportunities in law school, and, if your law school does not offer initiatives of this kind, be proactive and encourage the administration to initiate these efforts. You should also get involved with women's practice groups during your summer associate experiences and participate in programs sponsored by local bar associations. When you join a practice after law school, make sure that your firm or your public-sector practice provides this assistance. Again, if it is not available, become active in getting such programs started. Typically, large East Coast and West Coast firms developed these programs first as a result of the increased numbers of women in those practices. Firms in middle America typically have been slower in recognizing the need for these programs, and they have responded at a less aggressive pace. The good news, however, is that 95 percent of firms reported sponsoring a women's initiative (The National Association of Women Lawyers (NAWL) November 2007 National Survey on Retention and Promotion of Women in Law Firms), and it is almost a necessity today for successful recruitment of women.

Make sure that the content of these programs is responsive to your needs. It is helpful to have women lawyers come together to share their experiences and tell their stories about the realities of practice, but those discussions too often can be limited to topics of billable hour requirements and the pressures of a law practice. Descriptions of the differences between various types of practices and the relative impact on lifestyle choices, however, should not be overlooked. This is where the real mentoring is done, and you should try to get as much of this as possible during law school and in the early years of your practice.

Find Good Mentors

Finding the right mentor, or preferably the right mentors, is very important and will seriously affect the value of the mentoring. Having a mentor who can teach you and vouch for the quality of your work is critical to your success and upward mobility in a law firm. However, typically, law firms do not give enough attention to mentoring, and it will be up to you to make sure that you get it. Be on the lookout for an attorney you would choose as a mentor and volunteer to work with him or her. Select a mentor who is in a strong position in the firm and well regarded by his or her colleagues. Fortunes change, and you want to take your best chance on picking a winner. Be enthusiastic and let the attorney know that you are eager to learn. Perform well for that attorney, and you will get follow-up work. By developing a good working mentor-mentee relationship, you are likely to have someone in your corner when questions of case assignment, compensation, and promotions are addressed. Employees usually do not leave jobs, they leave managers. The value of a good supervising attorney cannot be overestimated.

You should set goals with your mentor and decide how to achieve those goals. Mentors will often have to deliver some bad news, and you should listen carefully to the message and learn from it. One of my contributors says it best: "Find and keep solid mentors. You need caring, thoughtful mentors to navigate you to success in this profession, and you can expect the best mentors to be those who are most critical of you. It's the constructive criticism that you learn from and that makes you a better lawyer. Your mentor would be lying to you if he or she gave you nothing but praise."

Informal mentoring is also important, and it will naturally occur in social settings. Success is usually at the "people" level, and this will require your initiative. Get involved with the firm members and in firm activities—even if you think they are silly or a waste of time. One of my contributors, a law school career counselor, reports that too many associates remain isolated in their offices and are content to produce good work while listening to music on their iPods. She reports that hiring partners object to this behavior and point out that it works to the detriment of the young lawyer in terms of perception by colleagues. It also is likely to interfere with the ability of the young lawyer to get clients, which depends on who you know and who you engage in conversation.

According to a law school career counselor, most young women lawyers today prefer to be mentored by another woman. It is part of the feminist overlay that still exists. However, by sheer virtue of the statistics, most of the supervising attorneys for young women will be older men. This is not a bad thing, but often the best result is to have both male and female mentors. If you want to succeed in the real, sometimes cold, law firm world, you need to be exposed to both styles of mentoring. Typically, the models are quite different. This contributor reports that men tend to be very direct, very particular in the way they want things done, and very "bottom line," whereas women mentors often tend to be more open to new approaches. Although opinions certainly will vary on this subject, it is undoubtedly true that you can benefit from having both male and female mentors. If you are unable to find a female mentor in your firm, find a woman lawyer outside the firm through your participation in bar associations or other professional groups. It is very important to have another woman lawyer to talk to about some of the difficulties that you are likely to encounter that are unique to women in the profession. Even women competitors are a good source. Don't forget that imitation is the highest form of flattery.

In addition to female mentors, you must also learn to accept the older male lawyer as a mentor. Do not let this be a problem for you. Young women have a tendency to view older men as father figures, and, in most business settings, that can lead to some disappointing results. Remember that your male mentor is not your father—or your husband, fiancée, or boyfriend, for that matter. Give up the unnecessary male-female baggage and understand that he is teaching you and not reprimanding and judging you.

I received some push-back from one of my contributors on this point. She said that she did not believe this to be a problem and thought that I was personalizing too much on this point. Maybe she is right, but I think that it is worth including. I can recall many conversations with older male partners where I felt that I was in the company of my father, and it was not going well! Maybe it was just me.

Ask for Help When You Need It

Women like to think that they can solve problems themselves, and they take on the weight of the world without asking for help. In this context, I am not referring to help with legal assignments or other substantive requirements of the job. Here I am referring to the help that you will need in navigating the difficulties of a professional career and family. In my experience, young women lawyers are reluctant to show their vulnerability and to ask for help, and this can lead to some very bad decision making. Although you will find a great deal of help between the covers of this book, you also will need help from senior lawyers to craft the right solutions to problems that are specific to the firm and to the practice. Do not hesitate to seek out this help. The problems are often too difficult and the consequences of unwise decisions too grave. You also will find that the wisdom of older, more experienced colleagues will help to make things clearer and that these lawyers generally are flattered to be asked and very willing to help. Fortunately, today you are likely to find both male and female senior lawyers in your firm or organization to help you out.

As this contributor found out, do not be too afraid or too proud to ask.

Case in Point

"I was returning from my second maternity leave, and the power structure of the law firm had changed while I was away. I was a part-time associate, and certain members of the firm did not support part-time work in my specialty. As a result, I was told by one of the managing partners that

I would not be allowed to continue my preferred practice and that I would have to transition to another practice. That put me in an untenable position because I knew that I would not enjoy the alternative practice and I did not have the option of working full time. I felt betrayed and decided that I would have to leave the firm. When I resigned and joined a competitor firm, some of my colleagues at the first firm were outspokenly disappointed that I had not enlisted their help to bring about a different result. The move to the competitor firm turned out to be a very bad decision, and it took me years to repair some of the friendships that had been affected by my decision. I think that many of these problems could have been avoided if I had just been willing to fall on my sword a bit, swallow my pride, and ask for help."

—**Brenda, 60-Something**

I have heard similar stories from other women, and I also have heard from senior lawyers who regret that young colleagues did not ask for help before making what appeared to be rash decisions. Career decisions are difficult and very often require objectivity and many different perspectives and suggestions. Do not be hasty in making these decisions, and do not try to make them alone. Each career decision is likely to lead to another, and you want to make the best and most informed decisions that you can. In most circumstances, there is no place in this process for pride, anger, and hurt feelings. Calm down, keep a cool head, and seek out some experienced sounding boards who you know have your best interests at heart. You will be happy that you did.

Remember That Law Is a Business

Managing partners will tell you that, first and foremost, a law firm must be a successful business, and most of the decisions that are made in law firms are business decisions. If the business does not succeed, there will be no place in that firm for the lawyers to practice their trade. Take care of the business first and the rest will follow.

One of my contributors, a woman who specializes in business and corporate law, believes that it is especially important for a young woman entering the legal profession to gain knowledge about the business side of a law practice. Most particularly, it is important to understand that opportunity and career advancement are tied to the "value" the lawyer brings to the firm. Value to a law firm is all about "rainmaking"—developing new clients, driving business within existing clients, and becoming known in the business community. Being a smart, dedicated, and hard-working associate who bills more than 2,000 hours a year will not guarantee personal success or a place at the partner table. You need to develop your own business within the firm's business. Figure that out, and you will be in good shape when promotion time comes.

Another of my contributors, a managing partner in Big Law, believes that many young attorneys do not understand law practice as a business. He explains that all firms have unique profiles, and those profiles are what eventually define the firm and affect most firm decisions. This manager has actually hired a psychologist to advise the firm about how to identify candidates who meet the firm profile and objectives. Finding attorneys who are a good match and who understand the firm profile is key and saves the firm money over the long run in terms of retention. The business of a law firm is a collaborative process, and the firm is looking for team players. To accomplish that objective, his firm looks for indications of team experience in prospective firm members, things like playing in the band, playing on a sports team, or other similar group experiences. This should remind you of the previous section in this chapter, "Be a Team Player."

This contributor also describes a typical successful law firm in terms of philosophy and organization. He says that a successful law firm must have the following: a desired position in the industry (often referred to as a "vision"—a hackneyed label that many current hard-core managers choose to avoid), a strategy based on the desired position, and a business model consistent with the desired position and the strategy. Pretty simple really, like Business 101.

However, as simple as it might seem, the contributor encounters many law firm participants who either do not understand the model or do not act consistent with it. He warns that not understanding your firm's business model or not acting consistent with it can trip you up in many ways. For instance, he says that if the business model needs to change to respond to new developments or issues, attorneys should think about the proposed change within the context of the desired "vision" for the firm and be constructive in the way that they approach management. The attorney who proposes the change should take a stakeholder's approach to the issue, and that approach is much more likely to win the point. The firm wants good ideas to make it easier to be successful and to recruit clients. Most firms love positive initiative. Be a part of the solution, not the problem.

Rather than take this constructive approach, the contributor claims that far too often the proponents of change approach the firm with the victim mentality. They have the attitude that it is "us against them." The contributor has a visceral reaction to this approach. He wants to see an attitude that sends the message that the proponent for change is part of the firm and will behave in a manner that helps to shape the firm in a good way. This attitude should carry over to the orientation to the problem, the way of analyzing the problem, and the way of presenting ideas and proposed solutions. In his experience, the victim mentality, where the proponent of change views herself or himself as different and tries to get special treatment based entirely on that difference, will not lead to job satisfaction. It will annoy the manager, and it will lead to a greater feeling of rejection for the proponent when the request is denied. The better approach according to this contributor is to embrace the notion that you are a member of a firm and that you are trying to bring about changes that will improve the firm and benefit other members of the firm, as well—the team mentality. But do not delude yourself into thinking that the firm can and will do everything for every interest group that makes the right approach. It is all about choices for firms, and those choices must represent a return on investment.

Most of all, this manager does not like the collective bargaining approach. He warns against going to management with a list of people in the firm who agree with your request. In other words, do not organize the troops! According to him, that approach fails to put an individual face on the request and takes away the opportunity for meaningful dialogue and communication. It will annoy management, and they will stop listening. Likewise, do not present a list of all the other firms that have adopted a policy that you are promoting. Management does not care who else is doing it. They only care whether it is a good thing for their firm and whether it fits into their business model.

There you have the message from Big Law firm management. Although it risks generalization, it is valuable for you to know to avoid some of the mines in the field. However, I cannot say that I agree with it in totality. It is certainly the approach that makes it easiest for management and allows managers to hide behind faceless policy statements and business models. It is certainly the "do not rock the boat" approach. However, I am not sure that such an approach would have brought about some of the significant changes of the past like flexible work schedules and reasonable maternity policies—after all, it took legislation to accomplish the latter. And, I am not sure that it works for all issues. Some issues need a more passionate approach than others.

This contributor's remarks, however, are particularly valuable in underscoring the fundamental truth: First and foremost, law is a business, and keeping the doors open for business is the primary concern. It is good to keep that in mind and to let it guide your conduct and presentation. Survival is key. Some day, when you have the power, you can change the rules and allow picketing in the boardroom if that suits your fancy. Until then, I have done my duty in delivering the party line.

Now let's try to relate the business context directly to women lawyers. Experience shows that business decisions can present particular challenges to some women. Stereotypically (and we must take that approach sometimes), women tend to take things more personally than men, and women are typically more emotional and personally invested in matters than men. Business decisions usually are not personal and should not be taken that way, but women very often do not recognize things as purely business matters, especially when they are new to the practice. You should watch out for this difference and try to make the distinction. Even matters of staffing cases are business decisions and often determine whether or not the client will be satisfied with the fee structure, the representation and, ultimately, the bill. A law firm cannot exist without its clients.

A male case manager tells this story.

> ## Case in Point
>
> "As a partner and chief of litigation, it was my responsibility to make staffing decisions on litigation cases. After reviewing the fee agreement that had been negotiated with the client on a matter, I decided to make a change of staffing and to substitute a junior associate for a more senior associate who had reached a higher billing rate. When I called the junior associate into my office to discuss this with her, she became very emotional and said that she could not work on the matter. I was stunned by her response because it was a very good case and would provide excellent litigation experience for a junior associate. When I asked her to explain her decision, she said that she was a very good friend of the senior associate and that the senior associate would be mad at her if she replaced her on the case."
>
> **—Charlie, 40-Something**

I am sure that you will agree that the associate's personal response to a business decision was inappropriate. Law is a business.

Understand the Conditions of Partnership

Most people will tell you that getting married is easy compared to getting divorced. Committing to a business partnership and trying to unravel it later presents a similar problem. Pay attention to all of the specifics of partnership, and avoid this result.

Partnership is the crown jewel of law practice for many. It represents acceptance, achievement, and prestige, and it can have very significant monetary rewards. It can be very satisfying for all of those reasons and is certainly desirable in many ways.

However, partnership is not available to every lawyer, especially every woman lawyer. Although law firms have changed radically over the years by allowing part-time schedules, flex time, and job sharing, there are many observers who believe that those concessions are the limit of what law firms can practically provide as accommodations to women who desire a work-life balance. As a result, most women, who desire the law firm partnership track, will have to choose a lifestyle that is heavy on the work side and will be considered an imbalance by many. The women lawyers who desire partnerships, especially in mid to large-sized law firms, can expect to give up much of their family lives to achieve their goals. Staying on partnership track and giving up a portion of family life is acceptable for some women, and there are many examples of successful women who have family and children and who become partners and firm managers. Many of these women change their personal life expectations to meet the realities of law firm life, and they are very comfortable with and satisfied by the result.

Partnership also is not for everyone. More and more associate lawyers today, both male and female, are finding that they are less interested in that career path than they might have expected before they experienced the law firm life. They have determined that they do not want their parents' professional lives, complete with the workaholic lifestyles and misplaced priorities, and they are satisfied to be senior associates, of counsel, or contract attorneys. In an article in *The National Jurist* (October 2008),

Deborah Epstein Henry is quoted as saying, "As Generation Y graduates, they are saying they don't want to practice law the old-fashioned way. They want a life. They want that balance" (at 31).

One of my contributors, a male managing partner, sees it this way. For him, the most important career goal for a lawyer is not necessarily to become a partner. He believes that there are many other objectives that you should want to accomplish as a lawyer, like being an excellent attorney, increasing your billable hours and client development to build an independent practice, performing important and rewarding civic and community work, writing and publishing on the law, participating in firm activities, and building alliances in the firm. If you do those things, you will have the foundation for a long, successful, and satisfying career, even without a partnership. He seems to be saying that partnership is not as significant as some lawyers think that it is and that building a valuable practice is the most important thing and will lead to a meaningful role in the leadership of a firm. He is not discouraging partnership, but he does not see it as the "end all." Some of you are shaking your heads and saying, "Easy for him to say." I know, but he presents some good points that are worth considering.

In addition, there are also some important business reasons that might make partnership less desirable than expected. Before we discuss this more, we need to get some basic terms straight. Let's concentrate on the partnership model, as compared to the corporation model. Although many law firms today are professional corporations and limited liability corporations rather than partnerships, the concepts of partnership are loosely transferable to those settings as well. What is important is that you understand the progression of a lawyer in a firm and what it can mean to you.

There are many classes of lawyers in a firm structure, as you know. Typically, there are associates, counsel, senior counsel, and primarily two categories of partners: nonequity partners and equity partners. Nonequity partners are treated like partners for purposes of committees and some management decisions, and they are expected to generate work and increase accounts. Although they usually do not share in the profits of the firm, they also do not share in the losses of the firm. They are paid a guaranteed monthly salary. Equity partners, by contrast, share in the profits of the firm, but also the losses, and they are responsible for all of the important management decisions in the firm, for generating work, and for keeping junior lawyers busy with that work. Partners, both nonequity and equity, usually are required to pay for their own health insurance, which is deducted from their paychecks.

Now let's focus on the big issues: money and responsibility. If you are promoted from associate or counsel in a firm to nonequity partner, the amount of pay that you actually take home on a monthly basis as a partner, after taxes and insurance have been subtracted, might be little more than what you took home as a nonpartner. Therefore, becoming a nonequity partner might result in little additional compensation but more responsibility for management and for generating work. If, as the scenario progresses, you are then promoted from nonequity partner to equity partner (although there is no guarantee of this), the compensation scheme becomes more complicated. Most firms require a "capital contribution" to the firm for equity partners, and the amount of that cash contribution can be significant and can amount to as much as $75,000 to $100,000. Most new equity partners find that they have to borrow the money to pay the capital contribution, which adds to their debt load and reduces the benefits of any additional pay received as an equity partner. In addition, many firms pay equity partners a "draw" or percentage of the projected income of the firm rather than a guaranteed monthly salary. The draw starts small and grows as the firm's fiscal year progresses and its profits are realized. As a result, a new equity partner's monthly draw could turn out to be considerably less than he or she was making monthly as a nonequity partner with a guaranteed salary, especially in a weak economy when the firm is not experiencing high receivables.

It is important that you think about these things and what they will mean to you. You do not want to be surprised because you did not understand or you did not ask the right questions. An article in the June 2008 edition of *ABA Journal* entitled "I Wish I Had Known . . ." chronicles these concerns and misunderstandings, as reported to the magazine by associates turned partner, and recommends that associates hoping to join the partnership ranks do the following:

- Learn what you can about what being a partner means at your firm.
- Find out whether your firm has an orientation for new partners.
- If the firm doesn't have new-partner orientation, highlight your leadership skills by offering to create one.
- Start asking questions of current partners you trust.

One of my contributors wishes that she had been better informed before making her decision.

Case in Point

"I was promoted to nonequity partner at my firm, and that promotion included increased responsibilities for a generation of new clients and pressure to produce more work. I languished in that status for years because there was no realistic structure to the partnership scheme, and the opportunities for promotion to equity partner did not come. I eventually decided that the trade-off had not been a good one. I had gotten the title of partner, which helped me to promote work, but I had not shared in the financial payoff from my efforts. I ended up regretting that I had not examined this issue to a greater degree before committing to the income partnership. I eventually came to believe that I could have done better at another firm that paid senior associates well and had only one level of partnership and well-established criteria for achieving that status."

—Lisa, 40-Something

This "languishing" in a status for years without promotion might be a little hard to understand, so let me try to explain. The truth is that once you are in any status except equity partner or shareholder (for professional corporations), it is very hard to move upward from that status. The reason can best be explained if you envision the firm and its income assets as a pie. The pie that represents the income assets of the equity partnership is a whole pie—it is 100 percent of the income assets, and the pie gets divided up among the equity partners. Every time a new equity partner is added, one of two things happens. Either the pieces of pie for all the other existing equity partners become smaller (an unattractive result for the other equity partners) or the newly added equity partner has business that converts to income to make the pie larger. In that latter event, the new equity partner is not diminishing the sizes of the pieces of pie for other equity partners. As a result, to make a compelling case for promotion to equity partner, you must be able to demonstrate that your participation at that level produces a bigger pie. That can be very challenging and requires a great deal of work and sacrifice and a lot of careful planning throughout your career. You also should be aware that the rules of partnership could change after you have joined the firm. Keep your head up and your ears open. Get all the information before you make a commitment.

Partnership for women lawyers presents additional issues, and the statistics on women partners are not very encouraging. The figures and how far we have *not* come in this regard may surprise you. According to the National Association for Law Placement (NALP) in its tracking of legal careers, only 12 percent of partners in law firms in 1993 were women. This might not seem unusual to you, but compare that to the figures for 2006 and 2007. In those 13 years, the figures rose to only 17.9 percent and 18 percent, respectively, and NALP and NAWL statistics show that, in 2008, approximately only 16 percent of equity partners nationwide were women. These are disheartening figures for women who desire partnership, and these disappointing statistics are more often than not the result of the work-life issues that women lawyers face and the choices that they make along their career paths. The National Association of

Women Lawyers (NAWL) has issued a new report entitled "Actions for Advancing Women into Law Firm Leadership" written by Linda Bray Chanow. In her report presented at the NAWL National Leadership Summit, Chanow presents practical action steps a law firm can implement to ensure that women lawyers remain with the firm and advance into leadership positions. In 2006, NAWL challenged the legal profession to double the percentage of women equity partners, general counsel, and law professors by the year 2015. This recent report is designed to help law firms meet their part of that challenge. The report is available at *www.nawl.org/Assets/ Summit+*

Report+2008. For more information on this subject, see *Creating Pathways to Success: Advancing and Retaining Women in Today's Law Firms* (Women's Bar Association of the District of Columbia Initiative on Advancement and Retention of Women, May 2006).

Although these figures are disheartening, there is some good news. As the result of competence, very hard work, and perseverance in a male-dominated profession at a time when women were not getting much help in the process, a minority of women rose to the level of partner because they figured it out for themselves. Fortunately, it is no longer necessary to figure it out all alone. Dedicated women attorneys, many of them partners, have made their counsel available to you between the covers of this book, and it is yours for the taking. Use it well, and and I will keep my fingers crossed for you.

The Elusive Part-Time Partnership

The concept of part-time partnership will be very attractive to many young women associates who are grappling with work-life issues. As discussed earlier, partnership in a law firm is difficult enough for a woman to achieve, if that is her goal. Quite predictably then, you can imagine that part-time partnership is even more difficult to achieve and is typically the result of a full-time partner cutting back to a part-time schedule or a very valued associate or of counsel being promoted as a part-time partner. Either way, it is very difficult to reach that objective, and I am always delighted when I hear that another of my colleagues has made it.

When my time for partnership came many years ago and at a time when I had young children and a litigator husband with a very busy schedule, I argued hard for a two-pronged analysis to the question of part-time partnership. One prong of that analysis was entitlement based on merit, including consideration of the quality of the lawyer and the quality of the work produced in the past and expected in the future. The other prong was compensation. I was confident that I met the test on the first prong for many reasons, most notably the acknowledgments from partners. However, I also recognized that becoming a partner would put me in a different salary category, and I was willing to negotiate salary commensurate with part-time hours. However, I did not prevail on those arguments. In fact, it was not until 20 years later that I finally successfully negotiated a part-time partnership to meet other needs. That partnership was a sweet reward, all the sweeter for what had come before. However, it was not the result of fate or serendipity. My success 20 years later resulted from my proven track record, a perceived need for my talents and services, and my familiarity with the key players and decision makers in a very specialized practice. Under those circumstances, I was able to make part-time hours a condition of my partnership. It was not easy, however, and I would not like to leave that impression. Any law practice is difficult to do part time, and this one was no exception. However, it did give me more flexibility than a traditional five-day work week, and that is what I needed at the time.

The statistics on part-time partners can appear discouraging and, of course, reflect the fact that many women do not remain in the practice long enough to climb the partnership ladder. At the same time, there is a "small yet burgeoning trend at law firms" for part-time partnership, according to *Working Mother Magazine* (*www.workingmother.com*, November 16, 2008). That article is quick to point out, however, that this new breed of partner is still the exception, not the rule. According to recent NALP statistics, part-time partners constitute less than 2 percent of partners in firms of more than 500 lawyers and only 2.3 percent at smaller firms. Those same statistics show that, in 2008, women made up only approximately 16 percent of equity and nonequity partners nationwide, and only 12 percent of women equity partners and 22 percent of women nonequity partners work reduced-hours schedules.

One of my contributors, a male managing partner, empathizes with the dilemma of women attorneys who are mothers and who also want to become partners. He is very candid in his assessment of the realities of the situation. He starts with the assumption that women attorneys are always balancing family responsibilities with their desire to be fully contributing members of the firm. He acknowledges what he considers to be "heroic efforts" by these women, but he also believes that the efforts cannot be sustained over time. According to him, "something has to give" in that scenario, and what women usually give up are leadership roles in the firm. Management takes time, and women with family and child care responsibilities typically do not have the time. Civic roles and writing and speaking also end up being compromised, and that means a reduction in business development and a reduced role in the firm. When the subject of part-time partnership comes up, the reaction of many male full-time partners is to ask "How can you expect to be a part-time owner of a law firm if you are not doing these things?"

This contributor says that the central problem is that senior women attorneys need to function as more than just workers. It is not enough to do good or even excellent work. Younger, less experienced attorneys can take some of that worker responsibility, and the firm can pay them less while they get valuable practice experience. According to him, senior women attorneys must be able to function as managers or they are not as valuable to the firm. There also is a limit to how many senior women on flexible schedules a firm can absorb, and these things can work against a woman who desires part-time partnership.

On the other hand, and in spite of these difficulties and impediments, the part-time partnership option is an important and attractive retention and recruitment strategy for a growing number of law firms. According to

Working Mother Magazine, which publishes the "Best Law Firms for Women" list each year, 100 percent of the firms that make the list allow reduced-hours lawyers to be elevated to partnership. Over the past five years, these firms have promoted reduced-hours lawyers to nonequity and equity partner positions at an average rate of two lawyers a year per firm, and the firms also offer mentoring, business development training, and back up child care to help these lawyers succeed. According to a recent publication of the Project for Attorney Retention, an initiative of the Center for WorkLife Law at the University of California Hastings College of the Law entitled "Positioning Law Firms for Long-Term Success: New Strategies for Advancing Women Lawyers," the firms with the best part-time partnership programs not only make part-time associates partners, but they also include the option of part-timers being made partners with their classes while continuing to work part time. In making these decisions, the firms consider at what point in her legal career the part-time associate reduced her hours and the amount of the reduction, and the firms delay the partnership decision only if the part-timers have not had sufficient experience relative to full-time associates in the firm. For more information on the Hastings Law Project, go to *www.worklifelaw.org* and *www.pardc.org*.

The importance of this reduced-hour path to partnership cannot be underestimated. For many women it may be a deal clincher, especially if they have experienced less than satisfactory career paths as of counsel in the past. However, partnership continues to require top-quality performance, substantive expertise, and solid revenue production. If those qualities are present, the part-time partnership can be a win-win situation for all parties. A recent online article in *Working Mother Magazine* discusses many of these successes and is worth checking out (*Working Mother Magazine*, "Focus on the Best Law Firms—Part-Time Partners," November 16, 2008).

There is evidence that a growing number of the biggest U.S. law firms are initiating policies that outline how an associate looking for work-life balance can move to a part-time schedule and stay on partnership track. (Product Liability Law 360 (*www.productliability.law360.com*, November 6, 2008.) However, experts say that the trick is to make these policies work in practice. In addition to having an effective part-time partner track as a critical retention tool and an important consideration in keeping talent from leaving the practice, as discussed earlier, the case for taking affirmative steps to retain women also is strong from an economic perspective. According to a November 3, 2008, article in *Legal Times* entitled "Patience Won't Make Women Partners," attrition is expensive, and the cost to replace an associate at a large law firm ranges from $250,000 to $500,000. Hopefully, this economic incentive will benefit women on the partnership track and will help to improve the statistics on part-time partnership.

The daily schedules for part-time partners vary significantly, but here are two models for your consideration. In "Part-Time Partner Works 9 Hours a Day" (*ABA Journal*, July 16, 2007), author Martha Neil profiles a part-time partner in a large Washington, DC appellate practice as starting work at 6 a.m. and leaving at 2:55 p.m. to pick up her children from school. She puts in nine hours a day, five days a week, and probably some time on the weekends. By contrast, one of my contributors is a part-time partner in one of the largest and most prestigious law firms in the world. She has three children and works three full days a week. Her days are typically 8 a.m. to 6 p.m., and she does some work from home on her days off. Surprisingly, she has a litigation practice, and it is her reputation with clients over the years of full-time practice that has contributed to her success as a part-time partner. She is also one of the smartest and most capable attorneys that I know, and she has an academic pedigree that makes her very desirable for the firm. In other words, she is a superstar, and, remember, we need superstars.

According to one male Big Law contributor, a "one size fits all" policy in terms of flexibility and promotion to partnership is not the best approach. Because there are many different individuals and practices within a firm, he favors accommodations and promotion decisions that are tailored to a particular individual and practice and that are consistent with the firm strategy and economic model. He stresses that women need to be thoughtful and creative when requesting flexibility and accommodations, and he offers this example. His firm generally requires that each attorney bill at least 1,950 hours per year. For partners, another 400 hours might be required to meet the needs of management, pro bono practice, and other management related responsibilities. The total hours required of a partner, therefore, is closer to 2,400 or 2,500 a year. If a woman partner needs flexibility because of family and child care issues, it is possible to reduce the number of billable hours required from 2,400 to 1,800 or 1,900 and add some additional responsibilities for teaching or mentoring to arrive at a plan that accommodates both the woman partner and the firm. In fact, this contributor has seen a similar model work successfully in his firm. Specifically, a woman partner with teenage children wanted to cut back her hours to allow for more time at home. The woman had proved herself to be very valuable to the firm, and the firm did not want to lose her. In tailoring a solution that would fit the needs of the firm and those of the individual lawyer, the discussion centered around the most important client relationships that both the woman partner and the firm wanted her to retain, and the nonstrategic responsibilities, typically required of all partners, that could be reduced or eliminated. The mutual solution was for the woman partner to retain all responsibilities for three key clients and for the firm to direct her nonstrategic responsibilities to others for a period of two to three years to help get her through the difficult years with teenagers. Her compensation, of course, was reduced commensurate with this plan. The objective of the plan was achieved: The management of certain internal firm issues changed hands, but the perception from the outside world was not affected by the change. Again, it was a win-win for all.

However, one of my contributors favors a more defined path to partnership for part-time attorneys and believes that the expectation created by such an established path would go a long way toward retaining female attorneys. She asks, "Why does one seldom, if ever, see a female attorney in private practice who is over 50 years of age?" She believes that most of the women attorneys that age have left private practice because of the uncertainty and impediments surrounding partnership and because it is still extremely difficult for women to work the number of hours required in today's elite law firms and also be successful in raising a family—and maintaining sanity through it all. She looks forward to the day when more law firms implement a number of defined "tracks" to accommodate women's desires to find the proper work-life balance and to fully embrace this kind of flexibility as a benefit to the firm.

As you can see, there is some progress being made on the important issue of part-time partnership. It undoubtedly will be harder to make a case for becoming a partner part time than for converting to a part-time schedule after partnership has been achieved. Good luck with your efforts on this issue. I still believe that it is very much a two-pronged analysis, and I understand the importance of meeting the needs of the law firm in making part-time partnership work. I hope that you can make a better case for it today than I was able to 25 years ago. Even with improvement, however, part-time partnership will continue to be very difficult and somewhat elusive for many women.

If working full time is a requirement for partnership, find out early when you can consider your options without entanglement. Men don't have to consider this like women do. They don't have the babies, and, typically, they are not the primary caregivers. They might not identify it as important to the partnership discussion, so you will have to be the one to address it. Make sure that the conditions of partnership that you agree to are worth it for you.

Case in Point

"I had been with my firm for approximately five years, and was on the path to partnership. I then became pregnant with my first child and decided that I would have to transition to part time. I discussed the option with one of the managing partners, and, during that discussion, he told me that I had 'shot myself in the foot' on the partnership issue unless I was willing to work full-time after my baby was born. Can you imagine? Often men do not understand the choices that women face. Men, more than women, define themselves by their work and cannot understand choosing personal life over professional life. Some of my female colleagues and support staff urged me to take the partnership and to cut back to part time later. Those women had watched me fight against the odds to rise to be the first woman to be considered for partnership, and they wanted me to be rewarded for all of the hard work and perseverance. However, I could not take this self-serving path. I was close to the partners in the firm, and I had become an excellent young lawyer through their example and teaching. It was just too new a concept for them."

—**Constance, 60-Something**

This contributor says that she never regretted that decision. She continued to practice law in a manner suitable to her family situation, and she valued the time that she spent with her children. Her husband, also a lawyer, was not able to assume much responsibility for home and children, and it was the model that worked for them. Others might have made a different decision. The point is that it needs to be a very informed decision and not just a rush to partnership.

Much is being written on this subject lately. Fortunately, the Project for Attorney Retention is going to help you keep up with recent developments on this issue. In response to many inquiries from part-time partners and from law firms about the best way to structure part-time partnerships in law firms, the Project for Attorney Retention is undertaking a new study. The resulting report will not only provide an overview of the current state of part-time partnerships, but also will provide best practices for law firms. (See *www.parcdc.org* for more information.)

Find a Comfort Zone for Promoting Work

Promoting work and building a portfolio of business is challenging for all lawyers. Ask most successful lawyers, and they will tell you that it is a chore, and it is often more difficult for women than for men. One of my contributors has suggested that this might derive from the fact that bravado is valued in men from the time that they are little boys. They are complimented for their bravery and competitiveness, and their own recognition of those attributes is not discouraged. Witness a bunch of guys playing pickup basketball and you will have enough examples of this to last a lifetime. Teenage boys are always bragging about how they are bigger, tougher, and faster than the others in their group. It is almost a rite of passage for boys and men.

Women, on the other hand, are more likely to be viewed as braggartly, conceited, and self-absorbed if they act in the same manner. Women discourage that behavior in each other, and often it is difficult for a woman to make the transition from personal promotion to professional promotion. Additionally, women historically have been taught that it is bad manners to ask for things. The taboo surrounding not asking a man for a date is a perfect example. Why, then, would it be hard to understand the reluctance of a woman to ask a potential client for work?

Women must get over these limitations and do what men do. Women must choose professional, social, and recreational settings where they are likely to meet potential clients. Those settings might be health and country clubs, parent activities, bar association events, and business and professional groups, to name just a few. Although it might not be advisable to immediately morph into your lawyer role at your child's play group, there is always an opportunity to work your profession into the conversation. You never know who you might be talking to. CEOs have children, too.

Another hurdle to promoting work is that women tend to understate, rather than overstate, their potential. Men are typically very optimistic, even overenthusiastic, when discussing how they can serve a potential client. Women should follow this example, as long as they are being enthusiastic about the possibilities of the case or matter and do not make any specific promises of success. Often it takes research and discussions with colleagues to determine whether it is an appropriate representation for the firm. If you discover problems, you can always discuss that with the client later. Do not lose a potential client prematurely over these issues.

A slightly different view is offered by one of my contributors. She believes that women are more realistic about their expertise than men. It might be a lack of confidence on the part of women, but she believes that women seem more likely to decline a representation if they are not experienced in the field or cannot adequately represent a client. She views these traits as positive for the woman practitioner. She states that, in contrast, she has often heard men claim expertise about matters in which they have no expertise, and she has observed situations in which male attorneys should have declined representation and referred the client to someone more experienced.

No matter which view you take, one thing is clear: Women must become proficient at promoting work. One of my contributors tells this story, which illustrates how little some young women lawyers understand this concept.

Case in Point

"I had taken a group of young women attorneys to an event with me to give them an opportunity to practice their promotion and networking skills. During the event, I was pleased to observe certain of the young women engaging other attendees in conversation. The next day at the office, I talked to each of the young women to discuss the experience, and I was amazed to find that not one of the women had passed out or collected a business card during the event! I also was surprised to hear that most of the conversation engaged in by the young women had been social and not business-related. I challenged these young women to do better the next time, including handing out and getting business cards and making follow-up contacts the next day."

—Sandra, 50-Something

163

Another of my contributors, a partner in a midsize firm, says that women must be intentional about building relationships, which includes everything from keeping track of law school classmates to keeping a list of people they meet in various business settings. These contacts can become critical to promoting and developing work.

The issue of promoting work and including women in the promotional effort is being positively affected today by corporations and other businesses that are demanding diversity in their teams of outside counsel. This initiative was addressed by the University of California Hastings College of the Law Project for Attorney Retention First Annual Conference in May 2008 at George Washington University. As panel members, associate counsel for Wal-Mart and DuPont Corporation explained their commitment to diversity and saw this commitment as a real benefit to retention of women attorneys in law firms.

Last, but not least, I want to share one of my favorite pieces of advice for promoting business: Learn to golf. More business than you can imagine is done on the golf course. It is an ideal place for attorneys to cement attorney-client relationships, generate business, and build their practices. Male lawyers, typically, feel comfortable on a golf course and take advantage of every opportunity to play with clients. The world of business pays great homage to this, and some of the best MBA programs in the country emphasize the value of learning the game. It is also a fact that many firms subsidize country club memberships to encourage this valuable means of generating business. Several of my contributors emphasize the importance of golf as a business development tool, and the subject was discussed at the WomenLegal 2009 conference in New York City in April 2009. I have seen the power of golf as a promotional tool up close and personal, as described next.

Case in Point

"A male founding partner in one of my firms was very successful, and his counsel was highly sought in a specialized practice. I was very often asked what I considered to be the reason for his success, and I am sure that the answer that was expected had something to do with his education, intelligence, hard work, personal characteristics, and an excellent win-loss ratio. However, to the surprise of the inquirers, my answer was always the same: 'He learned to golf.' And I meant it. Sure, he possessed all the other attributes, but I had observed him in many settings with clients, and he was never more effective than when he was on the golf course. He belonged to at least three country clubs, and he mined for clients in all those settings, with unprecedented success. He spent a lot of time out of the office and had a decent back swing and an even better tan. But, his way of generating work benefited everyone throughout the firm, and few complained."

—Susan, 60-Something

However, some of you will see this as a very stereotypical approach. One of my contributors takes particular issue with this, and for very good reasons. She cites the new women's initiatives, at firms like hers, in developing marketing strategies that are more tailored to what women like and feel comfortable doing. She finds the golf option to be very stereotypical and "old school," and she believes that it is not apropos to today's young lawyers. She prefers the new direction that is being developed, which capitalizes on women's strengths and doesn't require a "male-oriented" makeover. Contrast that with another contributor who says simply that "it is what it is—either there is an opportunity or there is not." Put another way, old school, new school—it really doesn't matter. It is all about generation and survival.

You can make up your own mind. I choose to keep the golf option on the table. It will not be a good fit for many of you, but I think it would be a mistake to dismiss it as simply "old fashioned" and "out of touch" with today's realities. If you are a woman who can play a decent game of golf with the boys at the law firm member-client golf tournament and also are able to take advantage of the more woman-friendly development opportunities that were addressed earlier, you could be unstoppable!

Golf as a means of networking and promoting work is hardly a novel idea. Hilary Fordwich, founder and CEO of Strelmark, LLC in Washington, DC, consults to companies and law firms on building relationships that market their business. She assists her clients in all aspects of business development, in particular gaining and retaining work. As a golf competitor who is active in tournament play, she is a strong advocate of golf as a business development tool, especially for women. She sees it as an opportunity for women to gain entry into the "Old Boys Network" and to turn a stereotype to their own advantage. She has built a business golf expertise and is a contributing editor on ABC affiliate News Channel 8's Capital Golf Weekly in Washington, DC and *The Washington Post*'s Metro Talk. For more information on Fordwich and Strelmark, LLC, see *www.strelmark.com*.

If the golf option appeals to you, keep in mind that it might not be easy at first. Be aware that men will be very happy to exclude you from this "jock" setting because it changes the dialogue and holds them to a higher standard than boys' night out. However, do not allow this result. Learn to play a respectable game. Take lessons so that you do not embarrass yourself and take advantage of every opportunity that comes along. This might be difficult in your early years of practice, but do not give up. Your work schedule is likely to get less hectic as you gain expertise, and you will find more time for recreational things. After all, it is well known that Justice Sandra Day O'Connor took golf lessons for a year before she ever teed off for a regular round to assure a respectable performance. If she can do it, you can do it! Get in the game!

Make a Graceful Exit

Hopefully, you will make a good choice and will not have to leave a law firm or employer that you have chosen. However, there are many reasons for leaving, and, as discussed earlier, the business of law has become very dynamic in recent years. This is especially true as firms merge and acquire and alter the complexion of the firm you might have joined. Changing firms or employers is not a bad thing, but it must be handled correctly.

No matter what the reasons for leaving a law firm or another law setting, departing can be very painful, and leaving the right way is critical. The right way is usually the graceful way, without jeopardizing your relationships. Remember that you will be in a position to get referrals from colleagues at a former firm if you do it right. Achieving a smooth transition will depend on whether the attorney has a good reputation in the firm, has developed good contacts, and is generally well liked. The last two will probably not be achieved if the attorney concentrates only on billable hours. It is essential that a young lawyer get her head out of the books for long enough to make valuable human contacts with colleagues. Seeking out a mentor and forming a solid relationship with that senior lawyer is essential to this situation, as well.

Do not leave too soon and without having another job lined up first. An unexplained six months out of work is bad for a professional résumé. There are times when the lapse can be explained by some kind of epiphany, but that occurs seldom and is usually part of a lawyer's decision to leave Big Law for the nonprofit world. In that case, it can be explained through a values discussion. In most cases, you must be strategic and line up your options first.

Most important, do not put off the decision to leave if the benefits analysis does not work to your advantage. Each year that you remain in a bad situation, leaving becomes more difficult. One way to keep flexibility in that decision is to pay off your student loans as soon as possible and avoid getting caught up in the Big Law lifestyle. I know that I have said this before, but it bears repeating. Getting caught up in the Big Law lifestyle benefits the firm more than it benefits you. The more dependent you become on the big salary for your chosen lifestyle, the fewer options you will have when it comes to leaving the firm. It can be a type of modern-day servitude!

I was summoned one day to the office of one of my partners. He told me that he was having trouble with a female associate, and he needed my help. He said that each time she came into his office she became sexually aroused and that it was a problem for him. I was astonished and asked him how he knew that she was sexually aroused. He said that it was because her nipples showed "hard and perky" through her clothing. I tried not to laugh. Then I responded, "I think that you have identified the wrong problem. Most likely this has nothing to do with your sex appeal or her attraction to you. It is like a meat locker in here. Turn up the heat and the problem will go away!"
—Woman Senior Partner

Critical Lessons

Dress Appropriately and Practice Good Etiquette

Hopefully, you paused long enough at the beginning of the book to read my bio (if not, just humor me), and you know that I am a little older than you are.

Now you might think that I am going to give you some Victorian views on how to be a lady and how to dress for success or to impress. Not so. I am fully aware that we are in a new millennium and that what was required of me and my generation of women lawyers is not as appropriate when applied to your generation. You indeed do stand on the shoulders of the women who came before you in the profession, and those women are proud of what they have accomplished and what is available to women today. We recognize that your generation of women will not tolerate being told to act like a man or to dress like one to be successful, even in a male-dominated profession like the law. We recognize that you want to be judged on your intelligence and competency and not on your appearance. We recognize that you do not want to conform for the sake of conformity. And, we applaud all of that because it is what we want for you. However, we also want you to survive in the profession, and that might take a bit of finessing on your part. It might require a little bit of checking the attitude at the door in some situations. In other words, it might require seeing the forest for the trees and recognition on your part that some axioms stand the test of time.

So, how should you deal with the issues of femininity that will inevitably become part of your professional life as a young female lawyer? The answer, I think, is to deal with them as a professional, as an individual who has been trained to use her intelligence and to recognize the reality of her circumstances. When expression of your individuality, either by the way you dress or the way you act, becomes a distraction from your professional self, it is not only bad for those observing you, it is also bad for you. That is what you should keep in mind when you determine the limits of your self-expression in a law office setting. If you do that, you will make good decisions on how to talk, how to dress, and how to interact with your colleagues and staff, and you will not limit your opportunities in the process. What is appropriate at a nonprofit or at the public defender's office might not be appropriate at a Wall Street firm. What is appropriate in a small law firm might not be appropriate at a large corporate firm with

Fortune 500 clients. What is appropriate at a firm that is predominately female attorneys might not be what is appropriate at a firm that is predominately male attorneys. What is appropriate in a practice in the North might not be what is appropriate in a practice in the South. What is appropriate before a young new appointee to the bench might not be appropriate for an appearance before an octogenarian judge. What is appropriate for corporate in-house counsel might not be appropriate in a private law office.

You are smart, and you can make the right decision. The issue is not your intelligence and wisdom once you address the question; the issue is whether you do address the question. Survival is key, and you do not want your ego and attitude to get in the way—no matter how entitled or empowered you might feel or how right you might be. Entitlement and empowerment will not pay back those student loans and might not support your chosen lifestyle. So, for a while at least, you might have to "play the game" until you are in a position to have your own law firm and come to the office in your cute lacy camisole and strut your stuff to your heart's content. Until that time, be smart and attentive to your circumstances and setting. When in doubt, risk being overdressed.

One of my contributors points out that we are now in what is referred to as the "third wave of feminism" and that young women, including young women professionals, are now embracing their feminism more than ever. They are proud of who they are and get satisfaction from expressing it in their actions and attire. However, the problem, according to this contributor, is that, although the women understand it, the men "are clueless" about these new attitudes. Unfortunately, these men are still at the controls and offending their sensibilities could be a high price to pay for euphoria and freedom of expression.

Now, here are the fundamentals, because I never want it to be said that I didn't tell you. Always dress appropriately for a professional office. This cannot be overemphasized. What is appropriate for a casual lunch with friends might not be appropriate for the office. You must look professional to be treated as a professional. There is nothing wrong with looking feminine as long as it is done in a tasteful manner. Always remember, however, that femininity and sex appeal are two different things. The office is no place to demonstrate your sex appeal.

I am always amazed at the stories that my contributors tell—tales of nipples peeking through sweaters and blouses and exposed cleavage. They recount the necessity to counsel young women attorneys to raise the necklines and lower the hemlines. This is very good advice, and you will be glad that you read it here and did not have to suffer the embarrassment of hearing it from a female partner or, even worse, a male partner.

Lately, similar observations by federal judges also have been reported. At a recent Seventh Circuit Judicial Conference, U.S. District Court Judge Joan Lefkow stated that she thought that some women attorneys should pay more attention to dressing appropriately for court, and she found support from her colleagues for that concern. In addition to Judge Lefkow's objection to women lawyers dressing for court in work-out attire appropriate to a gym setting, several of her male colleagues and male attorneys in the audience objected to "skirts so short that there's no way they can sit down and blouses so short there's no way the judges wouldn't look." One judge said that he wished that he could tell the offending female lawyers that, but for those distractions, he would really "like to pay attention to [their] argument[s]." This same judge stated, "You don't dress in court as if it's Saturday night and you're going out to a party. Dress as a serious person who takes the court seriously." When the subject was opened up for broader discussion, which included a discussion of inappropriate dress by male lawyers, some of the judges and attorneys blamed law firms for not giving lawyers enough guidance, and others said that law schools need to do a better job of educating young lawyers on appropriate dress ("Federal Judges Grouse About Lawyer's Courtroom Attire." *The National Law Journal,* May 21, 2009).

Fortunately women law students and attorneys have more choices in appropriate dress today. You no longer are confined to the dark pinstripe suits, cotton blouses, and little bow ties that were popular for women attorneys in the 1980s, probably because the style came as close to looking like menswear as possible. The choices for your generation of women lawyers are much more extensive and a whole lot more fun to wear. Pantsuits, jackets and slacks, and even sweaters and blouses without jackets are appropriate in the more relaxed styles of the 21st-century professional office. Miniskirts and low-cut blouses, however, are out and hopefully always will be. Don't go there. Remember, you never get a second chance to make a first impression.

Let me share what the law school career counselors have to say on the subject. Their advice is no breasts exposed, no panty lines showing, no visible underwear, and no thigh-length skirts. Mandie Araujo, Esquire, the Director of Career Services at New England Law | Boston is also the owner of PardonMe, a business etiquette consulting company (*www.pardonmeinc.com*). The need for her services grew out of what she observed in business and in law, and her services include not only etiquette and dress advice, but also tips for networking, dining interviews and other related topics. She finds her advice particularly valuable for young women and men who have not had the advantages of growing up in professional households. She reports that she is always surprised at how pervasive this problem is and tells the story of the male law student who arrived at the on-campus interviews without a necktie. I suspect that she now keeps a few odd ties in her drawer!

According to Araujo, too much perfume can also be a problem. This definitely struck a chord with me and brought back at least one painful memory from my law school days. While participating in the first-year moot court competition, the results for my partner and me were mixed. The good news was that we won the competition, but the bad news was that we were chastised by one of the judges for the distraction caused by the scent of my perfume! As I learned later, physiologically, a "little dab will do you" in high-anxiety situations because the body responds to stress with increased blood flow, which can accentuate the scent of perfume or lotions. Although I was outraged by the comments and suspected that the same would not have been said to a male student about his aftershave, it was a good lesson.

Araujo recommends that you also become completely comfortable with the rules of business etiquette, which reflect the military model and are based on rank. For example, men and women should be treated the same in terms of handshakes, assistance in opening doors, and the like. Do not let men treat you as a woman in the workplace; rather, make them treat you as a fellow professional, and you return the same respect to them. If a senior attorney, either male or female, is having difficulty opening a door, offer assistance. If a senior attorney requires assistance in putting on a coat, offer assistance. And, if a senior attorney needs help getting in or out of a chair, offer assistance. Workplace etiquette should be based on rank and age and not on gender. Araujo points out that students in MBA programs receive etiquette training or are provided with recommendations for etiquette consultants. Government officials, especially at the State Department, have similar instruction available to them. Law students and young lawyers do not get this in the traditional curriculum, and, therefore, many of them must go outside the classroom to learn how to present themselves as professionals.

If you think that these problems of proper attire and etiquette are confined to a particular socioeconomic class or a certain kind of law school, think again. I was amazed to hear similar stories from career counselors at upper echelon law schools that include many students of privilege from professional backgrounds. One career counselor at a top law school told me that she gets calls from hiring partners at major law firms complaining of attire and conduct, and a second counselor reported the same. On one occasion the partner asked, "Who told these young women that Friday business casual means cut-offs and flip flops?" And then there is the story about an associate looking to relocate to Big Law, who went to the interview in flip flops! My contributor got the follow-up phone call from an astonished partner who had been present at the interview. Yes, it seems to be a more universal problem than you might think.

> **Case in Point**
>
> "I was recently in court on a motions day. There were many young associates, including women, in court that day for the purpose of being introduced to the judge and for gaining permission to practice in that court. I was appalled at the dress of some of the young women lawyers. While it appeared that they all were wearing beautiful new suits, the skirts were too short, the necklines too low, the clothing too tight and the stiletto heels too high for a courtroom appearance. I could not help but think that these young women were denigrating the professional respect that I had fought for my entire career."
>
> **—Deirdre, 50-Something**

I have thought about this a lot since first hearing it. Of course, the contributor is right, and the dress was inappropriate. But, I think there is more at play in her remarks. She is an accomplished attorney and represents the feminist generation of the 1960s and 1970s. It is hard, indeed almost impossible, for the women who fought for those equality issues to set them aside, even in a world of changed circumstances. Although it is broadly acknowledged that young women attorneys today would not have the choices available to them without the efforts of these women, the social change that has occurred cannot be overlooked and it is important to the discussion. Women of my generation run the risk of "raging against the machine" too much, and it many times falls on deaf ears with the current generation of young women. Too often it is received as "Mom's news" or worse, "Grandma's news." The current generation views these things as old and settled, and with good reason. Take for instance, the propensity for women professionals to keep their maiden names after marriage as a way of heralding their independence. This does not seem to be as much the trend anymore, and it might not be necessary. Young women are focused on different things, and that is probably a positive development. For those of us who lived the struggle, it was big. For the current generation, it might not be today's reality, but we would like them to remember it. However, beating a dead horse is never a good thing!

Some standards of etiquette might be changing in a changing world. This is particularly true as technology has altered the circumstances that surround business in the 21st century. Recent technological advances have changed business norms, and that includes the business of law. A simple question may be, "Is it OK to e-mail a prospective employer after an interview in lieu of sending a formal letter or note?" The answer might have been "no" a year ago, but might be "yes" today. One law school career counselor at a top-tier school reports that he has changed his mind on that within the year's time span. He bases his opinion on feedback from the employers, many of whom now view e-mail as a more efficient use of their time. He opines that it is technology that has bred not only the informality of this situation but others, as well. Whereas it once was necessary to put in a requisite amount of "face time" at the office every day to communicate a level of dedication and professionalism, the advent of the computer and remote work sites may be changing that perception. These differences of opinion will be worked out in the debate and negotiations between members of the new and old generations, but a lot will depend on tailoring the response to particular circumstances. It will take a concerted effort to "gauge" the reactions of the prospective employer and law firm members to make the right decisions. For example, it might be that a woman of my generation, who grew up wearing white gloves and a bonnet on Easter, will prefer a written note to an e-mail after an interview. (For the record, I would not!) On the other hand, if the interviewer is clearly high-tech and clutching his or her Blackberry during the interview, it could call for another result. For information on preparing for job interviews and appropriate follow-up, I recommend that you consult *Nail Your Law Job Interview: The Essential Guide to Firm, Clerkship, Government, In-House, and Lateral Interviews,* by Natalie Prescott and Oleg Cross (Career Press, 2009). Do not assume anything. Do your homework.

Now for a huge caveat. Although technology has changed the way we look at the appropriateness of some etiquette issues, the use of Facebook and other Internet social sites can be particularly inappropriate and risky for a young professional. What an individual chooses to post on such a site communicates a lot about the individual. In many cases, the things posted on an Internet social site are not what you want a prospective employer or an employer to see, and it has been reported that Internet sites like Facebook have become popular tools for recruiters (*The New York Times*, "Job Hunting Is, and Isn't, What It Used to Be," September 26, 2008). Beware of this pitfall, as it could cost you a job.

Watch Out for Emotions and Temper

Demonstrating too much emotion and temper can be the "gotcha twins" for female lawyers. Whether you are a law clerk, a summer associate, or an associate attorney, your supervising attorney is likely to be a man, simply by virtue of the numbers. It is almost a given that he can have a temper but you cannot. It is an ugly double standard, but it is true. Yes, it is the 21st century, but some things never change. What is "assertive" in a man is too often perceived as "bitchy" in a woman. Stand your ground in the same way that he does, firm, but with as little emotion as possible.

At all costs, do not cry. This is a hard one for women because most women are more emotional than most men. Women tend to cry when they are happy as well as when they are sad, and women are comfortable with tears. Additionally, logic tells us that, for the most part, there is nothing wrong with tears. Tears have been a part of humanity throughout evolution because crying is an important emotional release. However, crying is not appropriate in all settings, and you have to make good decisions about where to cry. Generally, the office, in the presence of a male boss, is not one of those places. Men feel uncomfortable seeing a woman cry, and the conversation is likely to end prematurely and unsatisfactorily. Tears can also be interpreted as manipulation, and few people feel comfortable around a colleague who they view as Machiavellian.

> ## Case in Point
>
> "Crying is a no-no, particularly for a woman professional. I recall the political commentary when Hillary Clinton teared up during the days leading up to the 2008 New Hampshire Democratic primary. The debate over whether her tears were genuine or whether they were manipulative continues. There are equally compelling arguments on both sides of this debate. Contrast that to the tears shed by other male political candidates over the years or the tears of running back Terrell Owens of the Dallas Cowboys when his team was eliminated during the 2008 NFL playoffs. The discussion of those tears generally centered on the issues of strength and weakness, but rarely was that behavior seen as manipulative. Yes, the tears of a big, tough football player got less attention than the tears of a woman political candidate. Life is not fair. Get over it and, whenever possible, do not cry."
>
> —Beth, 50-Something

Understand That "No" Is an Answer

You knew this was coming, right? Let's face it, women very often need to have the last word in a disagreement. Even though this might be warranted in some situations, it does not work well most of the time with most male supervisors. You are taught in law school to "push back" in a debate, and I do not mean to say that women should relinquish their positions easily. However, you must keep the focus on the substantive issues and not allow the conversation to become personal. By beating a point to death, you will very often remind your male colleague of what he finds annoying about his wife, his sister, or his mother. You will give him the opportunity to characterize your behavior as "nagging," and it is difficult to win an argument that has become personal.

The better approach is to make it known that you do not agree and that you would like to continue the discussion later. Your male colleague will know that you are not walking away in defeat, and you will not have allowed the discussion to get out of control. You can return to the discussion at a later date, hopefully with a different approach or from a different perspective. "No" is not always "no" if you are clever in repackaging and representing the issue.

Case in Point

"One of the most valuable lessons that I ever learned centered around the meaning of 'no.' In conversations with my boss when we disagreed, I was often so confident of my position that I was certain that he either did not hear me or did not understand my point when he failed to come over to my position. So, of course, I tried to repeat and clarify. Fortunately and after some rather harsh words from him, I came to understand that he had not only heard me, but that he also understood my position. He simply did not agree with me, and he was the boss. Chapter closed."

—Charlotte, 40-Something

Support Your Female Colleagues

"There's a place in hell reserved for women who don't help other women." This quote has been attributed to the Honorable Madeleine Albright, former United States Ambassador to the United Nations. It just about says it all.

Always try your best to support your female colleagues. Do not intentionally work at cross-purposes with your female colleagues and don't sabotage them. In most cases, these women are your best friends at the bar, and you need mutual support to survive. Of course, there are many exceptions to this, and sometimes it is not possible to support certain behavior and motives. You will know the difference. Start out with the premise that you will support your female colleagues and work from there.

Avoid behavior that can be perceived as "catty" and back stabbing. Women have a reputation for this behavior, and television sitcoms, soap operas, and the movie industry have been cashing in on this theme for years. It is the product of jealousy and competition, often for men and attention, and it has no place in a professional setting. It is counterproductive to advancing women's causes, and it should be avoided at all costs.

Women lawyers have only just recently begun to realize the value of supporting each other. By recently, I mean within the last 10 to 15 years. Prior to that, there were very few female mentors in the profession, and many of the ranking females resented the young, energetic female associates. The established female lawyers were real trailblazers, and, in many cases, their personal lives had suffered as a result. Too often their behavior reflected the attitude that they had sacrificed under the old rules, and the younger generation would have to do the same. They showed no real desire to improve the situation for the generations of women to follow, and they enjoyed the exclusivity that came with having "made it" under the men's rules.

A 2006 ABA report entitled "Charting Our Profession: The Status of Women in the Profession Today" includes the following as part of the discussion of "The Generational Divide" (ABA Commission on Women in the Profession (2006) at 8):

Not surprisingly, a recurring theme among younger attorneys ... was their frustration with older female attorneys, particularly, on quality of life issues. [M]ost of the women are not realistic role models because they have never been married or do not have families or obligations outside the profession. . . . It was as if the more senior women in the firm had become a part of the good-old-boy network, rather than railing against it.

There is still some of this attitude present today, although there are many excellent women mentors in our profession, and the attitudes of senior women seem to have improved a lot. However, one of my contributors believes that women are still their own worst enemies because they do not help each other enough. That contributor reminds me that too often women still act like crabs in a bucket. Maybe you have been crabbing along the beach in the summer and will share the visual for this. The caught crabs are all in a bucket, at various stages of clutching and grabbing their way to the top of the bucket and freedom. Eventually one crab perseveres and makes it to the top. What comes next is key. The crab that has been successful in reaching the top of the bucket proceeds to knock down each and every other crab that subsequently comes near the top. It happens without fail, over and over again.

The reason for this behavior, which also has been referred to as the Queen Bee Syndrome by Rebecca Shambaugh, President and CEO of Shambaugh, a corporate leadership advisor (see *www.shambaughleadership.com*), is that the women who have become established at the top of business either don't think there is enough room at the top for more women (and are, therefore, threatened or unwilling to bring others along) or they simply believe that the young women should have to pay the same "dues" as the older women had to pay. If either is true, women are simply defeating themselves.

Women should not want to behave like crabs—or queen bees in any setting,—and it should not be tolerated in the legal profession. Women must stand together to create opportunities and to change establishment attitudes. If not, they will be divided and conquered. Most men are not motivated to change conditions for women, so women must stick together to create change. Women established in their legal careers must become effective mentors to young female attorneys. If there had been more good mentoring over the years, there likely would be much less need for a book like this one.

One of my contributors offers an example of how not to act toward your female colleagues.

> ## Case in Point
>
> "When I came up for partnership at my firm, I was advised by my male mentor to visit all of the partners in the firm so they could interact with me on my chances for partnership. I took this advice, and, among others, I met with one of the few women partners. After a ten-minute conversation that I thought went well and demonstrated some female 'bonding,' the partner said, 'We've talked for ten minutes now and you still haven't given me one reason to vote for you.' I learned an important lesson from this experience: Just because someone is a woman doesn't mean she is nice. I got that partnership, and I try to remember this lesson in the way I interact with young women lawyers."
>
> —Julia, 50-Something

Fortunately, we are now seeing an "Old Girls Network" develop in our profession. *The American Lawyer* article "Obstacle Course" by Amy Kolz (January 2007) points out there is such a network of former U.S. attorneys who make an effort to refer clients and legal matters to each other, and I am sure that it is happening in the private sector as well. In fact, you are experiencing such a result in the contributions of female lawyers and judges to this book, and I am gratified and proud to be part of the effort. Women are now referring work to each other and supporting each other in a way that has been unprecedented in the past. Perhaps there are now enough women in positions of control to bring about this result. Whatever the cause, I am happy to report that you and other young female attorneys will be the beneficiaries of this enlightenment.

The example of Deborah Epstein Henry is instructive here. Although today she is a highly sought-after consultant, who spends her profession life advising lawyers, law firms, and corporations on how to maintain a work-life balance, this was not always the case. Like so many of you, she wanted to be a litigator and had a successful career as a commercial litigator while raising three sons. She struggled with how to balance taking care of her family, practicing law part time, and staying on the partnership track. This is a common story, but what comes next is unique. Instead of sitting around worrying about this dilemma, Epstein Henry sent e-mails to three female lawyers in her firm and to several other women who were working part time. She invited them to a brown-bag lunch to discuss work-life issues. Within several days, she was flooded with e-mails, and she ended up holding regular meetings to discuss flexible hours, reduced schedules, and other work-life issues. She went on to found Flex-Time Lawyers LLC in 2002 and expanded the dialogue to include other issues like retention and promotion that also affected women lawyers. By 2007, her company had expanded so much that she left the practice of law altogether to concentrate on consulting. (See "Best Firms for Work-Life Balance," *The National Jurist* (October 2008).)

Although this is a great personal success story, it also is so much more. It is the story of a woman who saw herself as part of a group of women who needed to band together to prevail over some very challenging obstacles to success in their careers. It is the story of a woman who knew how to support other women. For additional interesting reading on this subject, I recommend the following books: *Tripping the Prom Queen: The Truth About Women and Rivalry* by Susan Shapiro Baragh (St. Martin's Griffin 2007), and *In the Company of Women: Deepening Our Relationship with the Important Women in Our Lives,* by Brenda Hunter, PhD (Multomah Press 2006).

Get It in Writing

If you are going to be judged by the expectations of others (like supervising attorneys and management), it is a good idea that you get the job assignment or description in writing. The last thing that you want is to be told that you did not do the job correctly when you cannot defend yourself with a description of the assignment. Although some supervising attorneys still send memos to junior attorneys setting forth the issues and matters to be researched and addressed, it is much more common to cover that ground with oral briefings and less formal means, including a brief discussion in the hallway. Although this might satisfy the needs of the supervisor, the lack of a written record might not work as well for the junior lawyer. Solving this problem is easier today with the liberal use of e-mail between attorneys in offices just 20 feet from one another. If the assignment is delivered orally, send an e-mail to confirm the conversation and to summarize the expectations. It could come in very handy for rebuttal along the way. This is particularly important for women lawyers and women summer associates. Some male professionals still question the competency of women in the profession and will take advantage of simple misunderstandings to prove their predisposition. Take this extra precaution and do not give them that opportunity.

One of my contributors learned the hard way.

Case in Point "I was preparing to accompany a male partner on a prelitigation trip. I was new to the case, and it was my understanding from conversations with the partner that I was going along to meet the client and get background on the case. In other words, this was to be a learning experience for me, and my role was to listen carefully and gain a full understanding of the matter to prepare myself to jump into the case at a level with colleagues who had been working on the case for years. So, that is what I did—listened and learned. Later, after returning home from the trip, I was called into the office of a named partner and told that he understood from the partner that I had acted 'like a secretary' on the trip because I had taken notes and had not participated in the discussions. Unfortunately, all of my conversations with the partner about my role at the meetings were oral, and I had no paper trail to defend my position. Do not let this happen to you. A confirming e-mail to the partner addressing my role on the trip would either have been evidence of our mutual understanding and my appropriate behavior or it would have given the partner an opportunity to clarify his intent so that the pitfall could have been avoided."

—Diana, 50-Something

This may be difficult for many women. Law school career counselors report that women are often reluctant to ask questions and seek clarification from their supervising attorneys. A contributor also observes that, for some reason, women are less inclined to ask questions about work assignments than men. Too often, women associates find themselves writing memos assuming wrong facts or making similar career-limiting mistakes. Ask, ask, and ask. The only dumb question is the one that you do not ask.

Treat Support Staff Well

Treating support staff well cannot be overemphasized. It is so easy, and it is an investment that will pay great dividends. Support staff can make you look good in certain situations and can help you avoid pitfalls by sharing a salient piece of information. Staff members are often the only ones who know how to send a fax, contact FedEx, remedy the copier paper jam, and set up a conference call. Staff members almost always know more about the office grapevine than the attorneys, and knowing an important piece of information can often come in handy. All of these things benefit you and make you look good. However, staff can just as easily sabotage you. Treat them well at all times.

Here is a story that I like to call "Who's Got the Power?" That is a game that I have played with my children from the time they were very young. They would come home from school and practice railing about the unfair teacher and the unfair coach, especially, and they would proceed to tell me

185

what they intended to tell that offending person. My question was always the same, "Who's got the power?" If you do not have the power in a situation, you had better temper your words and your actions or you could pay a high price.

Case in Point

"When I was an associate attorney years ago, I was in charge of the summer associate program. I noticed that one particular male summer associate was very condescending to support staff. One day I asked him who in the firm he thought was most important to his professional growth. He quickly responded by identifying a named partner. I took the opportunity to educate him on the realities of life at a law firm. I told him that he could be the most brilliant young lawyer ever to have graced the entrance to the firm; however, no one would ever know it unless he could get his thoughts on paper and to the important partner he had named and before the deadline. As a result, I told him, 'Your secretary may be the most important person in your life here at XYZ law firm. Treat her well.'"

—**Alicia, 60-Something**

You are probably scratching your head a bit. Let me clarify. In "the old days," lawyers did not use computers, and were totally dependent on secretaries and typing pools to turn dictation or handwritten memos into legal documents. Without a willing and loyal secretary, you were doomed. Even though most lawyers are completely computer savvy today, the rule still holds: Support staff provide myriad daily conveniences to attorneys, and they can make you or break you.

One of my young contributors points out what appears to be the flip side of this issue. She describes situations where support staff do not treat young associate attorneys well. Female secretaries often can be rude to young women attorneys, especially, based on the negative female–female dynamic discussed earlier, and often secretaries do not want to work for associate attorneys who lack the prestige and power of partners. This contributor describes a secretary who refused to do the associate's work and who identified herself on her telephone voice mail message as working for the partner only, with no reference to the associate. After talking to the secretary to no avail, the young woman attorney was forced to bring the matter to the attention of senior lawyers and management. Eventually, the secretary was terminated, but not before she caused a great deal of discontent and discomfort in the practice. If this happens to you, do not wait too long to resolve the issue or to bring it to the attention of someone who can. You should not put up with this behavior.

You are now ready for my personal favorites. The following few lessons—which I like to call "Lessons You Should Have Learned Along the Way But Might Have Forgotten"—should not be taken lightly, although I can understand the temptation. I realize that you are likely to view certain of the lessons as obvious and instinctive and not worthy of inclusion. However, failing to understand the importance of these things has precipitated more than a few doomed careers. I personally have witnessed young female lawyers, who should have known better, fail to heed these simple warnings and pay a dear price. So, I will risk boring you. It is better to review what seems obvious than to take a chance with your future. Remember, this is not a profession where asking forgiveness is more effective than asking permission.

Party Hardy at Your Peril

Loose lips do more than sink ships. They can demolish careers. Women typically cannot hold their liquor like men and can become very emotional when they drink too much. Women lawyers should avoid partying to excess with colleagues and risking tarnishes to their reputations. Again, there is a double standard, but that is not likely to change. The boys can party hardy, make fools of themselves, and survive without compromising themselves professionally. In fact, they might become more attractive because of these antics. I recall the story of a young male associate who was intoxicated after a Friday night happy hour and put his foot through the front door of his firm because he could not find his key. However, he continued to do well at the firm and is now general counsel of a huge corporation and has the former partners working for him! Unfortunately, "boys will be boys" is still the standard. Not so for women, who pay a much higher price for their indiscretions.

One of my contributors offers the following advice, "Have only one glass of wine in a business setting and drink it slowly." Good advice. I might add: Eat while you drink for best results.

Avoid Office Romances and Affairs

Not much should have to be said about this. Simply put, there is not much good that can come out of getting romantically involved with a professional colleague. It often encourages unprofessional behavior and leads to allegations of favoritism. There are plenty of fish in the sea, and you should be doing your recreational fishing in other waters.

One of my contributors tells this story from her experiences in law school during the early 1980s.

> **Case in Point**
>
> "On the first day of my ethics class, at a time when the students were eager to explore the lofty ideals of professional responsibility, the professor opened the lecture with the following remarks. 'There are only three things that you need to know about ethics. Don't sleep with your secretary, don't sleep with your client, and don't mess with the trust

accounts.' My classmates and I were very disappointed with what we thought was a trite and simplistic approach to a serious subject. In other words, we expected more. However, years later, most of us agree that it is some of the best advice we ever received."

—Molly, 50-Something

Here is a story about a young colleague who became involved in an office affair, as told to one of my contributors.

Case in Point

"Everything seemed to be going well. We were very discrete and had a good relationship until the partner that I was involved with changed his mind. The breakup resulted in a lot of office gossip and was very uncomfortable for me. I was astounded at the degree of resentment that both support staff and professional staff had toward me, and I was even more astounded at the level of loyalty they showed to the male partner who had treated me so badly. They defended his actions and found fault with me!"

—Courtney, 30-Something

This is an unfortunate story, and the associate ended up leaving the firm. However, office romances are sure to happen. Most young lawyers spend days and nights at the office and do not have much time to cultivate relationships outside the office. If it happens to you, be discreet, act professionally at all times, and work hard to keep the relationship a secret between you and Mr. Right-at-the-Moment. Even if you follow this advice, it will still be a great challenge, and it is likely to be much more of a challenge for you than for him. Again, there is a double standard that is not going anywhere fast.

There is only one way to avoid the sting: Don't get involved in the first place. As pointed out by one of my contributors, in almost every instance of office romance or affair, only Mr. and Ms. Right thought it was a secret!

Watch Your Mouth

Always remember that you can be tough and feminine at the same time. You do not have to talk trash to communicate your toughness and your resolve. In fact, you might find that you can disguise your toughness with your femininity just long enough to catch a male colleague off guard and make it work to your advantage. Trash talk by women does not have much appeal for men, who are typically uncomfortable with it coming from a woman, and it certainly does not appeal to most of your female colleagues. Your toughness would be better shown by thorough research, flawless presentation, and great delivery. If your colleagues and competitors know you can win, they know you are tough.

Some women learn the hard way.

Case in Point

"When I started practicing law, there were still not many women in the practice. I was surrounded by guys, and I talked like them. Reputations have a way of lasting, and it has taken me years to get the past behind me. I wish I had done things differently."

—Marie, 50-Something

Another feminine pitfall is talking too much. Typically, women love to talk, and they very often share personal information that can compromise them. This is true of what you talk about with your colleagues and also with the staff. Remember that secretaries and other staff generally owe their first loyalties to their bosses and supervisors. Confidences can become anything but private in this setting. It is better to find your soul mates outside the office.

*Expect the best mentors to be the ones
who are most critical of you. It is the
constructive criticism that you
learn from and that makes you a
better lawyer.*
—30-Something Woman Lawyer

The Working Bar
Speaks Out: As Heard
From the Best Friends

It is now time to hear more
from my "best friends at the bar."
Although many of their contributions and anecdotes have
appeared in earlier chapters, I
have included typical profiles
and certain of their responses here to familiarize you with their backgrounds and accomplishments and to highlight their advice to young
women lawyers and to law firms. These women bring experience from
several generations of lawyers, and they have demonstrated remarkable
dedication to this project to make sure that their opinions and advice are

included. It was not unusual to receive an e-mail or a phone call updating me on their progress and assuring me that, once the trial is over, once the merger talks are completed, once the judicial conference is concluded, or once the illness is improved, I would receive what they had promised. And, true to their words and their professionalism, they always came through. That is the quality of these women and their commitment to the next generation of female attorneys. This project started out as a labor of love for me, and that interest and dedication spread to the "best friends" in a way that has been truly inspiring. It became their project, as well. Once again, I applaud them and thank them for caring so much about you.

So, with pleasure I introduce you to my best friends at the bar. I hope that you now consider them to be *your* best friends at the bar, as well. There is no effective substitution for real-life stories and good, sage advice that has survived the test of time. Get ready for a variety of choices and results, as demonstrated by these women, and look for yourself in some of the stories they have to tell.

Typical Profiles and Work-Life Challenges

I start with the "old girls" in spite of the fact that many of you will find them less relevant to your situation. However, by now you know my penchant for past as prologue and the importance of gaining perspective. They are the trailblazers, and if nothing else, you might realize that it is now easier than it ever was for women in the law and you will take heart that you do not have to climb some of these same mountains and make some of these very difficult choices. You will be happy that the work-life balance is exactly that, more of a balance and that you do not have to cook every night and assume all of the responsibilities of child care to achieve an acceptable balance.

The 60-Somethings A 60-something, a judge, married with children, has this to say:

> Law school is not exclusively for the young. If you decide against law school at an early age, you can revisit the issue later. I began law school at age 35, with three children under six years old. I went to night school to fit my family schedule, which required that I be home with the children during the day. I experienced enormous challenges, little sleep, and few leisure activities. The largest hurdle for me was to overcome the concern that my children's lives would be irreparably and adversely affected by my distraction and absence from home. Eventually, I became a judge and my children turned out very well indeed! My best advice to young women lawyers is to make sure that you have a good mentor. I also recommend that you start as a law clerk to a judge, which gives you a year or two to make the transition from law school to private practice with a mentor who really understands the law. You also should take advantage of all networking opportunities, including young lawyers groups and women's groups, and you should learn to handle adversity with calmness and humor. Do not take things too personally or too seriously.

Is it any wonder that she is a great judge?

Another 60-something, a litigator, married with children, and partner in a large national law firm, responded that her most challenging issue was the travel demands of litigation, which often involved extended stays in other jurisdictions:

> Travel demands were really difficult for me when I was in both government practice and private practice. One particular incident sticks in my mind. I was on business travel from Washington, DC, to south Texas with a witness for a deposition at a time when one of my children was ill and not responding to medication. Although my son recovered from the illness, I felt that the work-life balance (although it was not called that then—or even identified as a concept—and certainly never discussed) was definitely "out of whack" on that occasion. My best advice is to develop a niche practice or specialty instead of being a generalist. This will provide a source of expertise and business over the years and allow you to tailor your working arrangement in private practice or a corporate environment. You should learn to be assertive within the limits of being polite and you should not let superiors treat you

paternalistically. Consider government and public service for great learning opportunities.

A 60-something, married without children, and litigation partner of a large firm, believes that one of the most challenging things for young women attorneys is standing up to male stereotypes:

> I have seen great progress over time on this issue, but I urge young women to be strong and purposeful and to nip those stereotypes in the bud as often as possible.

Another 60-something, a trusts and estates sole practitioner, responds that she had to establish a local practice near her home to deal with the work-life issues. It sounds as if she wishes she had made other choices earlier in her career:

> I recommend a career in the government, and I do not recommend that you leave a government practice without a lot of thought, especially if you are looking for flexibility and excellent benefits. This is particularly true of women who want work-life balance and a good pension that assures some life after career.

A 60-something, married with children, in a financial planning practice, describes her biggest professional challenge as coming to terms with "not having it all" after her children were born:

> You can't be the perfect attorney or business woman and go home and be the perfect mom. Something has to give both at the office and at home to make this work, and that is OK. I did not have children until I was established in my career, which made it easier to take time off when I needed it and at a time when I was not still trying to climb the career ladder as much. At-home child care, a husband who was willing to pitch in with family responsibilities, and a schedule that did not require much travel were all helpful to my success in those years with small children. My best advice to young women attorneys is to network, network, and network. Although you do not have to play office politics, you need to know where the power lies and make that information work for you. Women also need to be less reluctant to talk about their own successes.

Another 60-something, a former government attorney and current judge, found it very difficult when she began work as a lawyer in the 1970s:

> There were very few women in the profession and women were not readily accepted as "equal performers." This situation, combined with the need to care for small children while never losing a step, made things very difficult back then. Things are better now, but I know that it is still difficult. Young women attorneys must be professional in every respect and they must realize that a good reputation is critical to advancement. Get involved in local and statewide bar associations, both mandatory and voluntary. This is a particularly good approach if you are interested in a political career. Getting involved in industry and client groups also is important because it leads to new clients.

Another 60-something, with children, and partner in a midsized firm, recalls one of her greatest challenges when she began her practice in the late 1970s:

> I knew that I was not getting the same opportunities as my male colleagues, and I needed to figure out how to deal with that problem in a way that would not jeopardize my career. It was very challenging. My best advice is to always be in charge of your own career. It is extraordinarily unusual that any other attorney in your organization will take the time to express interest in your career to help you soar to the top. Unlike most experiences that you have had to date in your life, there is no roadmap, no blueprint guiding you to success as a lawyer. There is no recipe which guarantees achievement of your goals, hard work is only one of the factors of success, and you should not leave your future to fate. Be good to the young women coming behind you and pay very close attention to practice development from the very beginning. It is not enough just to do good work and to gain a reputation in your field. You will be able to attract clients with that approach, but you will not be able to attract the number of clients to give you the independence and status in the firm that you will probably want. You must promote you and your firm to gain and retain clients.

Still another 60-something, married with children, in an employment law practice, worked hard to be all things to all people, and it was not easy:

197

My most challenging issue was making sure that I had enough time to spend with my children. I handled this by being very efficient at work and prioritizing the things that I felt were important. For, example, I felt that dinner with my kids was important, and, yes, I did cook every night! As a result, I made sure that I left the office most days around 6 p.m. to make that happen. I also felt it was important to be involved in their schools and to make time for some field trips, school parties, and serving on the Board of Directors. I applied my lawyer skills to some of these things, like being very organized and delegating responsibilities to others. However, I also made sure that my partners and clients were well-served. I was responsive, and I always called and advised them when I was unavailable. I wish that I could say that I was totally honest in all of this, but I was not. I often referred to school events as "an appointment outside the office," but it worked for me. And, most important, I always met my billable hour requirements by working after my kids were in bed for the night. I would recommend a legal career to a young woman today as long as she is willing to commit to the practice and to her family. I think that the legal industry will be changing to be more accommodating to men and women who have an interest in having a life as well as a career. But, that doesn't mean that it will be easy. Women need to understand that the law is a demanding career, but extremely rewarding as well. Most of all, I hope that women will stay in large law firms. They get excellent training there, and they have the opportunity to do really interesting work. They also have the opportunity, if they take it, to gain power individually and through the firm to make important community and professional contributions. You can also make a lot of money to allow you to make a significant contribution to your own support and that of your family. A happy marriage is a wonderful thing, but financial independence is also very important.

The 50-Somethings Following the trailblazers of an earlier era, these women attorneys identified reasonable work-life balance as an issue that needed to be addressed.

One 50-something, married with children, former government attorney and current judge, says that the most difficult work-life issues surround the need to be all things to all people:

I resolved the issue by setting priorities and staying true to them, while recognizing that the difficult times would pass. I also learned that I could be less than perfect in the process and that my best under the circumstances would have to suffice. I am confident that most of you will find a balance between career and family. It is not easy, but, then, life is not easy, and it is all a part of life. I left my first legal job to join my husband who was posted in a foreign country and my colleagues warned that I was "sacrificing my career." I never saw it that way, and my life in a foreign country opened up many opportunities for me, including a position teaching law and observing another country's legal system at work. I knew that it was right for me, and I stuck to it. My best advice to young women lawyers is to have confidence to ask good questions and to look for challenges and not wait for them to come to you. If you do these things, you will be noticed, and it will be good for your career. Get involved in the local bar associations where you will meet other attorneys, learn from them, and develop a familiarity that will assist you when you come up against them in negotiation or litigation.

Another 50-something, married with children, and partner in a mid-sized firm, had a unique set of circumstances and took a different approach to the work-life challenge:

The greatest challenge for me was balancing the demands and desires associated with being a young mother and a young lawyer, even though I had advantages that many women do not. I had my children during law school. My first child was born between semesters my second year, and my second child was born a month after graduation. Although that schedule presented challenges, it was much more flexible than if I had been working full time. After graduation, I job shared and did not work full time until my children were three years and a year and a half in age. In addition, my husband has a great deal of flexibility associated with his job. He has always worked lots of evenings, and he was able to be home with the children during the day more than most spouses. He also did the lion's share of the household chores. Even though that might sound attractive, it was still a huge dilemma. The compromises I had to make meant that I did not feel that I was as good a mother as my neighbor, who was a stay-at-home mom and often made sure that my children were signed up for T-ball, and that I did not feel that I was as good a lawyer as I could be because I did not work as late as I needed to every night. Even with my advantages, the conflict was still very real.

Another 50-something, government attorney, single and without children, planned her life and career with a lot of soul-searching to determine her personal and professional goals and what was important to her:

Get to know yourself and your priorities on quality of life issues. Does it include a high salary? Does it include dealing with constitutional issues? Does it include representing the public sector or representing nonprofits? Is it a career that allows time for family life? Is it a job that involves significant travel or only limited travel? A woman may know that her work will be her life, that she does not want to marry and have children and that she wants to pursue the partnership track in a large firm. Another woman may decide that she prefers more of a 9 to 6 job, does not want to have to keep track of billable hours or have the pressure to bring new business to a firm, and wants to be able to pursue hobbies and interests outside the office. That woman may want to explore government and in-house counsel jobs with nonprofits or with corporations.

Another 50-something, a judge, married with children, says that "Chance favors the trained mind," and she urges you to study and work hard and know your subject area very well. She also counsels you about how to treat the men in the profession who might not value you as much as they should:

> I have seen men have a tough time when women consistently outperform them. Then the personal attacks and the subterfuge begin. Women just have to be tough. If you let bullies bully, they will just continue to bully. You have to fight back.

Another 50-something, married with a child, and partner in a financial practice, cautions women not to take criticism too personally and to learn the value of delegating responsibilities to strike an acceptable work-life balance:

> Women have a tendency to become immobilized and resentful over criticism, and it can be a great impediment to career advancement. Women lawyers also must learn to trust others with tasks that they do not need to do themselves so that they can focus on their professional responsibilities and find more time for family, friends and community.

Another 50-something, married with children and partner in a national law firm, has very encouraging words for young women lawyers and some excellent advice:

> I absolutely recommend a legal career to a young woman today. I have a big advantage as a woman lawyer in many ways. Very good women attorneys

really make an impression on clients and judges. However, you should remember that you should not take yourself too seriously. Life goes on, win or lose. Women tend to put too much pressure on themselves to be perfect. Do your best and then accept the result. Don't gossip and always keep your cards close to your vest. Winning a single case is great, but the challenge is in maintaining the respect of your peers and clients. Working with male colleagues and male judges can be a challenge. I refuse to deal with colleagues who are uncivil, and I get everything in writing if I am dealing with a difficult colleague. However, with judges all you can do is grin and bear it. A judge once told me that I could sit anywhere in his courtroom that I would like except in the jury box or on his lap!

Another 50-something, also married with children, who has achieved remarkable status in a very competitive field, cautions young women lawyers to be realistic about law practice and to recognize that it is very time consuming, stressful, and requires a "pretty thick skin." Her best advice is to seek out practice opportunities and not wait for them to be presented. According to her, "The people who come up for partner have common characteristics—they fully exploited their eight years as an associate to get the best opportunities." She also warns young women to take credit for their accomplishments and to lose the self deprecation.

A 50-something judge, who is married with children, describes her most difficult challenge as leaving a young infant at home after maternity leave and the daily separation from that child:

> After my second child was born, the separation was actually even more difficult because I had spent several months at home with two young children and knew how difficult it would be to find quality child care for them. Even though I did it a third time for a third child, it never got easier and, if I had to do it over again, I would have taken off a few years from practice during the preschool years for my children and would have looked for a part-time position in government or academia to accommodate my personal needs at that time. My best advice to young women attorneys is that they be prepared to put in long hours and hard work at the beginning of their practice because it will pay off in the long run. It is imperative to acquire the necessary analytical and writing skills early on because bad habits will deter advancement and improvement. Learn the value of professionalism and "plain, old-fashioned courtesy" and understand that having a working lunch at your desk once in a while can buy you an extra hour at home at the end of the day.

When you consider this advice about taking time off for children, you should be aware that the most important time to spend with children is a subject of great debate. Whereas some women, like this contributor, consider it to be the time when the children are very young, others think that the most challenging years are the middle and upper-school years. Those women advocate for flexibility when children are teenagers. Undoubtedly, the debate will continue and will be very dependent on the individual and the facts of her situation.

Another 50-something judge chose marriage but no children to meet the needs of a highly charged litigation career:

> I am aware of some women who seem to have "done it all," but I think this is very difficult for the average woman. My experience is that most women make an election between career and family responsibilities. My best advice to you is candid and blunt. You have to be tough to be a woman lawyer. Law, especially litigation, is aggressive and is a winner-take-all endeavor. You need thick skin to compete. Mentoring and networking are essential. While career plans are important, a woman must be open to new possibilities and challenges. It is important to recognize opportunities when they arise and be ready to take them on—even if they are a little scary or risky.

Yet another 50-something, married with children, and partner in a labor and employment practice of a large national law firm, sees the work-life balance issue a little differently:

> The most challenging thing for me was building a law practice while raising three children, trying to preserve some time with my husband and doing some volunteer work. I practiced part time for a number of years and found it helpful to view things as choices instead of trying to achieve "balance." Any balance in my life lasted for all of about 30 seconds! I preferred to focus on choices, make the best selection I could, and then not feel guilty. That was my coping mechanism. Sometimes I chose the school play, and sometimes I chose the client meeting. My best advice to young women attorneys is to check out all of the employment options before you commit yourself. Law firms look alike from the outside, but they are culturally diverse. Legal jobs outside of private practice are very different from each other. You need to find mentors who can help you understand all of these options and why you might prefer one over the other. Young women lawyers should not be shy about asking for

career assistance, but I typically get more questions from young men than from young women. Learn to network, and always take credit for your ideas. I was in a meeting once where a woman said something that was ignored, followed by a man, who offered the same comment and received accolades. Do not let this happen to you. Speak up and take credit.

Another 50-something, married with children, and partner in a mid-sized litigation practice, responds that she was shocked by the complexity of the work-life balance:

Until I had my first child, I had grown up with only encouragement from the outside world. There was no limit to the educational and job opportunities for me, and everyone supported my choices. However, after having a child while I was a law firm associate, I felt that everyone was second-guessing me. No matter what decision I made, people were ready to criticize me. Society in general seemed to suddenly have an opinion on my career and family decisions and did not hesitate to express those opinions. My response was to try to allow my professional life to evolve in parallel with my home life. I never was afraid to alter my approach from month to month or year to year, and I had to stay flexible. It worked over time as I went through the following life phases: Law firm associate with a small child and supporting a law student spouse; law firm part-time associate; six years as a stay-at-home mother of two; return to practice as a part-time associate for seven years; conversion to full-time associate and election to equity partnership. Two years later, I was chosen managing partner of my firm. I am proud of my career path and my resolve to stay in the profession. Another factor that contributed to my success was the flexibility of my husband's schedule. He worked from home for much of the time that the children were young and took a great deal of responsibility for child care—much more than most attorney-husbands. My best advice to young women attorneys is to consider a broad array of professional opportunities without limitation or preconceived notions and to order only one glass of wine at dinner when traveling with male colleagues and clients. Although we have come a long way, we have a long way to go.

Yet another 50-something contributor, a government lawyer, married with children, takes a little different approach to work-life balance. She is a tenacious litigator, and her emphasis was always on perfection in her practice:

To me, work-life means opportunities for equal work and an emphasis on the dignity of life. This was a particular challenge for me in the early years of my practice with the government when there were very few women in practice and my area of practice was entirely dominated by male attorneys. In the first days of affirmative action in 1976, I was one of six attorneys hired in my agency and the only woman. The male attorneys challenged my dignity with inappropriate advances, crude language, and off-color jokes. My youth and gender worked against me, and, even when the men were indulging in acceptable behavior, they did not know whether to open the door for me or watch me struggle with heavy litigation cases and suitcases. It was awkward for everyone in those days. So much has changed for the positive in my 30-year career, and my best advice for young women lawyers is to consider public service for its supportive and inclusive environment and seek out a mentor who is well respected and with whom the young attorney feels a connection.

Another 50-something, married with children, and partner in a national law firm, focuses on the work component in describing her greatest work-life challenge:

I think that, as a professional woman and mother, my greatest challenges centered on the "extracurricular" activities which can be so central to career development—client entertaining, industry and bar association activities and events, and the entire plethora of business development activities—and how to incorporate those activities into your life. Those activities not only take time away from family, but it is particularly hard to take off the "mom hat" on the weekends or in the evenings and put the professional hat back on to attend these functions or to finish up office work at home. While it is easier to compartmentalize life during the work day, at other times it is not as desirable or comfortable. As I look back, I am not particularly pleased with the way I handled the dilemma. At first, I did not recognize the problem for its importance, and I convinced myself that it was alright to just decide "not to play" at the extracurricular professional activities, but I learned that there are consequences to that decision. I would not necessarily do it any differently today because my family responsibilities were very important, but I would make a conscious decision that did not include as much denial or naiveté on my part.

These women are pouring their hearts out, and I hope you are listening. This same contributor offers some very sound advice:

I urge you to take responsibility for your own career because no one else will take the same interest in your future or know what is right for you. Check at certain intervals to make sure that you are on track with your career plan and make adjustments, if necessary. If that includes asking for more or different work or opportunities, do not hesitate to do that. Men do it all the time. Do not put off what you want in terms of a personal life until you have accomplished certain career goals. In other words, do not wait to be happy. If you wait for the big case to settle or the promotion to materialize, you will miss out on too much. Relationships and family are important and can only make you a better lawyer. Also, be nice to everyone you meet—truly live by and practice The Golden Rule. Forming relationships makes you a better, wiser, stronger person. Find a good mentor and be a good mentor and keep in mind that, as a young lawyer, you can provide mentoring to more seasoned lawyers by sharing your experiences, your ideas, your energy, and your idealism. You young lawyers help us "more mature" folks recharge our batteries.

You have to love this woman!

The 40-Somethings The 40-somethings demonstrate divergent choices. You will note as you read these profiles that flexible work schedules still were not available for most of these women early in their careers. Fortunately, that is not the case today and you have other choices available to you.

One 40-something, single without children, and formerly of large law firms and currently in a very specialized solo practice, works nonstop and underscored the power of choices:

> I took advantage of the fact that I did not have children to surpass other women who were perceived as not putting their careers first.

Another 40-something, married with children, and former litigator turned business lawyer, described her work-life challenge as a 100 percent overachiever:

> Because of my age or the way that I was raised, I only know how to give 100 percent to my clients and to my work, and I have to keep aware at all times that I also am a wife and mother. As my two children approach the end of their high school years, the need to maintain a proper balance has become even more important to me. That balance became easier once I left the large

law firm practice and committed to making the weekend a time for family, friends, and activities. I protect this time as my own, and I rarely let work interfere with it. That commitment has helped me to keep focused and true to myself and my family. My best advice is to follow your passion. For those of you who do not know yet where your passion lies, I advise learning as much about the various areas of law as possible and seeking out other lawyers, both male and female, in your areas of interest and asking them to tell you their stories. Do not stay in a job or area of law that isn't a good fit for you, and do not fail to listen to your inner voice because of obligation or fear of being seen as a quitter. In my opinion, the best time to try new career experiences is in the first five to seven years of your career. If you are lucky enough to have a mentor, use that person as a sounding board as you seek to make a transition. The bottom line is not to be afraid of change. And lastly, be tough. Do not compromise your femininity, but remember that a steady, firm, and no-nonsense attitude is essential for success. And take more courses in school related to business and finance. In the end, it is the business and financial issues that drive the ultimate decisions in any business environment, and the knowledge is invaluable.

Another 40-something, married with children, and part-time partner in a large litigation firm, describes a struggle with work-life throughout her career:

I had three children in four years, and one of them is still preschool age. In trying to balance family and career, I sometimes think that I do not do either very well. I feel guilty about work creeping into the time that I should be spending with my kids, and that puts additional stress on me. I think that the life of a working mother, who is an attorney, is difficult for the children and that the times when I have to travel for work is especially hard for them. My best advice to young women attorneys is to figure out what makes them happy and to follow that path. If you are not happy in a job, then change it. You will end up working long hours so it is wise to really enjoy the subject matter you work on and the people that you work with. Finally, you need to have a great mentor and balance in your life that allows you to pursue other interests so that you do not focus entirely on law. The memories that I hold dearest are the ones created by activities and events that I have shared with family and friends, not the fact that I worked until 8 or 10 p.m. on a case. Consider clerking for a judge or working as a United States Attorney before starting private practice. I was in too much of a rush to get to a law firm, and I believe that I would have benefited from observing other trial lawyers and learning from the different styles of litigation. My greatest accomplishment is a pro bono case where I represented the female employees of a prison in a class action sexual harassment suit, and we won. The conditions for these women were terrible, and we changed the way business was done and helped these women in a material way.

This is another amazing story, particularly because this woman has achieved so much in her career, including the elusive part-time partnership in a very prestigious law firm. I think that you can see why she has been so successful.

Another 40-something found that her career was shaped at least partially by her status as a racial minority:

I consciously opted for career over marriage and children. My career combines both politics and law and includes significant time demands for work and travel. These commitments posed serious challenges to dating, marriage, and children. In addition, as the first African American woman to secure many of the positions that I have held, the time and work demands also included other challenges related to gender, race, and class. My best advice is that you believe in yourself and keep your options open. Pursue your career as if it is a business and you are its best-selling brand. Understand that business, brands, and people must be willing and able to adapt to market changes. Therefore, your focus should be on developing as many skills as possible in your early years of practice and establishing a strong network of mentors and associates that you can engage over a period of years. What you know and who you know should be symbiotically rooted objectives in any long-term career strategy. But, most important, know who you are and what you believe in. Reaching your greatest aspirations, in part, will be determined by how well you embrace your fondest dreams and whether you are willing to do the research, prepare the written product, hit the streets, and attend the events needed to expose you to others and them to you. You also must market yourself internally. Early on in my career, I was ignorant about that particular need. I worked long hours and got the work done, but I failed to keep my ear to the ground and to assess how others on my team perceived me. As a result, I failed to identify persons who were out to discredit me because they were in competition with me for promotion and the attention of superiors. Keep your "antennae up" and network internally, as well as externally.

The 30-Somethings These 30-somethings, especially those in their early 30s, are just beginning to grapple with the work-life issues. One woman, married with very young children, and a partner in a national midsized litigation practice, simply states that work-life issues are SO COMPLEX!

> My best advice to young women lawyers is to always give 110 percent and consider every contact you make to be a potential source of business or referral. Use mentors to help you with this business development because you do not learn it in law school. Expect the best mentors to be the ones who are most critical of you. It is the constructive criticism that you learn from and that makes you a better lawyer.

Another late 30-something, married with children, and currently off-ramp, warns of making career decisions solely on the goal of paying off student loans:

> I joined a large litigation firm after graduating from law school with the singular focus of paying off my mountain of student loan debt. I did not feel like I had the freedom to pursue a career in an area of law that really interested me. I also accepted the perception of my fellow law students that following other paths, like becoming a civil or human rights lawyer, were limiting. My best advice is to be in charge of your own career at an early time before law school, define yourself and consider a broad array of factors in making an important decision about your first job out of law school. Seek out relationships with lawyers who can help you, gain their confidence, and communicate openly with them about your expectations. Most of all, if you join a large law firm, go in with your eyes wide open.

Another late 30-something responded to the work-life issues by taking five years off from her law practice:

> I made family a priority for much of the time that I was in practice, and I consider myself to be fortunate to have worked in a number of different venues where my priorities were respected. At times, however, I had to place limits on myself professionally to ensure that family remained the top priority. My best advice to young women attorneys is to always remember that self-promotion is not a bad thing and that planning ahead is always useful but must be done with flexibility. Today very few women or men work in the same job for their entire careers, and a young lawyer should always be open to interesting opportunities that will form the foundation for very interesting work as the lawyer gains seniority.

Another 30-something, newly married, and without children, is an associate in a small firm. She finds the work-life balance to be very challenging:

> When I was single, I could work late and not worry about needing or wanting to be home for anyone, but now that has changed. I need to put the right amount of time into my marriage, and now I get into work earlier, work through lunches and try to leave the office to have dinner with my husband, who is not a lawyer and has a more flexible schedule. Often, I have to work late at home to manage this balance. This is all very new to me, and I find that I must be realistic about how many hours there are in a day. I have learned not to be afraid to ask a case manager whether something can be completed a little later than originally desired. Women, particularly, fall victim to false deadlines because they aim to please and hesitate to ask. My best advice to you is to throw yourself into practice when you first start and to learn as much as you can, as quickly as you can. I always was commended on how I would really try to understand a complicated document rather than taking the shortcut and relying on accepted forms. And you should request more work from your managers. Build your career and your reputation in the first years when you know that work is going to be your life. It will pay off. Work hard, play hard.

I am so glad that this young woman was so candid about the importance of spending time with her spouse in the early days of their marriage. Building a relationship with a spouse is every bit as important as caring for children. It takes time and attention if the marriage is going to be successful and last. I completely understand the challenges of these young people, and I am pleased that they recognize the commitment. On a related subject, one of the 30-somethings also advises a young woman lawyer who wants to have a family and will require a work-life balance to look around at the partners in the firm for models of that balance. "If you do not see such models, beware!"

Another 30-something, married with children, and partner in a midsized firm, is constantly juggling:

> I have important committee positions in the firm and head up the flexible work program. I live the work-life struggle and also mentor many others who do. It is important to talk to others who are working a flexible schedule

if that is what you think you want to do. It is often difficult to tell who they are in a firm because many part-time lawyers like to stay under the radar so that they do not call too much attention to their special circumstances. However, you can find them if you try.

Another 30-something, married with children, identifies having a lawyer spouse as adding to the challenge:

> The most challenging issue I wrestle with is trying to excel professionally while maintaining a happy home life with my lawyer-husband and our three young children. I am fortunate to have a very understanding employer who honors my commitment to my family while permitting me that flexibility to fulfill my work duties. It has not always been like this. After several years of working for a 150-attorney law firm, I decided to make the switch to a different career path that would allow me to have a family. My best advice to young women lawyers is that they do not worry about the right decision forever— make the decision that is right at the moment and reevaluate when the circumstances of your life change. Also, preserve all of your relationships— professors, classmates, and colleagues—because you never know when you will cross paths with these people again and in what setting.

Another 30-something, married with children, and part-time partner in a midsized national firm, advises you to take advantage of alternative work schedules if you need them and to take charge of your career as early as possible. "I also put a high premium on the work environment, and I believe that a happy lawyer is a more productive lawyer."

The 20-Somethings These young women attorneys are just starting their careers. Although they have not had to face the work-life issues involving children, they understand the dilemma, and they are supportive.

One 20-something, unmarried with no children, in a business litigation practice in a midsized regional firm, responds:

> Sometimes I work longer hours than my female colleagues with families, but that is a choice that I make and it works well for me. I hope that it will serve me well when the shoe is on the other foot one day. I relocated after a relatively short time in my first private practice experience, and my best

advice to you is to find the right balance for yourself and do not stay in a job that you know is not right for you. Do not view leaving as a loyalty issue. It is a business decision, and you should treat it that way.

Another 20-something, married with no children, working in a litigation practice in a satellite office of a large firm, expresses certain reservations about being in a satellite office:

I would like to have more access to the women's initiative programs and other practice development opportunities that are available at the home office. I try to take advantage of the programs electronically, but it is not the same. I miss the dynamics of being in a larger group of associates.

Another 20-something, not married and with no children, has chosen a very independent career path. After a judicial clerkship at the state supreme court and several years as a law firm associate, this woman followed the beat of a different drummer and formed a virtual law firm:

Because of my independent nature, I enjoy working for myself and find it much more rewarding than working for a law firm. In my contract work, I do all of the things that I did as an associate attorney, but I do them as my own boss. I can pick and choose what I want to do, and I always seem to have work. My best advice to young women law graduates is to explore a lot of areas of the law and law-related activities in your quest to find what is right for you. When you find what interests you that is also rewarding, stay with it even if the pay is less or the situation is less prestigious. Also remember that it may take a few years at a less-than-perfect job before you secure your ideal job.

Another 20-something, married with no children, is an associate in the business practice of a large national law firm. She emphasizes prioritization and efficiency and finds the double standard in acceptable socialization to be problematic:

The biggest challenge for me has stemmed from the value that the law firm places on socialization. Certain socialization activities are acceptable. Going home to cook or taking care of pets all may be socially acceptable reasons to leave the office in certain settings. On the other hand, having drinks with colleagues or networking or going to board meetings appear to be less than acceptable in other settings. The difference in treatment seems to be rooted in the law firm's belief about what it means to be a lawyer. If they want you to become a rainmaker by creating new clients, then networking and speaking events are seen as positive investments of your time. On the other hand, if they do not expect you to become a rainmaker, or believe that the work will be passed down to you from others, some of these socialization experiences are seen as unnecessary and not to warrant the time off. It is confusing and can be disappointing. My best advice to young women attorneys is to find a good mentor and to be flexible in your substantive area of practice to stick with the right guide. It will be well worth the trade-off.

Yet another 20-something, not married and with no children, an associate in a midsized litigation practice, left her first very prestigious practice to clerk for a federal judge. She saw such value in the clerking experience that she took a leap of faith:

I am glad that I took the time off from my practice to clerk for a federal judge, and I think that the experience has made me a better litigator. I enjoyed clerking more than anything else that I have done to date. There is not the same pressure as there is in a law firm, and the goal is to achieve the most legally correct and equitable result. There was a lot of variety in my case load, and the legal issues that I dealt with on a daily basis were very interesting. As an associate in a law firm with a "big case" practice, I regularly encounter fewer issues. I have done both litigation and corporate work so far, and, although I find the work in litigation more challenging, I have a lot less client contact than I did as an associate in the corporate practice.

The biggest challenge for me in private practice is the work-life balance and figuring out the right timetable for starting a family. I look at the female partners in my firm, and they have all waited until after making partner to start a family. I don't know whether that will work for me. Another major challenge for me has been practicing in specialty areas where there are few women lawyers. It sometimes limits my opportunities for socialization and business development. My best advice to young women lawyers is to have a career plan. I think that I should have gone to the government prior to entering private practice because I think that background opens a lot of doors in the private sector. When you start from a position of power, you have more leverage in negotiating future work.

Another 20-something, not married with no children, and working in a large firm, advises that you not be afraid to ask for what you want.

As firms begin to consider formalizing new work-life policies, don't be afraid to ask for what you want. After four years of developing a reputation as a diligent and committed associate, I discovered that my firm is more receptive to reduced-hour arrangements than I had thought. However, be aware that many large law firms continue to value "face time" over quality of work, and senior partners equate lower billing tiers and reduced-hour work arrangements with a lack of ambition. You have to try to dissuade them from this predisposition. This might also be a problem for you in finding good mentors among your female colleagues. Reduced-hour schedules are often stigmatized at law firms, and therefore, women who work those schedules are reluctant to share the details of these successful arrangements with their colleagues.

This contributor also has some interesting information on alternative billable hour requirements.

Last year, my law firm implemented a tiered billing system that allows attorneys to remain "full-time" employees while selecting one of three billing tiers with adjusted compensation. The new tiered system provides a unique opportunity for greater flexibility in developing a legal practice and allows attorneys to individualize their own work-life balance. Many of my colleagues are considering taking advantage of these reduced-hour tiers, but most of them remain reluctant because of the past stigmas associated with part-time tracks.

Another 20-something, married and with no children, an associate in a small firm, has faced some significant challenges and has learned a lot in her short career:

I absolutely loved clerking for a judge, and the experience was invaluable. The judge I worked with was an incredible mentor. She provided a wide-ranging education and strove at making the learning process fun, but also very challenging. I consider myself lucky to have had the opportunity to train under such a well-respected member of the judiciary, who was also a highly respected litigator prior to joining the judiciary. During my three years, she spent a considerable amount of time attempting to prepare me for the rigors of practicing law and being a litigator. Although I have left chambers, she is still a mentor and someone I turn to for advice and help.

After leaving my clerkship, I spent a year "in turmoil." The firm I joined was not a good fit for me, my philosophy on practicing law, or my values in general. In addition, the firm environment was very toxic. There was no interest in training or mentoring. Often large cases were "thrown" at me, with little guidance or assistance. When a question arose, I was left on my own to tackle the issue. If, however, I did not handle the matter in the way "expected," I was yelled at and chastised.

I have always considered myself to be a confident person. However, after a year of practicing in this environment, I had lost all confidence. While I had been quite successful in my education and at my clerkship, I could not trust myself to do the simplest task, and I was seriously contemplating leaving the profession. Thankfully, I was able to speak with trusted peers outside the firm about my experiences. With their help, I realized that it was okay to leave the job and find a firm where the philosophy and values were more consistent with my own. I successfully made a transition to a new firm, and it was amazing how different two firms could be! My "home" now focuses on a team effort from the attorneys down to the support staff. I finally feel like I am getting the guidance and support for which I had been looking. I finally came back to the love and enthusiasm I had for the law when I graduated from law school. A positive practice environment is crucial to job enjoyment, and I wish that I had realized it earlier and asked the right questions at my first firm before accepting the job.

My best advice is that you really check out your future employer and that you ask the right questions during job interviews. Do not assume anything. There are so many questions I did not think to ask during my interview. Also, as I practice in a small area, I should have done a better job of vetting my firm with other attorneys in the area. It's amazing how after I left the firm, I was constantly receiving statements like, "I knew you would not like it there" or "I knew you would not fit in." And, if you make a mistake, don't be afraid to leave a job and look for something that is a better fit for your philosophy, values, personality, and goals. Really examine what you want in your life and find something that fits your needs and your dreams.

So, there you have it. Choices, choices, choices. There are many different career paths and models. It is not necessary that any one fit you perfectly or that you agree with all of the decisions, observations, and career paths of any one contributor. What is important is that you understand the "yin and yang" of it all and the choices that you will have to make during your years of practice. Go to school on these women and develop a personal career strategy. You will be better off for it. Listen to your best friends at the bar!

Advice to Employers

The contributing attorneys are quite consistent in their advice to employers. I include this information for two purposes. First, it gives you an idea of the things that you should be looking for in an employer. Second, it will serve as a guide as you advance your career and are responsible for making decisions that affect other young women in the practice.

The questionnaire that was sent to contributors asked them to identify three things that are essential for an employer to consider in establishing a positive, healthy working environment for young women lawyers. This is how the contributors responded.

- Have open and competitive hiring practices where women are viewed in the same way as their male counterparts—no better and no worse. Maintain an approach to hiring that recognizes the importance of diversity. It is important for firms to find a balance between the genders and to take steps to maintain the balance to combat female attrition. Have an effective women's initiative or include women's issues as a topic within the diversity committee. Make sure that program addresses benchmark career development goals. Also recognize the importance of diversity in the staffing of cases. Clients have diversity in their ranks, and they expect to see it in their legal team.
- Create a work environment that fosters respect for staff at all levels, men and women alike. Do not allow an environment that makes women professionals feel like they are required to prove themselves as professionals more than men. Employers should remember that they need to provide healthy working environments for all lawyers and that women lawyers must be respected for their

intelligence, passion, and compassion. Marginalizing women within historic gender parameters does them a disservice. Employers should recognize that one size does not fit all (all associates do not want to make partner), positive incentives work better for women than negative incentives, and incentives can come in the form of better hours and flexible schedules, as well as money, and that the former is sometimes much more important to women.

- Establish effective mentoring programs for young women attorneys. Strive to have women in senior positions so that young women lawyers have role models and mentors with whom they can readily identify. Coach young lawyers on how to work in teams and how to communicate with each other. Be candid about expectations so that there are no surprises later.

- Encourage regular communication between young female attorneys and supervisors, especially male bosses, to send the clear message that both genders are respected. Do not leave all the communication with female lawyers to female supervisors. Have an open door policy.

- Provide immediate constructive criticism to all young lawyers and provide positive feedback when work is done well. Take the responsibility to help young lawyers get to the next level of practice. It is good for the young lawyer and good for the firm.

- Be concerned about your employees' lives, not just their work. Establish policies that permit flexible work arrangements, including job sharing and teleworking, to accommodate personal and family responsibilities, and do not punish women (or men) who take advantage of those policies. Lawyers who have child care responsibilities should not be made to feel like they are second-class attorneys. Include a well-accepted and well-implemented balanced hours/part-time program for working mothers. Keep up with industry trends. Send the message to young women that you understand their lives and want them to be long-term members of the organization.

- Offer generous maternity leave for birth and adoption and have a caring response to family emergencies. Be prepared to be flexible with women who are experienced and have proven their worth to increase the possibilities of those women returning to work after maternity leave. Include support for workload coverage during the leave period and support during the reentry stage of any maternity program.

- Provide on-site or nearby exercise and child care facilities.

- Establish networking programs that are responsive to women's lives and experiences.

- Provide reasonable work and billable hours standards. Also provide options to the billable hour fee structure and give favorable consideration to those options in evaluating young attorneys. Get rid of the lock-step advancement in favor of measurement by competencies. Consider providing well-defined formal policies for multiple billable hour tiers with adjusted compensation, rather than the traditional part-time and full-time categories with associated stigmas. Consider a similar flexible approach to the partner track.

- Invest time and effort in professional development, especially for women with children, and ensure equal access and opportunity for client interaction. Promote the efforts of women lawyers outside the day-to-day practice of law, including membership on bar association committees, networking in business and professional venues, and speaking engagements. Do not take the "wait and see" approach with women or you will lose them. As a part of these efforts, help women see a path to success in the firm.

- Offer a social aspect to the firm—happy hours and lunches, for example—to get people comfortable with each other. Having that familiarity can increase communication and comfort levels and fend off problems.

Meeting those basic needs should not be controversial and will encourage more lawyers, men and women alike, to stay in the profession.

The controversy will be over what comes next—beyond the "right" thing to do to the "expected" thing to do. This is a new generation of lawyers, a generation that does not want to practice law like their mothers and fathers. To some degree, this is a generation that is rebelling against the old models that robbed them of time and attention from parents and grandparents. In their own way, albeit somewhat awkwardly, the members of this generation are saying that there has to be another way and that they are entitled to it. They will be pushing the envelope for a more genteel lawyer model that recognizes the need for rest, relaxation, and refurbishment as well as time with family and friends. The success of that initiative will be determined by the degree of resistance from clients and Big Law and the effects of that resistance on law practice generally. At the very least, it is likely to be a compromise, with the new generation of lawyers gaining some ground while law firms make whatever accommodations they can within the context of the business model. It is a process that will be interesting to follow.

7

The Solution

By now you know that there is no one solution to the issues addressed in this book. The solution for you is unique to you, and that solution will be the result of the choices that you make. It is all about informed choices: choices as part of a career plan, choices to make you happy, choices to make you proud, and choices to give you power. Your choices. Choices to make you *you*. Choose well and often, if necessary. Your career is a continuum, and the right choice at one juncture might not be the right choice at another.

The solution for the profession is more complicated, but that solution will be easier if more young women lawyers stay in the practice to rise to levels of decision makers and use that power to improve law firms and other practice settings and bring about better conditions for all women lawyers. To accomplish this, women who want to have families must plan careers that will sustain them during the challenging childrearing years or the years of caretaking for an elderly or ill family member. Those career plans, if crafted carefully, also will allow them to stay connected to their professions until they are able to advance to senior levels where they can fulfill the goals of their own careers and positively affect the futures of the women to follow. It also will be incumbent on law firms and other employers to critically review their procedures and practices with the goal of improving conditions for women who are particularly challenged by the work-life dilemma.

Finding these solutions and accomplishing these goals will take time and effort. Not all things work for all people; much of it is a matter of style. Find your own style and try to avoid the pitfalls that have been identified for you. My guess is that you will be wildly successful.

With success comes responsibility. Your responsibility will be to spread the word and to reach down to younger women entering the profession and mentor them to assist in their own success. You must be willing to "pay it forward." This is the step that too often is missing for women, and women must change that. Women lawyers must band together to remove the obstacles and to level the playing field so that not only our junior colleagues but our own daughters and granddaughters can experience success in the profession. It is a profession that not only demands a lot of us, but also gives a lot to us, and our goal should be to improve it and to make it even more attractive to the young women of the future.

Thank you for your attention to this book. It has been a labor of love for me and, I think, for all those who contributed to it. My own experiences mentoring women started when I was in law school and have continued throughout my career. Most of my contributors have similar stories. We all would have benefited from a candid look at the experiences of women lawyers, and we all feel honored to share our experiences with you.

As I think of the proper way to end our conversation and say goodbye to you, I recall a friend of mine who once owned a Doberman Pinscher dog. I was intimidated by that dog every time I was at her home, and one day I told my friend that I thought her dog was "really scary." She responded by saying that he was a wonderful dog but that he just needed "to be managed." She said that she would not think of having any other kind of dog.

That, it seems to me, is a lot like a career in the law, especially for women who want more than just professional lives. It can be a little scary, but it is a wonderful profession and one that I hope you all will find very satisfying. The key is learning to manage it.

As for my friend, she has given up on Dobermans and now owns Yorkshire Terriers! Her decision might have had something to do with failed management skills. You should want a different result. You need to make sure that you manage your career well so that you do not have to make radical adjustments and sacrifice your dreams.

So, good luck, *buena suerte, chuc may man*, or whatever salutation you choose. It is all about choices, and I know that you will choose well. You are ready to launch exciting and rewarding careers and to make the legal profession a better place for women. As you do, remember to become someone else's best friend at the bar.

Epilogue: The Male Perspective

There is another perspective, and I know you understand that. You need to consider the male attorney's perspective on these issues and prepare yourself for the debate. Because the majority of management today, especially in law firms, is male, it is fair to anticipate the male perspective in many of the critical conversations that you will have about your career. In preparation for those conversations, you must prepare your arguments well, and, to do that, you must be familiar with the perspective of your male colleagues and managers. You need to prepare yourself for the arguments you might hear against the "privilege" of a flexible schedule, the resistance to altering the established conditions of partnership, the justification for exclusion from traditional male promotional venues, the accusations of "bitchy" behavior rather than recognition of aggressive practice, and the many other issues addressed in this book that will continue to challenge women in the profession. Be prepared and be a force. Make your best case.

The advice and counsel of male law firm managers are included throughout the chapters of this book. Their participation as contributors was critical to a balanced approach and a true and accurate message. They have been remarkably candid and thoughtful to achieve that result, and they were very eager to participate because they recognize the challenges you face and they want to help you be the best and most successful lawyers that you can be. You might not always like the message, but you should appreciate the messengers. They are helping you to be better prepared than any generation of women lawyers before you. Take advantage of their thoughtfulness and candor; work hard to embrace what you agree with and to change what you do not.

However, I know when I am in over my head. I recognize that I lack credibility to present the male perspective. Interviewing male managing partners does not equip me to effectively articulate their unique perspectives. To remedy that, I am joined by Sheldon Krantz, Esquire, Partner, DLA Piper, Washington, DC, a specialist in corporate and white collar criminal defense and the Director of New Perimeter, DLA Piper's unique affiliated nonprofit that provides global pro bono services. Mr. Krantz is the former Dean of the University of San Diego School of Law and professor of law and the Director of the Center for Criminal Justice at Boston University School of Law. He was named the DC Bar Pro Bono Lawyer of the Year in 2004 and a District of Columbia Super Lawyer in 2008. I am sure that you will agree that he is more than qualified to present the male perspective on some of the issues addressed in this book.

Here is his "take" on the future of women in the law and his best advice for young women lawyers for achieving success in their careers:

> Susan Blakely has written a timely and important book about women and the legal profession. It accurately captures the barriers women continue to confront in progressing up the ladder in larger, more traditional law firms. While many of the barriers are slowly breaking down, most law firms are still not effective in supporting women in their ongoing struggles to compete on equal terms and balance professional and family obligations. The author skillfully presents alternatives to the traditional law firm practice and

encourages women to assess career options more broadly. This is good advice and should be heeded. This book is particularly helpful in assisting young women in thinking about ways to develop an appropriate work-life balance that will allow them to remain in a profession that sorely needs them.

In addressing the issues identified in this book, it would be a mistake to focus entirely on the legal profession and its failures, particularly at this moment in time, without recognition of the potential for positive change. The profession has not been immune from the current devastating recession and it might never be the same again. Law firms are likely to undergo seismic changes in spite of their resistance to them. It is becoming increasingly apparent, for example, that corporate clients are no longer going to permit law firms to unilaterally control the rates they charge. This, in turn, will compel firms to reassess how they are structured. New competitors to the traditional law firm model are also emerging in the marketplace. They will likely offer alternative fee arrangements and more flexibility to their lawyers in the way they practice law, where they practice, and how much time they devote to it. This, too, will put pressure on more traditional firms to challenge the precepts under which they have been operating for years.

These developments should open up opportunities for women who want to work in law firms but under different arrangements. Women (and men), however, must recognize that change will have other implications: The days of increasingly higher starting salaries, sizable increases and bonuses with each passing year, and partnerships as the likely ultimate reward for those that do well might be over for all but a select few. This will be unhappy news for law students who were counting on the "way things were" and who are graduating with suffocating college and law school loans. In sum, there should be more alternatives in the future for women (and men) who want a more sensible work-life balance, but the salaries under these arrangements will be lower and the positions will be less secure. These changes will be similar to what has been happening in other professions, such as the medical field, and should not come as a surprise to those who have been following these recent developments.

More important, we are at a moment in history for the profession where there are few givens about what happens next. This provides unique opportunities for creative thinking about our profession. The message for law firms is that the landscape is changing and those firms that remain static will risk being left behind. The one certainty is that the current traditional law firm model has serious flaws. I anticipate that women in law firms today will help lead the debate on how lawyers can better serve their clients, how firms can expand their commitment to pro bono services without putting the involved lawyers in jeopardy, and the changes that are needed to make law firms better places to work and to grow professionally.

The next generation of women lawyers also must recognize, however, as the author notes, that limiting the options within the legal profession to law firm practice is far too restrictive. Women lawyers must realize that what they view as their unique situations might call for unique solutions and more realistic views of their options. In that analysis, they are likely to discover that lawyers often feel more gratification, even with less pay, when they work in one of the three branches of federal, state, or local government; for non-profits and NGOs that are seeking ways to improve the human condition and the rule of law both here and abroad; in legal departments in the corporate sector; or even in nonlegal positions where they can put their valuable law school training to use alongside other disciplines that address intractable public health, environmental, or economic development problems.

It is fair to say that, in many ways, this is the "worst of times" for graduating law students in general and for the women among them in particular. And yet, because the profession is in the throes of change, it can also oddly enough be the "best of times." Polls consistently report that lawyers today have long been an unhappy lot (in spite of the money they make). The challenge now is to figure out why that is so and how to get our profession back on a more honorable course. The next generation of lawyers should welcome this unique opportunity, and women lawyers should embrace the central theme of this book—women helping women. It is a powerful theme that cannot and should not be ignored if women are going to have an important role in reforming the profession in ways that benefit them and the profession alike. I will be watching with great interest to see how women, particularly, help stimulate the necessary changes while staying true to the goals of the profession. Clients still have to be served and the business bottom line still has to be reconciled. Within these essential parameters, however, the possibilities are countless and the professional journey can be very gratifying.

BIBLIOGRAPHY

Books

Linda Babcock & Sara Laschever, *Women Don't Ask: The High Cost of Avoiding Negotiations and Positive Strategies for Change* (Bantam, 2007).

Susan Shapiro Baragh, *Tripping the Prom Queen: The Truth About Women and Rivalry* (St. Martin's Griffin 2007).

Joan Biskupic, *Sandra Day O'Connor: How the First Woman on the Supreme Court Became Its Most Influential Justice* (Ecco 2005).

Carol Fishman Cohen & Vivian Stein Rabin, *Back on the Career Track: A Guide for Stay-at-Home Moms Who Want to Return to Work* (Business Plus, 2007).

Phyllis Horn Epstein, *Women-at-Law: Lessons Learned Along the Pathways to Success* (American Bar Association, 2004).

Betty Freidan, *The Feminine Mystique* (W.W. Norton, 1963).

Sally Gunz & Robert V. A. Jones, *The New Corporate Counsel* (Carswell Legal 1991).

Mark Harris, *So You Want To Be Corporate Counsel* (Infinity Publishing.com 2002).

Sylvia Ann Hewlett, *Off-ramps and On-ramps: Keeping Talented Women on the Road to Success* (Harvard Business School Press, 2007).

Bruce R. Hopkins, *The Law of Fundraising* (3d ed., Wiley 2008).

Brenda Hunter, *In the Company of Women: Deepening Our Relationship with the Important Women in Our Lives* (Multomah Press 2006).

Emma Gilbey Keller, *The Comeback: Seven Stories of Women Who Went from Career to Family and Back Again* (Bloomsbury USA, 2008).

Deborah M. Kolb, Judith Willams, & Carol Frohlinger, *Her Place at the Table* (Jossey-Bass, 2004).

Alan B. Morrison & Diane T. Chin, *Beyond the Big Firm—Profiles of Lawyers Who Want Something More* (Aspen 2007).

Natalie Prescott & Oleg Cross, *Nail Your Law Job Interview: The Essential Guide to Firm, Clerkship, Government, In-House, and Lateral Interviews* (Career Press, 2009).

Terrance Real, *How Can I Get Through to You? Closing the Intimacy Gap Between Men and Women* (Scribner, 2002).

Lauren Stiller Rikleen, *Ending the Gauntlet: Removing Barriers to Women's Success in the Law* (Thomson Legalworks, 2006).

Ronald M. Shapiro & Mark A. Jankowski, *The Power of Nice: How to Negotiate So Everyone Wins—Especially You!* (Wiley, 2001).

State Bar of Wisconsin, *Balancing Work and Personal Life: Developing Flexible Work Options for Lawyers* (State Bar of Wisconsin, 2004).

Leo Tolstoy, *Family Happiness* (London: Pitman, 1945).

Kimm Alayne Walton, *Guerilla Tactics—Legal Jobs of Your Dreams* (Gilbert Law, Thomson West, 2008).

Joan C. Williams and Cynthia Thomas Calvert, *Solving the Part-Time Puzzle: The Law Firm's Guide to Balanced Hours* (National Association for Law Placement 2004).

Reports

ABA Commission on Women in the Profession, *Charting Our Profession: The Status of Women in the Profession Today* (ABA 2006).

ABA Legal Education Statistics, *Enrollment and Degrees Awarded, 1963–2007 and First Year and Total J.D. Enrollment by Gender, 1947–2001.*

Linda Bray Chanow, *Actions for Advancing Women into Law Firm Leadership* (National Association of Women Lawyers 2008).

Commission on Women in the Profession, ABA, *A Current Glance at Women in the Law* (ABA 2007).

Law School Admission Counsel, *Volume Summary: Applicants by Ethnic & Gender Group* (2008).

National Association for Law Placement, *Toward Effective Management of Associate Mobility* (National Association for Law Placement 2005).

National Association for Law Placement, *Jobs and JD's, Employment and Salaries of New Law Graduates, Class of 2007* (National Association for Law Placement 2008).

National Association for Law Placement, *Starting Salaries: What New Law Graduates Earn—Class of 2007* (National Association for Law Placement 2008).

National Association of Women Lawyers, *National Survey on Retention and Promotion of Women in Law Firms* (Nov. 2007).

Project for Attorney Retention, *Balanced Hours: Part-Time Policies for Washington Law Firms* (Project for Attorney Retention 2001).

Project for Attorney Retention, *Solving the Part-Time Puzzle: The Law Firm's Guide to Balanced Hour Programs* (Project for Attorney Retention 2004).

Project for Attorney Retention, Positioning Law Firms for Long-Term Success: New Strategies for Advancing Women Lawyers: The First Annual Conference of the Project for Attorney Retention, Washington, DC (Project for Attorney Retention 2008).

Report on the Conference, Advancing Women in the Profession: Action Plans for Women's Bar Associations Conference (June 2007 Boston).

Jean E. Wallace, *Juggling It All: Exploring Lawyers' Work, Home and Family Demands and Coping Strategies* (Law School Admission Council 2002).

Washington College of Law, *Balanced Hours: Effective Part-Time Programs for Washington Law Firms* (*www.wcl.american.edu/gender/worklife/publications/ Balancedhours*, American University).

Women's Bar Association of the District of Columbia Initiative on Advancement and Retention of Women, *Creating Pathways to Success: Retaining Women in Today's Law Firms* (Women's Bar Association of the District of Columbia May 2006).

Articles

Number of Students Applying to Law Schools Jumps 3.8 Percent, ABA Journal Law News Now, www.abajournal.com, April 29, 2009.

Best Defense? Seeking a Haven in Law School, www.wsj.com (March 19, 2009).

Best Firms for Work-Life Balance, The National Jurist (Oct. 2008).

Bureau of National Affairs, Inc. (BNA). *Interview with Jacquelyn Finn and Paula Campbell Millian of Finn and Associates, LLC*, Corporate Counsel Weekly (Dec. 31, 2008).

Focus on the Best Law Firms-Part-time Partners, Working Mother Magazine (Nov. 16, 2008).

Deborah Epstein Henry, *What Makes a Best Law Firm for Women?* Working Mother Magazine (Aug. 21, 2007).

Investing in Women Lawyers' Success Begins in Law School, 4 Raising the Bar 4 (2008–2009).

I Wish I Had Known . . . , ABA Journal (June 2008).

Job Hunting Is, and Isn't, What It Used to Be, N.Y. Times (Sept. 26, 2008).

Amy Kolz, *Obstacle Course*, The American Lawyer (Jan. 1, 2007).

Law Firms Offering More Flexible Schedules, Law 360 (Aug. 22, 2008).

Lawyers Want More Time, Less Stress, Not More Money, ABA Journal-Law News Now (Oct. 7, 2008)

Martha Neil, *Part-Time Partner Works 9 Hours a Day*, ABA Journal (July 16, 2007).

Patience Won't Make Women Partners, Legal Times (Nov. 3, 2008).

William P. Quigley, *Letter to a Law Student Interested in Social Justice,* 1 DePaul Journal for Social Justice (2007).

The State of the Legal Profession, Georgetown Law Res Ipsa Loquitor (Spring/ Summer 2009).

With the Downturn, It's Time to Rethink the Legal Profession, N.Y. Times (April 2, 2009).